Colin Fraser was a pioneer in the use of communication for development, founding this area of work in the UN's Food and Agriculture Organization and running it for 17 years. Now a consultant, he has worked in communication for agriculture, rural development, the environment, and children's health and rights. He has worked in more than sixty countries and with most development agencies.

Sonia Restrepo-Estrada has specialized in communication for health and nutrition, and for women's and children's rights. She has designed and implemented innovative strategies for putting children onto political agendas. After several years with UNICEF, she is now a consultant and has also worked in communication for natural resources, agriculture, and rural development in various countries.

'If my analysis is roughly correct, the forces for change facing the world could be so far-reaching, complex, and interactive that they call for nothing less than the re-education of humankind.'

Paul Kennedy, *Preparing for the Twenty-First Century*

COMMUNICATING FOR DEVELOPMENT

Human Change for Survival

COLIN FRASER AND
SONIA RESTREPO-ESTRADA

I.B.Tauris Publishers
LONDON · NEW YORK

Published in 1998 by I.B.Tauris & Co Ltd,
Victoria House, Bloomsbury Square, London WC1B 4DZ

175 Fifth Avenue, New York NY 10010

In the United States of America and in Canada distributed by
St Martin's Press, 175 Fifth Avenue, New York NY 10010

A full CIP record for this book is available from the British Library

A full CIP record for this book is available from the Library of
Congress

ISBN 1 86064 347 7 (hb)
ISBN 1 86064 238 1 (pb)

Library of Congress catalog card number: available

Set in Monotype Garamond by Ewan Smith, London

Printed and bound in Great Britain by WBC Ltd, Bridgend,
Mid-Glamorgan

Contents

Abbreviations

ACPO	Action for Popular Culture, Colombia
AIDS	acquired immune deficiency syndrome
BBC	British Broadcasting Corporation
BKKBN	National Family Planning Board, Indonesia
CADRI	Centre of Support for Rural Development, Mexico
CMC	Community Media Council, Philippines
CMTC	Community Media and Training Centre, Philippines
CNA	National Water Commission, Mexico
CSDR	Child Survival and Development Revolution
DANIDA	Danish International Development Agency
Ejido	unit of a communal land ownership system, Mexico
EPI	Expanded Programme of Immunization
FAO	Food and Agriculture Organization of the United Nations
FGD	Focus Group Discussion
HIV	human immunodeficiency virus
IBTA	Bolivian Institute of Agricultural and Livestock Technology
IEC	Information, Education, Communication
IMTA	Mexican Institute for Water Technology
IPCC	Intergovernmental Panel on Climate Change
LDP	Local Development Plan, Mexico
NGO	non-governmental organization
ODA	Overseas Development Administration, United Kingdom
ORT	oral rehydration therapy
PRODERITH	Programme of Integrated Rural Development for the Tropical Wetlands, Mexico
RCUT	Regional Communication Unit, Tamuin, Mexico
SAHR	Secretariat for Agriculture and Water Resources, Mexico

UCI	Universal Child Immunization
UCT	Technical Cooperation Unit, Mexico
UN	United Nations Organization
UNDP	United Nations Development Programme
UNESCO	United Nations Educational, Scientific, and Cultural Organization
UNFPA	United Nations Population Fund
UNICEF	United Nations Children's Fund
USAID	United States Agency for International Development
WHO	World Health Organization

Acknowledgements

We were privileged to receive generous support and help from many sources to write this book. UNICEF, UNFPA, and UNESCO provided grants with no strings attached. In addition, FAO and the Government of Mexico contracted us to write a case study of rural communication in that country which would also appear, in shortened form, as a chapter in the book (Chapter 4). Finally, the consultancy company for which we work, Agrisystems (Overseas) Ltd of the United Kingdom, supported us and gave us the time we needed for the task. We are deeply grateful to all of the individuals in those organizations who had enough faith in the project to back us in this way. We particularly want to mention Mehr Khan, Stirling Scruggs, Carlos Arnaldo, Silvia Balit, and David Hopkins.

Before starting the book, we were fortunate to be commissioned by UNICEF and WHO to carry out a survey among decision-makers in international development agencies to ascertain their opinions about communication for development. We interviewed about forty very high-level staff for this survey, and we subsequently found that many interviewees had made comments or expressed ideas that were of significance for the book. We thank them all for the time they devoted to talking to us and for their valuable opinions, but in particular, we must single out Ismail Serageldin and Kathryn Marshall of the World Bank, who are extensively quoted in this book, David Nabarro of ODA, and the late James P. Grant of UNICEF.

We received help from numerous other people. The interviewees and others who provided information for the various case studies that make up Part II of the book are unfortunately too numerous to mention by name, for they run into the hundreds. The contributions of all were vitally important to us, but for their particular commitment in providing us with information and opinions when we asked for them, and sometimes spontaneously, we would like to mention the late Patricia Anzola, Hernando Bernal, Manuel Calvelo, the late Erskine Childers, Santiago Funes, Luis Masias, Sergio Sangines, Haryono Suyono, and O. J. Sykes.

Our thanks are also due to the organizations that allowed us to include material that was originally written for them. Chapter 3 is an abbreviated version of a case study written for UNICEF, and Chapter 4 and the part of Chapter 5 describing *The Archers* were first written for FAO.

We wish to make special mention of two fundamental works that we drew on as source material for Chapter 1. They are *Preparing for the Twenty-First Century* by Paul Kennedy and *The Third Revolution* by Paul Harrison. The enormous research efforts that went into both of these outstanding books compel profound admiration. Other basic sources of information were UNICEF's annual publications *The State of the World's Children* and *The Progress of Nations* as well as UNFPA's annual *The State of World Population*.

The bibliography was created for us from a suitcase of books and documents we dropped on Eugenia Pieschacon's doorstep. We thank her for this labour of love.

We wish to give special thanks to Céline Baker, Rosemarie Clarke, and David Hopkins for the time and trouble they took to read the first draft of this book and for their valuable comments.

Emma Sinclair-Webb, our editor, deserves our gratitude for her support and interest in this book from the stage when it was just an idea. She was always a source of encouragement, but at the same time, she helped to keep us on track with her comments and probing questions.

The printing of the paperback edition of this book was made possible through advance purchases by UNFPA, UNICEF, UNESCO, Deutsche Gesellschaft für Technische Zusammenarbeit (GTZ), and Worldview International Foundation. We are particularly grateful to them because the existence of a paperback version and its distribution by these institutions will allow the book to reach many more people than it would have as a hardback only.

Authors' Note

In this book we envision how communication could help societies engender the changes and development necessary for a better and more secure future on earth. We do admit to a certain professional bias, but this is probably a natural consequence of our combined total of more than fifty years of work in development, and in communication for it.

Perhaps some readers may find our views Utopian, but we believe that they should be put forward because we are convinced of the need for radical change by people at all levels and in various walks of life. We trust that these views will at least provide food for thought; if they also lead to action, especially among some influential people, so much the better. In hoping this, we quote the memorable words of Margaret Mead: 'Never doubt that a small group of thoughtful, committed citizens can change the world; indeed, it is the only thing that ever has.'

Change for the Next Century

Part One will identify the need for human change and development at different levels of society for creating a sustainable and better future on earth and the role of communication in these processes.

CHAPTER I

The Panorama for Change

Any rational reflection about the present and future, as we approach the end of the twentieth century, must conclude that humankind faces unprecedented threats to its well-being, and perhaps even to its survival. The growing numbers of people on earth and the way we are already making demands on natural resources are undermining the ecosystems that support us. Global warming, damage to the ozone layer, and acid rain have implications for the whole planet, while at the more local level, pollution of air and water are creating serious harm, including to health. Furthermore, at a time when there are already more than 800 million malnourished people in the world, and when there is an urgent need to produce more food for the burgeoning population, poor land use practices, soil erosion, and deforestation are degrading the natural resources on which that food production depends.

Social systems are also in disarray or decline almost everywhere. Present trends are for the rich countries to get richer and for the poor to get poorer, and the same applies to people. According to the 1996 UNDP Human Development Report, 1.6 billion people in 89 countries are worse off today than they were ten years ago; the gap in per capita income between the industrialized and the developing world tripled between 1960 and 1993; and the net worth of the world's richest 358 people is equal to the combined income of the poorest 45 per cent of the world's population – 2.3 billion people. Such growing disparities threaten the stability of societies, with unpredictable consequences. In addition, violence, human rights violations, drug abuse, AIDS and other phenomena are tearing at the social fabric almost everywhere.

Massive changes are going to be needed if we are to avert the threats to our future. We cannot continue complacently to live and work as we have. This point has been made in several authoritative books, published between 1993 and 1996, in which their authors

3

express deep concern about the future. Among the first of these was Paul Harrison's exhaustively researched work *The Third Revolution*. The essence of Harrison's thesis is that humanity has so far accomplished two major revolutions: the first was the shift from hunting and gathering to agriculture, and the second was the use of fossil fuels, which opened the door for the Industrial Revolution. The third, and current, revolution involves the urgent changes to adapt our production systems and consumption patterns, and the demands made on natural resources by the growing population, to the needs of creating a sustainable world. Failure to achieve this third revolution would have dire consequences.

Richard Leakey, in *The Sixth Extinction*, written with Roger Lewin, states:

> Through continued destruction of biodiversity in the wake of economic development, we could push the natural world over a threshold beyond which it might be unable to sustain, first, itself and, ultimately, us. Unrestrained, Homo sapiens might not only be the agent of the sixth extinction but also risk being one of its victims ... I believe we face a crisis – one of our own making – and if we fail to negotiate it with vision we will lay a curse of unimaginable magnitude on future generations.

Perhaps the view that relates most closely to the theme of our book is that expressed by the historian Paul Kennedy. Towards the end of his book *Preparing for the Twenty-First Century*, he writes: 'If my analysis is roughly correct, the forces for change facing the world could be so far-reaching, complex, and interactive that they call for nothing less than the re-education of humankind.'

In effect, Kennedy's words 're-education of humankind' imply attitudinal and behavioural change on a massive scale; for there can be no doubt that the will and the ability for change among people are of the essence for solving the problems facing humanity and for creating sustainable development, in both developing and industrialized countries.

A prime factor in fostering change and development can be the planned and systematic use of communication to help individuals, communities, and societies to accept and introduce change in a democratic way. Communication is the basis for creating awareness, for consensus building, for generating participation in processes of change and development, for making informed decisions, and for resolving conflicts. It can help individuals to change their attitudes and their behaviour patterns, and it can introduce new ideas and practices into their lives that will improve their economic and social situation, at the same time making a positive impact on society in general.

As Mrs Gro Harlem Brundtland, the ex-prime minister of Norway and chairperson of the World Commission on Environment and Development, said in an interview for a video produced by the Food and Agriculture Organization (FAO):

> Sustainable development is a major challenge for the next century. People are central to that task. The only way we can work for common cause, for common interest, to improve our condition, is really through communication. Basically, it has to do with democracy, with participation, with spreading of knowledge and insight, and ability to take care of our future.

Yet despite such important opinions, the fact that we are living in a period of a communication revolution, and the fact that the theme of this book may appear obvious, in practice the purposive use of communication for change and development remains one of the neglected issues of our times.

Clearly, communication alone is not enough, because resources of infrastructure, new technology, investment, and so on, are also needed. However, in the final analysis, there is hardly a change and development challenge that can be successfully met without attitudinal and behavioural change by people. Whether in population programmes, protection of the environment, proper use and conservation of natural resources, or increasing food production, it is change by people in the way they live and work that in the end will make the difference. And the same is evidently true for curing social ills such as lack of respect for human rights, poverty, violence, drug abuse, and so on.

A typical change and development situation usually calls for attitudinal and behavioural change among different broad sectors of society, beginning with policy- and decision-makers, for on them depends the political will that usually creates the conditions that can favour change in other sectors of society. The service providers, such as health or agricultural extension workers, often need to change as well to become more effective in promoting change among their client populations. And it is, of course, change among large numbers of individuals in society in general that must be the ultimate aim. Communication processes for change involve all these groups in an interrelated way, creating interaction and influence within them and between them.

Let us look at some of the needs for change that appear to exist in the scenario for creating a better and more secure future in the next century and beyond.

Change among Policy-makers

When high-level policy-makers embrace a social objective, many of the factors required for success tend to fall into place, beginning with government structures and services. And endorsement and support from national figures can be used to bring the objective to the attention of the general public as a way of mobilizing their active involvement. But how is such political will created? Sometimes, politicians just need full information about the realities of a situation and the possibilities for improving it to create the will. The task will, of course, be made easier if launching and pursuing a specific social objective will also enhance the politicians' own public image.

In fact, some international development agencies have had considerable success, through communication initiatives with high-level government policy-makers, in setting the scene for concerted social action. This has been the case with UNICEF's interventions at high political levels in favour of children. Child immunization, described in Chapter 3, is one example. Subsequently, the 1990 World Summit for Children – itself achieved only after intense information and communication work by UNICEF – resulted in 150 governments formally committing themselves to set and meet a series of goals for children by the year 2000.

For population, too, information and communication have been the basis for creating policies in many countries, especially since the mid-1970s. Prior to that, many governments in developing countries were in favour of larger populations, and it was only after widespread communication activities, often linked to international conferences, that decision-makers in country after country introduced population policies. As a result, family planning programmes, both governmental and non-governmental, began to flourish, as we shall see in Chapter 6.

However, even if good progress has been made in population programmes in some countries, many others are lagging behind. Decision- and policy-makers often need to be made even more aware of the developmental and environmental implications of population growth in order to reinforce their commitment and determination.

The coming decades are going to see the greatest population growth ever, especially in developing countries, where 95 per cent of it will take place. An illustration of the exponential process of population increase is the number of years taken to add each billion people since humankind originated. The first billion took thousands of years and was finally achieved in about 1820; the second took about 110 years and was reached in 1930; the third took 30 years and was reached in 1960; the fourth took 14 years and was reached in 1974; and the fifth took 13 years and was reached in 1987. The sixth billion will take only 10–11 years and will be reached in 1997–98. According to UN projections, population stability will be reached only in about the year 2050, when world population will be at least 7.9 billion and could be as high as 11.9 billion. Achieving the lower of these two projections would make an enormous difference to the possibility of creating a sustainable world, and political will must be an essential factor in doing so. Africa, already the poorest continent and the one with the highest population growth rate, has the most critical situation. Its present population of just over 700 million could more than double to reach 1.58 billion by 2025.

The UN International Conference on Population and Development held in Cairo in 1994 produced a Programme of Action which points out that efforts to slow population growth, to reduce poverty, to achieve economic progress, to improve environmental protection, and to reduce unsustainable production and consumption patterns are all mutually reinforcing. Even the difference of a single decade in achieving fertility rates – the number of children a woman bears in her lifetime – that stabilize the population in a country can make a considerable difference in reducing poverty, in protecting and repairing the environment, and in laying the foundation for sustainable development. Governments hold the prime responsibility for putting this Programme of Action into effect. Its impact will be nil without their commitment and active involvement in mobilizing resources and their societies around population and its related issues, as spelled out in Cairo.

Solving the problems of environmental protection and the sustainable use of natural resources calls for much more political will than governments have generated so far. The USA, with 4 per cent of the world's population, burns 25 per cent of the world's production of oil. New taxes on energy use, beginning with gasoline, have been discussed as a first step to doing something about this disproportionate consumption and the atmospheric pollution it causes. But no recent American administration has had the political will to take such a step.

Similarly, the United States is the biggest producer of the greenhouse gases that are responsible for global warming, accounting for more than 20 per cent of all the world's output. It would therefore seem logical for the USA to take a lead in proposing and adopting measures to reduce CO_2 emissions, but the opposite was the case until recently. During the run-up to the UN Conference on Environment and Development (the 'Earth Summit' held in Rio de Janeiro in 1992), many other industrialized countries indicated their willingness to set binding targets for CO_2 emissions, but the Bush administration refused to accept any need for such targets. It was only in July 1996, during a meeting of the Intergovernmental Panel on Climate Change (IPCC) in Geneva, that the US administration changed its stance and urged firm commitments and quicker action to curb greenhouse gas emissions.

Of course, many industrialized countries have now introduced legislation and are making large investments to clean up their air and waters. Today, it is the countries of Asia, with their enormous populations and needs, who are at the forefront of rapid and environmentally damaging development as they follow the patterns that created jobs and wealth in Europe, the USA, and Japan in the past. As countries like China and India press ahead with their industrial development, they cannot afford to invest simultaneously in environmental protection measures.

More political will is needed to curb the effects of industrialization on the biosphere. One school of thought is that the rich countries should provide support and technology to developing countries whose industrialization is becoming a major factor. However, controls on greenhouse gas emissions are needed everywhere, but this is a politically sensitive issue because they are bound to be unpopular with the electorate and with certain business interests. Perhaps another reason many governments have been hesitant about taking action is that, for the early part of the 20 years since global warming as a result of human activity was first identified, scientists held divergent opinions about it. But erratic weather patterns since the 1980s have given the global warming theory added credibility, for they are what many scientists had been predicting it would cause.

Furthermore, the IPCC, created in 1989, held a meeting in Rome in December 1995 at which scientists from more than one hundred countries affirmed that human activity was playing a notable part in climate change. In addition, the Climate Research Unit at the University of East Anglia in Great Britain states that the average surface temperature of the earth has already risen more than 1.5°C since 1860. Some scientists say that this is still within the range of normal variation, or that the computer models are wrong, but on balance, evidence is accumulating that the greenhouse effect and global warming are real and threatening.

If no solutions are found, the consequences could be disastrous. Most specialists agree that world food production would be reduced by lower rainfall in many of today's major grain-growing areas and by the spread of pests curbed until now by cold winters. And the issue of rising sea levels, caused by the expansion of water as it gets warmer, and by the addition of melt water from glacial rivers, has been attracting much attention. About 90 per cent of the earth's ice is in Antarctica. There, probably because of warming that has already taken place, a huge piece of the floating Larsen Ice Shelf – measuring 48 miles by 22 miles and 300 feet thick – broke off in 1995 and drifted out to sea.

Such an event does not, in itself, cause the sea level to rise – floating ice displaces the same amount of water as it contains. The real concern is about the huge amounts of ice now resting on top of the Antarctic land mass. At present, they are held in place by the damming effect of the floating ice shelves close to the land. If these begin regularly to break off, as did the piece of the Larsen Ice Shelf, their stabilizing influence would be removed and the ice lying on the land would be free to flow gradually, like glaciers, into the sea.

If present warming trends continue, the IPCC has forecast a rise of 1°C to 3.5°C in the earth's surface temperatures by the year 2100. This would cause sea levels to rise at least 15 centimetres and possibly as much as 95 centimetres. If the highest prediction were to be fulfilled, people living on atolls such as the Maldives would be displaced, as would about 10 per cent of the population of Bangladesh, which the UN expects to have increased to 196 million by the year 2025. Overall about 200 million people from low-lying delta areas and atolls would lose their homes. Vast areas of land would be lost everywhere, in industrialized countries too. The USA could lose 20,000 square kilometres of land worth about US$650 billion, and Britain could lose much of its prime farmland in East Anglia. Even a 50-centimetre rise in sea level would wipe out 15 per cent of Egypt's farmland, and it does not have enough to feed its people even today.

Despite this potentially threatening situation, the voluntary and modest target set by many industrialized countries during the Rio de Janeiro Earth Summit of reducing greenhouse gas emissions to their 1980 levels by the year 2000 will not be met. The political will actually to introduce the necessary changes still seems weak, with governments preferring in practice to believe those scientists who say that nothing needs to be done for the moment and that even the year 2020 will provide time enough to reduce emissions. The opposite view is that it would be better to begin earlier, with gradual changes, than wait until a crash programme is necessary. Some experts are also concerned that climate changes could accelerate suddenly and not leave time for the necessary adjustments.

Lack of political will, leading to inadequate government policies, may also be implicated in the degradation of natural resources that is taking place all around us. Soil erosion in Bolivia is one example. A drive through the highlands in that country shows hillside after hillside so barren that they can no longer produce crops. And the degradation process continues as farmers go further and further to find land to cultivate, often on even steeper slopes. Yet despite the horrific erosion problems in the country, the Bolivian Institute for Agricultural and Livestock Technology (IBTA) has no programme in soil conservation – and this is the national agricultural research organization that has been receiving major support from the World Bank.

The gravity of environmental degradation in rural areas needs to be better communicated to all concerned. Understanding should begin with government echelons because urgently needed measures of conservation farming will not be put into practice unless there are policies and mechanisms to support them.

Land distribution and agricultural production policies can also cause degradation of natural resources. In Honduras a few years ago, one of us (C.F.) saw a fertile and flat valley floor taken up by an enormous ranch with fenced fields and magnificent Santa Gertruda cattle. Just a few kilometres further on, in a village clinging to the slopes above the valley, the underemployed peasants were scratching a living from steep plots hacked out of the forest. The erosion damage was clearly evident, and the malnourished children and general poverty of the villagers were heart-wrenching.

The ranch was owned by a general who was exporting prime beef to the United States where it could be sold slightly cheaper than the home-produced equivalent. Since beef ranching requires very little labour, the general was not even providing jobs for the local people. In such a situation, the people have no choice but to degrade natural resources in their search for survival.

The case of Brazilian government policy in favour of agricultural development is well known. For many years, subsidies were paid to people to start ranching and farming in the interior, in effect promoting deforestation. The policy was changed only quite recently, as a result of pressure that used information about the global importance of the Brazilian rainforests.

Food production and the elimination of hunger and malnutrition are other areas in which there is an evident lack of political will, as emerged during the World Food Summit organized by FAO and held in Rome in November 1996. The technical background documents drawn up for that summit estimated that today some 841 million people, or about 20 per cent of the population in developing countries, are 'food-energy deficient', or in plain words, hungry. The cause of so much hunger is generally the fact that the poor do not have the buying power to purchase the food they need, rather than a global food shortage.

However, even the question of total food availability in the future is subject to doubt. Although FAO predicts that global food production can probably increase more or less in pace with the extra demands of growing population, other specialists like Lester Brown of the Worldwatch Institute are less optimistic. They believe we are running out of technologies for raising crop yields, that there will be insufficient water for irrigation, and that social disintegration, political instability, and environmental degradation will adversely affect agriculture. In fact, recent years have brought a deteriorating balance between world supply and demand for cereals, so there have been less carry-over stocks in reserve each year. FAO itself, taking this into account, states that it is legitimate to ask whether the 'fundamentals have changed significantly, whether ... even the limited progress foreseen for up to 2010 can be achieved', and identifies the 'strong risk of outright stagnation or reversals in several of the most needy nations'.

The political and social implications of hunger, especially the relationship between food and peace, have been recognized for millennia, as witnessed by the Old Testament of the Bible: 'And it shall come to pass that when they shall be hungry, they shall fret themselves and curse their King and their God' (Isaiah 8: 21). And as Lord Boyd Orr, the Scottish nutritionist, great crusader against hunger, first director-general of FAO, and winner of the Nobel Peace Prize in 1949, said pointedly, 'You can't build peace on empty stomachs.' Yet despite the political, social, and economic implications of so many hungry and malnourished in the world, the Action Plan from the World Food Summit agreed to by world leaders sets the objective only of reducing the number of hungry to around 400 million by the year 2015.

Fidel Castro, one of the many heads of state who spoke at the summit, was the only dissident voice. He scorned 'the modesty of these goals as shameful'. He called into question the ethical values and conscience of a world that still spends US$700 billion a year on arms, even after the end of the Cold War, yet fails to invest properly in eliminating hunger and poverty and in reversing the degradation of our natural resources. He finished his unusually short, but impassioned, plea with the words: 'The bells that presently toll for those starving to death every day will tomorrow toll for the whole of humanity, which did not want to, know how to, or have the wisdom to save itself from itself.'

According to FAO, it would need just US$13 per hungry person per year to abolish the problem, hardly an impossible target. The Action Plan of the World Food Summit puts much stress on creating the political, economic, and social environment that could eradicate poverty and ensure food for all. However, to achieve this will require major structural, economic, and social changes in many countries, and once again, this brings us back to our original issue of attitudinal and behavioural change. And until the political will is there, based on a vision similar to that of Castro, it will be impossible to agree on the more ambitious objective of providing food for all, and at the same time helping to set the scene for peace and stability.

Food security for all could be widely assured if poverty could be eliminated. Even during famines, food is usually available if people have the money to buy it. This was the case in Ethiopia in 1984–85, and also during the great Irish famine of the nineteenth century, caused by blight in the potato crop, when Ireland continued to export grain and meat to England. But poverty has been increasing rather than reducing. At least in part this is because policy tendencies of recent years towards market economies have the built-in factor of what the UN calls 'social Darwinism', or survival only for the most able. This is widening the already enormous gulf that separates rich and poor everywhere; even in the USA, according to a Labour Department report of February 1996, the median wage for full-time workers, adjusted for inflation, had dropped 3 per cent compared to 1979. It was also reported in 1996 that the top pay for corporate executives in the USA was almost two hundred times the pay of the average worker, whereas 20 years earlier it was 40 times more.

With regard to poverty in developing countries, James Gustav Speth, the administrator of UNDP, wrote in an article published in 1996 that it is a myth that 'the early stages of economic growth are inevitably associated with growing inequality within a given country. There is no iron law of development that makes this so. Equitable growth is not only ideal in the abstract, it is efficient – and it is possible in the real world.' Speth cited economies in Asia that have had rapid growth and relatively low inequality. Malaysia, for example, has boosted its income by more than 7 per cent a year during the past two decades, but it also took steps to achieve equity, and it reduced its incidence of poverty from 49 per cent of the population to 14 per cent between 1970 and 1993. He also wrote that 'there is no automatic link between growth and human development – a simple fact that is often forgotten by growth advocates. Such a link must be deliberately forged by governments and regularly fortified by skilful and intelligent policies.' Speth concluded: 'If current trends are not quickly corrected, economic disparities will move from inequitable to inhuman, from unacceptable to intolerable.'

There are about 1.3 billion people wordwide living in absolute poverty, that is to say people who cannot meet their basic needs. About a third of the population in developing countries are in this category, and even in the USA and the European Community, 15 per cent of the population are living below nationally determined poverty levels. On the face of it, the problem of poverty might appear insoluble, but the World Bank has estimated that it would require only 1 per cent of developing countries' consumption to abolish extreme poverty, which it defines as an income of less than US$275 per person per year. Furthermore, it would require a transfer of just 3 per cent of the total consumption in developing countries to eliminate poverty in general, defined as an income of less than US$370 per person per year. Poverty and its related social disintegration were key themes at the World Summit on Social Development held in Copenhagen in 1995. That summit called for changes in policies to tackle the problem of poverty seriously.

It is not uncommon for policies and budgets of specific social services to be completely out of tune with the basic needs of most of a country's people. Nigeria in the early 1980s provides an

interesting example of this. At that time, only 2 per cent of the
national budget was being devoted to health, and 80 per cent of this
was being allocated to 12 teaching hospitals that catered for only 6
per cent of the population. High-technology health services were
benefiting mainly the elite in the cities, and primary health care hardly
existed. It was not surprising that four children out of ten were dying
before reaching five years of age. UNICEF used a communication
strategy to help the government redefine some of its priorities and
favour actions for child survival, as described in Chapter 3.

   This type of process is not easy, even when working with a theme
as appealing as children. And if the theme involves hard and perhaps
unpopular decisions from policy-makers it is even more difficult, for
in democratic societies, political leaders often seem to shun taking
decisions and establishing policies that might negatively affect their
chances of re-election. Ricardo Díez-Hochleitner, the president of
the Club of Rome, which first gained renown for its 1972 publication
The Limits to Growth, made some interesting comments on politicians
in a 1997 interview with journalist Michael Gleich. Díez-Hochleitner,
while stressing the radical and dramatic change needed for our future,
said that politicians hardly played a leading role in his scenarios for
that change. 'They are just hostages to the electorate, always ready
to present the public with simple solutions that are as convenient as
possible and don't hurt anybody,' he said.

   However, if one looks at that statement from the other side, it
becomes evident that politicians will also feel the need to respond
if they are pushed by their electorate. In fact, democratic societies
often function and adapt to needs and circumstances through the
influence of pressure groups. In the past, such groups have sparked
the fire of great movements that have radically changed the way
whole societies perceive a social issue and behave about it. One
early example was the movement against slavery led by William
Wilberforce in Britain at the end of the eighteenth century and in
the first quarter of the nineteenth. More recently, we have seen
mass movements that have had radical impact in changing attitudes
and action in areas such as colonialism, women's liberation, civil
rights, and apartheid. Governments therefore need to be helped to
take hard decisions by pressure from voters.

   Information and communication about major issues are the means
by which political will for change can be generated, either by direct
intervention with policy-makers or by empowering people who can
then exert pressure to force changes in national policies.

Change among Service Providers

Teachers, health workers, agricultural extension – or assistance – staff (referred to as extentionists) and others whose job is to act as agents of change have a key role, for they have continuous contact with the people and are, in effect, the front-line troops in the struggle for development. Yet their importance is seldom recognized, so they are usually on the lowest rung of their ministry's career ladder, and are paid accordingly. In addition, they seldom have the background or support they need to do their job properly. They rarely have formal training in human relations and communication skills, in principles of adult education, and in group work and dynamics.

These, of course, are issues of government policy. However, both governmental and non-governmental service providers involved in helping people towards change and development often need to change their own attitudes and behaviour to be fully effective. Traditionally, technical staff working to help communities, especially the underprivileged, have shown attitudes of superiority and a lack of empathy that have been an obstacle to effective work. A crucial element for more success in future will be to eliminate the essentially autocratic – or in development jargon 'top-down' – approach that has dominated most past work by technical staff with the people they are supposedly helping.

Without changes in attitude and behaviour among service providers, proper communication with their 'clients', and creation of the necessary trust and confidence between them, will not be achieved. We, the authors, have lived at first hand many of the problems that exist between technical advisers and their clients. In 1995, for example, we worked in a team conducting a study for the design of a new technical assistance – or extension – system for farmers in Bolivia. As a first step, and so that the system could be based on farmers' real needs, we decided to find out what their experience had been with agricultural technicians who worked with them and what they would expect from a new system.

We trained a small team of Bolivians to do what are called Focus Group Discussions, a qualitative research method to determine people's attitudes, ideas, experiences and opinions about a certain topic. After 80 of these Focus Group Discussions, involving almost a thousand farmers in different parts of the country, we had detailed and remarkably homogeneous information about the experience that farmers had with technical advisers. The farmers were in agreement on the following points:

- Technical advisers thought that only their own opinions had value, and they did not listen to farmers' opinions and experiences.
- They did not understand the culture of the farming communities they were working with, and they rarely spoke the local language.
- They did not understand the farming conditions in which they worked.
- They were too theoretical in their advice and training work.
- They were unreliable and did not fulfil their commitment to visit the community on the day agreed during their previous visit, so farmers lost much time waiting around for them.
- They spent too little time with the farmers when they did come to the community.
- They persuaded farmers to buy expensive inputs but then failed to follow up to ensure their correct use.
- They usually ignored the women farmers and worked only with the men.
- They tended to work with privileged farmers, for example those with irrigation, and ignored the rest.

In Uganda, where we did similar research with farmers in 1993, the same sort of criticisms emerged, but they were even more strongly expressed. The Ugandan farmers had two additional complaints: the first was that they hardly ever saw an extensionist, and when one did turn up, it was only to count their livestock or coffee bushes as a basis for calculating the tax they had to pay; the second was that some extensionists tried to persuade farmers to pay them for visits and advice when they were already being paid a salary by the government. From field experience in many countries, we believe that similar research would produce similar results almost everywhere.

The health sector suffers from the same sort of problems with its staff. In Bolivia in the early 1990s, when one of us (S.R.-E.) worked there in communication for safe motherhood, research showed that many mothers did not come to the clinics for the birth of their children because of the attitudes of the medical staff. Traditionally, rural women in Bolivia deliver their children at home with their husbands present, in a squatting position, and in cosy surroundings. But in the clinics, the medical staff were working against these cultural traditions: they forbade the husbands to be present at the birth, insisted on a supine position for delivery, and did nothing to alleviate the cold, white-tiled, and brightly lit atmosphere. Not surprisingly, women were rejecting the clinics' services, preferring to run the higher risks of their traditional ways of childbearing.

We have found similar situations in quite different parts of the world, sometimes in countries that have invested enormous amounts in health services that remained under-utilized because the design of the services, as well as the attitudes of the health workers, did not take into account the cultural context. For example, Algeria used much of its gas revenues to build hospitals and clinics all over the country. You can be driving through the desert, come over a sand dune, and see the palm trees and traditional dwellings of an oasis spread before you, but the scene is dominated by a large and recently built hospital. For many years, people were reluctant to come to these new hospitals because the appearance of modern medicine, the white coats and the white-tiled walls, made for a strange and intimidating environment. This was worsened by the attitudes of the staff, who had never received the training in human relations and interpersonal communication that would have helped breed confidence among the population.

In truth, this sort of situation has been commonest in government health services, whereas NGOs have often been more sensitive to the needs and perceptions of their client populations. This is certainly the case of the community clinics in Indonesia run by an NGO called Yayasan Kusuma Buana, which can be translated as 'Harmonious Family Foundation'.

We visited one of their clinics in late 1994, in a residential area of low-to-medium income level in Jakarta. It had been set up in a family house, and it had been deliberately left to look like one because consultation with the community had shown that this was what they wanted. So the clinic has no hospital atmosphere; no one wears a white coat; there are no white tiles; the staff have been trained to listen to people and talk with them; consulting hours are set to meet people's availability before or after work; members of a patient's family can bring meals from home if they wish; mothers can give birth in the clinic or be attended at home if they prefer, and so on. In this way, the facility, although well equipped to provide modern medical care, maintains a homely familiarity.

The guiding spirit behind this initiative is Dr Firmin Lubis, who emanates human warmth and understanding. His total commitment to providing health services to families in the way *they* want them is impressive. As one sits with him in easy chairs in the entrance area, drinking tea, people from the community wander casually in and out. They are obviously at ease, enjoying the friendly atmosphere and a chat with the staff. The psychological barrier that so easily separates high-technology medical services and staff from the lowly educated has been overcome by a deliberate strategy of consultation with people and responding to their needs, with the result that the clinic has become a valued part of their lives.

Communication between technical specialists and those receiving their services is fraught with inherent difficulties that can prevent the building of a successful working relationship. This is especially so in the case of agricultural extension, when a first and serious obstacle may well be differences in age and experience. Extension workers are often young and without any real practical skills. In the field, they may find themselves with older farmers who have had a lifetime of practical farming and who have an instinctive mistrust of book learning. Furthermore, age commands respect in many societies, and so the young extensionist may easily feel himself at a disadvantage. Extensionists may also feel isolated and underprivileged within their ministry of agriculture and have very little job satisfaction, so they may need to find gratification and self-esteem in other ways. Because of this, extensionists may try to establish their authority by dressing more formally than the farmers, and by assuming an attitude of superiority, a poor start for establishing a working relationship.

Differences of educational level are another cause of the communication problems, especially if the farmer is illiterate. A barrier is created by the fact that a technician's logic normally comes from his education, whereas a farmer's logic comes mainly from his traditions and experience. Getting on to the same wavelength will need special skills and efforts. In fact, to understand the farmer's logic and way of thinking is one of the main challenges that face a technician, and it is not always easy to find out what is in farmers' hearts and minds. They may be reluctant to express themselves to outsiders and have difficulty doing so. One of us (C.F.) had an experience that is a good example of how difficult it may be to get true information from farmers, and of how important it may be to have it.

For many years, I trained mid-career professionals, mainly working for their governments, who were attending courses in various aspects of agricultural development at a centre in Northern Italy. During my sessions on communication, I routinely made the point that if farmers *do* something, or do *not* do something, there is always a good reason in their minds. When I made that pronouncement in one course, a man from the Ivory Coast said that he did not think this was always true. He said that there was a valley in his country where it had been demonstrated that rice could be grown with good results, but that despite a good market for rice, the farmers refused to grow it. He said that they must be stupid.

I replied that I was sure they were not stupid and asked what had been done to find out why they would not grow rice. With great emphasis to drive home the importance of the event, the course member said that the national director of agricultural extension in person had spent two hours in the village talking to the people, but that they would not tell him anything. I told him that I thought his director of extension was probably about the last person the villagers would talk openly to, but that there was surely a good reason. I suggested that they send two young extension workers, or graduate students in social sciences, to spend some time in the village, to establish a rapport with the people, and to do some gentle probing.

I heard no more until about six months later when I was again in the Italian training centre with another course, and again there were participants from the Ivory Coast. I remembered what had happened in the previous course and asked if they had found out why people in that valley refused to grow rice. One of them replied, with an embarrassed laugh, that they now knew the reason, but he hesitated to tell us because of the mixed company. However, the whole course was soon howling for him to continue, so he explained that they had sent two young extension workers to live in the village. One evening, after about three weeks, a group of villagers and the two extension workers were sitting around drinking beer and talking when the subject of rice-growing near the river came up quite naturally.

Immediately, a woman in the group said emphatically that if her husband went down to the river to grow rice, she would go to another village to find another husband. From the conversation that followed, it became clear that all the women of the village believed that if their men grew rice by the river they would become sexually impotent. There was great merriment in that lecture room in Italy. I remarked that, in their minds at least, the people had a very good reason for not growing rice. The fellow from the Ivory Coast asked what they should do next, and I suggested they try to find four or five couples from the village who could be persuaded to grow rice and demonstrate that the fear of impotence had no basis in reality.

A few months later, I was in Tunis helping with a course in

communication for health. One day at lunch I was sitting next to a man from the Ministry of Health in the Ivory Coast, and I remembered what had happened in the two sessions in Italy with his colleagues from the Ministry of Agriculture. I told him the story in full, and when I had finished, he said dryly,

'The women are right.'

'You must be joking!' I exclaimed.

'No, I'm not,' he answered. 'I know that area very well. It is full of bilharziasis and anyone paddling around in water to grow rice would be certain to pick it up. One of the main effects of that parasite is to make people feel tired and listless. Their sex life would certainly suffer.'

If the Ministry of Agriculture staff had had the proper respect for those villagers, instead of dismissing them as stupid, and if they had had the communication skills needed to do qualitative research, they would have found out much earlier what was causing the resistance to rice growing. Perhaps a joint venture with the Ministry of Health to eradicate bilharziasis and promote rice production at the same time would have produced the results the government was hoping for.

Fundamentally, that problem in the Ivory Coast was caused by a lack of respect for the values and beliefs of rural people. This is quite a common attitude in developing countries. Technicians with modern training often forget that rural people living in areas such as the fringes of the Sahara or high in the Andes have managed to survive there for centuries, against all odds and in extremely adverse conditions. So they must have been doing something right, using traditional technology that has developed over centuries.

This traditional technology and way of doing things should arouse interest and respect among modern agriculturists, but all too often it is dismissed as backward or not worthy of attention. There is a tragi-comic example of this from our experience in Bolivia. The Bolivian Institute for Agricultural and Livestock Technology (IBTA) was asked by an NGO to conduct field demonstrations in an area of the Altiplano with some new varieties of quinua that IBTA had developed. (Quinua is a cereal that is native to the high Andes and has a far higher protein content than most other cereals.) IBTA technicians duly turned up and quickly sowed several demonstration plots with the new varieties.

Quinua is particularly sensitive to rainfall after sowing, and if the soil dries out in the days after it has germinated, it dies. In the case of the demonstration plots, it rained shortly after sowing, the seeds germinated, and then dry weather killed the seedlings. The farmers, of course, were not impressed by these new and 'wonderful' varieties. But what the technicians ignored, or perhaps never knew, was that precisely because of quinua's need for consistent soil moisture in the period after sowing, the peasants of the Andes have developed a centuries-old insurance strategy of always planting their quinua in three phases spread over several weeks. In this way, they try to ensure that at least one of the sowings will get the right rainfall conditions to survive and produce. Once again, a lack of communication – or more precisely an attitude of unwillingness to listen and learn from farmers – was the cause of the setback.

Similar lack of genuine interest in farmers' ways of doing things and of consultation with them may also affect agricultural research programmes. Researchers often work in their own scientific world, more interested in earning prestige among their peers than in learning about farmers' problems and trying to resolve them. For example, there is the case of a high-yielding variety of sorghum developed in Ghana. Like all high-yielding cereal varieties, it had short and stiff straw, or stems, so that large quantities of fertilizer could be applied to it without it growing so tall that it would lodge, or be beaten to the ground by wind and rain. However, the researchers were surprised to find that, despite its high grain yield, almost no farmers wanted to grow it. They had not taken into account that sorghum stems are an important and valuable building material in rural Ghana, and the short-strawed variety was useless for this purpose. In summary, research and extension systems have often been the antithesis of true communication, with very little participation from farmers in determining what research work is needed.

Similar examples could be cited for health and other development sectors. Hierarchies and attitudinal problems are often the root cause. In most developing countries, respect for hierarchy is extreme, so people working at the field level feel inferior to their supervisors and more highly trained technicians. And in fact, the field workers are usually treated as inferiors. In many government services, therefore, common sense and reporting on the reality of a situation are thrown to the wind if to speak out could possibly upset a superior. Special efforts are needed to break down these hierarchical attitudes and to create a sense of mutual respect, teamwork, and joint ownership among all levels involved in change and development.

Sometimes this may involve only one development sector, say

health, but very often it means bringing together a variety of sectors. Traditional bureaucratic rivalries need to be overcome to create coordination and a shared sense of purpose in which each sector and its role is properly recognized and appreciated, a team that will share the sense of achievement when the programme succeeds. Some examples of how hierarchies were broken down and multidisciplinary coordination and teamwork created for child immunization and for integrated rural development are described in Chapters 3 and 4.

In conclusion, technical and managerial staff need excellent communication skills and appropriate attitudes to work successfully for change and development. Training in communication skills could considerably improve technicians' abilities to relate to their client populations, and also improve working relations among colleagues of all levels and sectors.

Changes among Individuals in Society

The purpose of change among policy-makers and service providers is, of course, to set the scene and promote change among the population in general, for it is only when societies change that the real benefits in sustainable improvements in the quality of life can begin to accrue. Changes in the way individuals work and produce is one obvious need, and the use of water in farming is one good example. According to Ismail Serageldin, the vice-president of the World Bank for Environmentally Sustainable Development, of all the water used by humans, about 70 per cent goes to irrigation. But 45 per cent of that water never reaches the plants in the field because of poor irrigation techniques.

At present it takes 2,000 tons of water to produce just one ton of rice, yet at the same time, 80 countries are already facing water shortages, and 40 per cent of the world's population does not have access to supplies of safe water. In addition, there is serious concern about water availability for future food production. Irrigated areas now produce 40 per cent of the world's food on 17 per cent of the cultivated land, and experts believe that 80 per cent of the extra food required in the coming years will have to come from irrigated farming.

According to Serageldin, farmers must learn to use irrigation water better, and people in general need to change their attitudes towards water. It can no longer be taken for granted, as it too often is. People need to understand the water system of our planet, and water issues need to be debated among the various stakeholders.

The way farmers use land is also a major cause of degradation all over the world, and it is continuing at a rapid pace. In Ethiopia, the African country with the most serious erosion damage, the highlands have been degraded by overcrowding and poor land use. At the end of the last century, 40 per cent of the country was covered by forest; by the middle of this century, this had been reduced to 16 per cent; and today it is only about 1 per cent. In the mid-1980s, an FAO/World Bank study estimated that an average of 100 tons of soil per hectare were being washed into the Nile every year. The degradation is so rapid that for today's children, over a third of the highlands could become incapable of producing crops in their lifetime.

Even in areas of the world already ravaged by erosion, and where peasant farmers have to go further and further from their homes to find land to till, most of them still plant their crops up and down the slopes. In fact, farmers' use of land resources is critical for sustainable agriculture and future food supplies, but their behaviour patterns may be deep-rooted. For example, we were once travelling along a road in Bolivia that crossed high on a mountainside with aerial views across the valley on to a potato research centre. All the land of the centre was cropped along the slope contours, but despite this demonstration, the farmers' plots surrounding the centre were all tilled up and down the slope in their traditional way. But erosion does not only exist in developing countries, and with 'backward' farmers: even in the USA, almost half of all cropland is losing soil faster than it is being created by nature.

Changes in production and technical areas are no more important for the future than the ability of societies to adapt and grow. As Jean-Claude Paye, the secretary-general of the Organization for Economic Cooperation and Development (OECD), wrote in an article published in the *International Herald Tribune* in June 1995:

> Lasting economic growth is built on productivity, which depends on innovation, the ability to adjust, to restructure and to streamline – all of which involve people. People need to acquire new skills, find new jobs, be flexible and mobile. Society needs to be cohesive and adaptive. The human mind is our greatest hope for more security and a better standard of living. It can be an equally powerful break. Leaders ... need to focus on society's fraying fabric. If the warp of societal well-being is economic growth, the weft is people who embrace and anticipate momentous change.

In the end, it is change by individuals that could bring the societal

changes necessary for greater security and well-being. In the case of
population growth, for example, it is decisions taken by couples that
will finally make the difference. They need to be helped to make
informed choices about the implications of family size, unwanted
pregnancies, and methods of contraception, but this involves much
more than just sending out messages. Rather, it involves learning
from people and their leaders how to make such issues socially
acceptable and worthy of urgent action.

In all social areas, communication research is needed to gain
insight into people's underlying attitudes before they can be helped
to change them for their own benefit and that of society. Then,
based on these insights, carefully tailored communication and information activities are required to help to bring about change.

Drug abuse certainly lends itself to much more communication
work. Over the last 30 years, there has been a dramatic worldwide
increase in the access to drugs and their use. Statistics about the
drug industry are hard to obtain, but the UN Drug Control Programme (UNDCP) estimates that it has an annual turnover globally
of about US$500 billion, which puts it in the same league as the
petroleum industry. Only the arms industry is significantly larger.

Drug abuse is expanding especially rapidly in developing countries.
For example, in Pakistan in the mid-1960s, drug abuse was mainly
limited to traditional opium smoking. But in the mid-1980s, heroin
addiction began to take hold, and starting from about 10,000 addicts
in those years, the number grew to 1.5 million by 1994. According
to the UNDCP estimate of an 8 per cent annual growth, it will top
2.5 million by the year 2000.

Most of the current war on drugs is based on reducing supplies
rather than on reducing demand. If one has worked and lived in
countries that produce drug crops, and where the small farmers
who grow them have little alternative for gaining a decent livelihood,
one must have sympathy with those who say that as long as there
is a demand for drugs, someone will produce and deal in them. But
illicit drugs worsen many of the world's problems. They impact on
employment, productivity, the spread of AIDS, the environment,
local armed conflicts, and on social well-being and stability in general.
In addition, they distort economies, political and judicial systems,
and moral and social values.

Surely, the drug problem can best be tackled by investing more
money and effort in information, communication, and education to
reduce demand. Furthermore, purposive communication could be

used to help mobilize individuals, communities, and societies against drug abuse and trafficking. Interdiction is not winning the war against drugs, and it must be won because of the future social consequences if it is not. Already today, about a third of black men in the United States between the ages of 20 and 29 are in prison or under the supervision of the criminal justice system, most of them for drug offences. And youth, especially the growing numbers of street children in many parts of the developing world, are addicted to sniffing glue and solvents, which are cheap, easily available, and have a powerful effect. Demographic pressure and the rural exodus are turning many cities into warrens of destitute children caught in a circle of poverty and drug addiction. For them, with no prospects of employment or a productive and decent life, trafficking in drugs offers a means of economic survival, and abuse of drugs offers a temporary escape from reality.

Many countries have indeed devoted resources to trying to reduce demand, and in April 1997, the Clinton administration announced plans to seek an increase of US$818 million, bringing the total it will spend on the drug war in 1998 to a staggering US$16 billion. Of this new money for 1998, it plans to spend some US$620 million on demand reduction through education and treatment. Much more is spent everywhere on interdiction than on education, but in 1995, interdiction succeeded in seizing only 230 metric tonnes of the estimated 780 metric tonnes of cocaine produced worldwide, and 32 of the 300 or so metric tonnes of heroin. This left more than enough to satisfy the markets, and so perhaps much more emphasis should be placed everywhere on demand reduction through communication and education.

Less complex than drug abuse is the prevention of AIDS, a classic case of the need for communication, because with no universal vaccine against HIV available, the only way to block its transmission is through changes in behaviour patterns. Only massive information and education programmes to create more awareness and knowledge about AIDS, and the virus that causes it, can limit transmission. Such programmes have already been taking place in industrialized countries, with some success, but much less has been done in developing countries, where the main threat from AIDS lies.

Communication about AIDS needs to be stepped up everywhere and refined because the problem is expanding rapidly. Even though it was recognized as a specific disease only as recently as 1981, by late 1995 there were already about 18 million adults and about 1.5

million children worldwide infected by HIV. Of these people, about 6 million had actually developed full-blown AIDS. About 6,000 people a day are now becoming infected with HIV, and WHO predicts that among those who carry the virus, only one person in 20 will survive more than 15 years.

WHO forecasts for the future spread of HIV are that, by the end of this century, about 40 million people will be infected, with the number of women infected rising to about 50 per cent of the total, whereas it was only about 20 per cent in the 1980s. The full effects of AIDS in society are still around the corner, but one of the greatest social threats is the number of orphans that it is creating. WHO estimates that worldwide there will be about 8 million children who will have lost their mother, or both parents, by the year 2000. The cost of looking after them – if they are looked after – will be enormous. And if they are not looked after and live in cities, the chances are that they will become street children. In rural areas, especially in Africa, many families who were barely surviving from their subsistence farming are now in a desperate situation after taking in the orphaned children of family members. WHO predicts that by the year 2000 about 95 per cent of the world's HIV carriers will be in developing countries, those that can least afford to deal with the problem.

The complications of AIDS prevention caused by some social behaviour patterns are indicated by a study carried out among male workers in Harare, Zimbabwe, in 1987. It showed that four married men out of five had lovers, and that married men, even when living with their wives, frequented prostitutes more often than single men. AIDS is already the main cause of mortality in Harare, causing 25 per cent of all registered deaths. However, it is not only among the labour force that HIV is rampant. In many African countries, successful men in government or commerce consider it a privilege of their position to enjoy sexual relationships with multiple partners. Many of these economically important people are now dying.

Some beliefs in developing countries lead to behaviour that spreads HIV. For example, one is that a man suffering from AIDS can be cured by having intercourse with a virgin. Another is that women can only become infected by HIV if they are sexually promiscuous. Thus there is no risk, they believe, if they are married and faithful to their husbands. In fact, however, more than half of the women in the world who test HIV positive have been infected by their husbands.

To illustrate the type of belief problem that is common in some countries, there is an example of a 25-year-old woman in Morocco who married a widower of 48. She had never been to school, and she had almost no knowledge of AIDS. From the little she had heard, she believed that it was a 'dirty disease' and that only 'dirty' women could contract it. She thought she was not at risk because she was 'clean'. Her future husband asked for a doctor's certificate of her virginity before marrying her. He knew he had AIDS, but he did not tell her. He died quite soon, leaving her a legacy of HIV.

In one Moroccan hospital, over half of the women being treated for AIDS have never been to school. Messages about AIDS are broadcast by radio and television, and there are also press articles on the subject, but the broadcast information is usually incomprehensible to women with no schooling. Furthermore, the messages are mainly aimed at men, because society is indulgent towards male sexual promiscuity, and also because men have a virtual monopoly on decision making. We suspect that Morocco is far from being the only country in which AIDS information and communication are insufficiently researched and professionally tailored to audience needs.

Behaviour patterns related to intravenous drug abuse also play an important role, either directly or indirectly, in HIV transmission. For example, as a result of direct transmission from infected needles, in Thailand some 40–50 per cent of drug injectors are HIV positive. The indirect role of drug abuse emerges from research in New York City, which showed that in over 80 per cent of the cases of HIV infection through heterosexual relations, there had been a drug injector earlier in the chain of transmission.

The position of women and children in society is mainly determined by attitudes and behaviour towards them. Even where women's rights are recognized by civil and religious laws, in practice, cultural traditions and men's ingrained attitudes towards women often deny them their proper status. For example, under Muslim law, men and women have equal rights in marriage, and in almost all Muslim countries, education for both boys and girls is obligatory. In addition, some countries have introduced laws to offer better job opportunities for women in the public sector. However, these laws have not generally made much difference to the status of women, and little will change as long as the attitudes and behaviour towards women in a society remain as they are.

These problems are certainly not confined to Islamic countries. During a recent assignment in Ecuador, one of us (S.R.-E.) was with a group of trainees practising Focus Group Discussions on the subject of family planning. Given its very personal nature, this is always a difficult subject to handle, but on this occasion, eight lowly-educated, rural women rose to the challenge magnificently. They were forthcoming and frank. Among the things they said was that they were tired of their husbands treating them as sex objects, without any right to decide about the number of children they had, or about the spacing between them. They wanted communication about family planning to be directed at their menfolk, as well as to male adolescents, implying that it was there that attitudinal change had to begin.

Although progress has been made in promoting women's rights, much change is still needed. Globally, about 32 per cent of the work force is made up of women, but only 6 per cent of posts at cabinet level in government are occupied by them. There are 116 countries with no women at these levels of political power, and in Kuwait, Bahrain, and the United Arab Emirates, women can neither stand for election nor vote. The attitudes of men have allowed discriminatory legislation to remain in force in some countries. Women may not be allowed to own property in their own names; they may have no access to credit; they may not be able to negotiate contracts; and sometimes they cannot even exercise their legal rights to inheritance. And this is despite the fact that in many developing countries, rural women produce between 50 and 70 per cent of the nation's food.

The authoritarian attitudes and disrespect of many men towards women is reflected in domestic violence. According to UNICEF, about a quarter of the world's women are violently abused by their husbands or male partners. Community-level surveys put the figure higher: up to 50 per cent in Thailand and even 80 per cent in Pakistan and Chile. In the United States, domestic violence accounts for more hospital admissions of women than rapes, muggings, and road accidents combined. Similar attitudes among men often result in fathers not sending their girl children to school or curtailing their education. According to UNICEF, there are 60 million girls, compared to 40 million boys, not enrolled in primary education in developing countries, and only 36 per cent of girls enrolled in primary school continue through to secondary education.

In the area of health, UNICEF estimates that at least 500,000 women a year die during pregnancy or while giving birth, virtually all of them in developing countries. The vast majority of these deaths could be prevented through relatively simple behavioural change, particularly through women paying more attention to pre-natal health care and to nutrition. During pregnancy, iodine and vitamin A deficiencies and anaemia are very common and may cause health complications for the mother and child. In countries of the Sahel, lack of vitamin A so often causes night blindness among pregnant women that most people consider it a normal condition. They are unaware that it is symptomatic of a serious health condition and that it can be overcome quite simply by regularly eating green vegetables, carrots, or paw-paw, or some liver from time to time. USAID has been supporting a nutrition communication project in several countries to promote this and other behavioural changes. And in its safe-motherhood projects, USAID has been devoting much of the resources to information, education, and communication directed at policy-makers, health staff and the general population.

UNDP, in its background document for the Fourth World Conference on Women, held in Beijing in 1995, stated that sustainable development could not be achieved without the full empowerment, participation, and contribution of women and men, in conditions of equality. In effect, this calls for education and information to promote changes by both men and women: men obviously have to adopt different attitudes, but women must also be prepared to assume their proper role in an equitable relationship with men. In addition, women must learn to stop perpetuating male dominance through the way they bring up their sons.

UNICEF, the most active of all of the UN bodies in communication for development, has been trying to make a dent in the ingrained attitudes of discrimination towards women, beginning with the girl child in certain societies. For example, one of its recent initiatives is the production of a series of cartoon films about a little Asian girl called Meena. She is drawn in such a way that she appears to be generically Asian, to allow her to pass for a local child in a number of countries. The episodes show her being discriminated against in typical everyday situations just because she is a girl. It is hoped that the emotionally moving scenes will start to change attitudes and values concerning girl children.

The UNICEF and USAID communication efforts mentioned here are drops in the bucket, but they are moves in the right direction. Much more will need to be done in the future to bring about the attitudinal and behavioural changes in society that will allow women to develop and use their potential and to play a proper role, in full partnership with men.

The situation of children is just as critical as that of women, and it obviously impinges even more directly on the future. UNICEF achieved wonders in its promotion work with governments to create the policy and legal framework for improving the situation of children, embodied in the 1989 Convention on the Rights of the Child, which has now been ratified by virtually all countries. The issue at stake today is having the provisions of that Convention respected by adults, for they are still being widely disregarded. The Pope made this point in one of his Sunday addresses in April 1997, appealing for respect for commitments entered into, and particularly condemning the involvement of children in armed conflict.

Indeed, the way guerrilla movements, and some governments too, cynically exploit children as warriors is an abomination. Even a 10-year-old child can use today's lightweight but deadly assault rifles, and children have natural advantages as combatants: they can be intimidated and disciplined into doing what adults want; they seldom desert; and they do not demand pay. Alone, often orphaned, frightened, bored, frustrated, and with little – if any – education, many end up adopting armed conflict as a way of life. What alternatives do they have to improve their own circumstances and make a useful contribution to society?

The dimension of the problem is significant. In Angola, a 1995 survey reported by UNICEF showed that 36 per cent of all children had accompanied or helped soldiers in combat, and 7 per cent of them had fired a weapon at a human target. The Renamo resistance movement in that country had about 10,000 children in its army, some of them only 6 years old. In the last decade, the governments of El Salvador, Ethiopia, Guatemala, and Myanmar, among others, have recruited children into their armies, in some cases forcibly. Guerrilla movements have done, and still do, the same, in countries as varied as Afghanistan, Sierra Leone, Liberia and Uganda, to name a few. Both the Convention on the Rights of the Child and the Geneva Convention of 1949 debar children who have not reached 15 years from direct participation in armed hostilities. And in civil wars, age seems to be increasingly irrelevant. Children are captured and tortured for information, imprisoned, maltreated, and often sexually abused too.

Street children, already victims of behaviour patterns in society, are often victimized further by 'decent' people who see them as 'vermin'. For example, in Brazil in the 1980s, people began taking the law into their own hands and organizing hit squads to gun them down. This was in addition to the police harassment and repression they had been subjected to for years. The phenomenon of street children is growing in many of the world's cities. Governments are not enthusiastic about divulging statistics about them, but UNICEF estimated in 1990 that there were about 50 million of them worldwide.

Although the problem of street children is growing, it is not intractable, as has been shown by efforts in some countries to change attitudes and behaviour towards them. In Brazil, for example, pressure and campaigning by NGOs, beginning in the mid-1980s with support from UNICEF, led to the creation of a National Movement in Favour of Street Children which is making progress in improving their situation, even if some are still being murdered today. Furthermore, communication campaigns led to the incorporation of a special statute in the national constitution that legally binds the government to ensure the protection and the rights of children and adolescents. Children participated in the process leading up to the constitutional changes through their presence in meeting after meeting in Brasilia. At the end of the process, children were invited to occupy the Senate, an emotional occasion with many politicians in tears as they offered their seats to them.

In the Philippines too, and also with UNICEF support, a communication programme was organized to arouse general awareness and understanding about the problem of street children. People were helped to realize that street children are victims of a breakdown in society, and that they are not evil or delinquent by nature. Furthermore, since society was responsible for their existence, society was equally responsible for helping them out of their situation and of their dependency on crime as a way of life. This communication work was a first step in creating awareness and mobilizing support for programmes to rehabilitate street children. Other countries could be tackling their problem of street children in similar ways.

Even if poverty is the driving force behind child labour, attitudinal and behavioural patterns in society are also involved. For example, efforts by the government of India to raise the minimum age for factory work to 14 were resisted by employers, who threatened to shut down their activities if they could not hire younger children. According to a report by that same government, in the mid-1980s, children made up 37.5 per cent of the workforce in the country's carpet industry. Some of the abuses of children in these factories are horrendous. According to a 1995 UNICEF report, in one small carpet factory in Asia, children as young as 5 were found working from 6 a.m. to 7 p.m. for 20 US cents a day. Similar conditions exist in the garment industry with children sewing shirts for 10 US cents each which are later sold for US$60 in industrialized countries. Such labour takes an enormous toll, often resulting in stunted intellectual and physical development and in afflictions such as chronic lung diseases and ruined eyesight.

Pressure groups in countries that import 'sweat shop' products are now beginning to have major success in influencing working conditions in the factories where they are made. This needs to be complemented in those producing countries by creating awareness among employers, parents, and the general public – and also among children themselves – regarding children's rights and needs and the long-term effects on society of abusive child labour. This is another case of countries not yet living up to the obligations they assumed under the Convention on the Rights of the Child.

Recent years have brought major advances in child health and, as we shall see in Chapter 3, information and communication have been central to this success. However, there are still many common disorders that can impede a child from ever becoming an adult who is fully able in mind and body, but which can be prevented by simple behavioural measures. Some of these require government actions, or legislation, such as iodizing salt supplies to prevent iodine deficiency, which impairs mental and physical capacity and can lead to cretinism. According to WHO, there are already about 75 million young people and 150 million adults in the world with reduced mental and physical abilities because of this deficiency, and there are 5.7 million cretins. Yet, despite the fact that iodizing salt is simple and only costs about 5 US cents per person per year, many governments did little or nothing about it until quite recent years and when development agencies began actively promoting it.

The prevention of many other child disorders depends on behavioural change in the household. Vitamin A deficiency, which in the early 1990s was causing blindness or severe eye damage in 500,000 children a year, can be prevented simply and cheaply by adding green leafy vegetables, carrots, paw-paw, or liver to the diet, or by giving children a vitamin A capsule, costing 2 US cents, three times a year. UNICEF estimates that more than 230 million children, about 40 per cent of the world's children under 5, have inadequate vitamin A intake, which in addition to blindness and eye problems, lowers their resistance to disease and increases their mortality rate by 20–30 per cent.

Dietary and feeding habits, rather than shortage of food, often cause chronic malnutrition, which permanently reduces intelligence and capacity for learning, as well as physical development. For example, in many countries, the male head of the household eats most of the available meat and other high protein foods, while his children and pregnant wife take second place. Life and work styles play a role too. A UNICEF nutrition programme in Tanzania found that the women were so busy collecting firewood or water, and working in the fields, that they did not have the time to prepare the four or more meals a day needed by their infants. With the two, or at most three, meals they were actually getting, their small stomachs could not absorb enough nutrients.

Taking into account that more than one child in three under 5 years of age in the developing world suffers from malnutrition, a third of tomorrow's adults in those countries will not have achieved their full mental and physical potential, hardly a conducive situation for a better future. In addition, UNICEF specialists now state that over half of the 13 million child deaths each year are caused by a stealthy partnership between malnutrition and disease.

Even children's education is subject to behavioural change if it is to be improved for the future. Although the vast majority of the world's children do now start primary school, too many drop out before finishing. In South Asia, for example, where most of the world's children live, 96 per cent enrol but only 57 per cent finish. One factor in this high drop-out rate is that parents and children do not see the existing content of primary education as relevant to their futures. UNESCO makes the important point that progress has been made in providing skills in literacy and numeracy, but little progress has been made in providing life, social, and value skills. We would add that the potential of the mass media to impart such skills and support non-formal education has been tapped to a very limited extent, although two outstanding examples are provided in Chapter 5.

Victor Ordoñez, director of UNESCO's Division of Basic Education, wrote the following in an article for UNICEF's 1995 *The Progress of Nations* report:

> We can produce experts in information technologies, but we seem unable to improve a capacity for listening, for tolerance, for respecting diversity, for harnessing the potential of individuals to the social good, or for strengthening the ethical foundations without which skills and knowledge bring little benefit.

In almost all countries, young adults are faced with unprecedented tensions, challenges, and temptations for which their school years have done little to prepare them. Often, the very structure and the role models set before them in schools stress one-way communication in an atmosphere of rigid repression and uniformity, rather than participation and diversity, so reinforcing patterns of demagoguery and conflict, rather than of openness and tolerance. This is poor preparation for life in the 21st century; it meets neither the personal needs of individuals nor the developmental needs of their societies.

The article goes on to state that where fundamental reforms in education have been successful, community involvement has been the key. Treating the community and its children as passive recipients of education, without promoting their inputs, involvement and commitment, has led to alienation and a common feeling that education in its existing form is irrelevant to the people's real needs. Returning ownership of education to the community naturally leads to a re-examination of its purpose and content, and of its relationship to employment, increased productivity, local opportunities, and the development of life skills.

So, as for most development fields, even improving education depends on democratic communication processes at the community level to analyse the situation and the needs, and to reach decisions for change.

International Conferences Call for Communication

There have been a series of world conferences on various socio-economic issues in recent years, and they have all implicitly called for major change and development and the use of communication to help achieve them. This is the case of Agenda 21, the action programme that emerged from the Earth Summit of 1992 in Rio de Janeiro. Its opening sentences set the scene:

> Humanity stands at a defining moment in history. We are confronted with a perpetuation of disparities between and within nations, a worsening of poverty, hunger, ill health and illiteracy, and the continuing deterioration of the ecosystems on which we depend for our well-being.

Then, almost all of the 38 chapters of Agenda 21 devoted to tackling various aspects of the environmental crisis implicitly recognize the critical role of communication in achieving results. They call for: 'raising awareness', 'promoting public participation', 'empowering communities', 'sharing knowledge and experience between communities', 'promoting participation in decision-making', 'education and public awareness campaigns', 'promoting the involvement of the local population', 'disseminating information', 'awareness/training campaigns ... through existing national mass media facilities', 'generating discussion at all levels ... through media programmes, conferences and seminars', and so on. All of these required actions that appear repeatedly in Agenda 21 need purposive communication strategies.

Chapter 36 specifically deals with the subject of 'Promoting Education, Public Awareness, and Training'. One of the objectives set out in this chapter is to 'achieve environmental and development awareness in all sectors of society on a world-wide scale as soon as possible'. It also states,

> Both formal and non-formal education are indispensable to changing people's attitudes so that they have the capacity to assess and address their sustainable development concerns. It is also critical for achieving environmental and ethical awareness, values, attitudes, skills and behaviour consistent with sustainable development and for effective participation in decision making. [Education] should employ formal and non-formal methods and effective means of communication.

The chapter goes on to recommend creating a special cooperative relationship with the media, popular theatre groups and the entertainment and advertising industries to mobilize their experience in shaping public behaviour and consumption patterns. It also recommends that 'countries establish ways of employing modern communication technologies for effective public outreach'.

The Programme of Action of the UN International Conference on Population and Development held in Cairo in 1994 also stresses communication when it states:

> Greater public knowledge, understanding and commitment at all levels, from the individual to the international, are vital to the achievement of the goals and objectives of the present Programme of Action. In all countries and in all groups, therefore, information, education, and communication activities concerning population and sustainable development issues must be strengthened.
>
> Information, education and communication efforts should raise awareness through public education campaigns on priority issues such as safe motherhood, reproductive health and rights, maternal and child health, family planning, and discrimination against ... the girl child. More

education is needed in all societies on the implications of population–environment relationships, in order to influence behavioural change and consumer lifestyles and to promote sustainable management of natural resources. The media should be a major instrument for expanding knowledge and motivation.

The World Summit for Social Development in 1995 devoted much attention to rectifying social disintegration and the ills it causes, and recognized the role of communication for doing so. The UN defines a socially integrated society as one that is capable of providing space for the aspirations of individuals and of different and divergent groups within a flexible structure of shared basic values and common interests. Social integration is synonymous with greater justice, equity, material well-being, democratic freedom, and more equal opportunities and rights for all.

The Summit's Declaration and Action Plan committed governments to promote respect for democracy, law, order, pluralism, diversity, non-violence and solidarity through educational systems and the mass media. Governments also agreed to promote access to education, information, technology, and specialized knowledge as indispensable means of improving communication and increasing participation in civil, political, economic, social, and cultural life. Furthermore, the Social Summit recognized the importance of giving everybody access to a wide range of information and opinions concerning issues of public interest. In this context, governments agreed to use mass media to improve understanding and public awareness of all aspects of social integration, and at the same time to promote the fight against poverty.

The Platform for Action of the Fourth World Conference on Women, held in 1995, identifies the mass media as having 'a great potential to promote the advancement of women and the equality of women and men'. It states that 'television especially has the greatest impact on young people and, as such, has the ability to shape values, attitudes and perceptions of women in both positive and negative ways'. A whole section of the Platform devoted to women and the media urges more gender sensitivity and the elimination of gender stereotyping in programming, as well as the incorporation of more women at decision-making levels in media operations.

In other sections, the Platform calls for education and information programmes, 'particularly in conjunction with the mass media, that make the public, particularly parents, aware of the importance of non-discriminatory education for children and the equal sharing of family responsibilities by girls and boys'. It also signals the need 'to modify the social and cultural patterns of conduct of men and women, and to eliminate prejudices, customary practices and all other practices based on the idea of the inferiority or superiority of either of the sexes and on stereotyped roles for men and women'.

In the agricultural sector too, the Action Plan from the 1996 World Food Summit calls for communication to help achieve sustainable development. Echoing the principles of a 1991 conference held in den Bosch, Holland, on the subject, it reaffirms that sustainable agricultural development will be achieved only if technology and policy are accompanied by participation, equity, dialogue, enabling mechanisms, empowerment, and incentives. The Summit Action Plan, in addition to stressing the need for participation, calls for campaigns in favour of 'Food for All'.

The examples quoted above hold in common the belief that change in people's attitudes and behaviour, whether they are policy-makers, service providers, or individuals, are at the heart of achieving sustainable production and consumption patterns and of improving quality of life, equity and stability in societies.

Communication and public debate provide the avenue by which, at least in democracies, individuals and societies become aware of the issues at stake and adopt new behaviour patterns, in their own interests and in those of society. Communication can also help them acquire the life and technical skills that are needed to implement change and development. Furthermore, even if human ingenuity comes to the rescue and produces solutions for humanity's problems, as many people believe it will, that will not create stability if billions of people do not have access to those solutions and continue to be marginalized.

Equity is the basis for stability, and what the Vatican calls 'development in solidarity' is needed to achieve it. In its 1996 document *World Hunger* the Vatican states that there are often traditions of solidarity among the poorest sectors of society, whose members are always willing to come to the rescue of relatives in distress. Such traditions need to be expanded, making those who are better off aware of the needs of the less fortunate, and persuading them to share the burden of reducing the gap, in the interests of all.

Yet, despite the evident need for communication to facilitate change and development, and despite the agreement on its importance in the recent international conferences, it is still a neglected field when it comes to action by most governments and development agencies. The situation is well illustrated by events since the Rio de Janeiro Earth Summit. The five subsequent years are enough to see whether its expressions of good intent have been followed up with deeds. In fact, progress has been disappointing, to the extent that, in 1997, the International Union for the Conservation of Nature (IUCN) prepared a paper called 'Education and Communication ... the Forgotten Priority of Rio?' The paper stresses that the role of education and communication is central to creating the social responsibility necessary for the building of sustainable societies and achieving virtually all aspects of Agenda 21. Despite this, IUCN states that education and communication have such low political and financial profiles in government agendas that, in terms of concrete action, they risk becoming the forgotten priority.

There is also the risk of a similar lack of follow-up to the other major, and more recent, conferences that called for communication. Indeed, one of the purposes of this book is that, perhaps, it will help to draw attention to what has already been done, and could be done, with communication in the future. The issues covered in this chapter are becoming increasingly urgent, but human beings have the capacity to change, if the will is created.

As Speth concludes in his article, quoted earlier: 'The script for human development in the 21st century will begin to be written by the choices we make today. We should not let it be said of our times that we, who had the power to do better, allowed the world to get worse.'

CHAPTER 2

Why Communication?

Communication for social change is as old as organized society. The great philosophers and teachers, the custodians of people's spiritual well-being, and the leaders of great social movements in the past, have all used communication in various forms to influence the values and behaviour patterns of the societies in which they lived. Today, as we have seen, there is an unprecedented need for change to assure our future well-being on earth. But who plans such change, and how? And how do individuals, groups, and societies come to an awareness of the need for change and act accordingly? Communication through interpersonal, group, and mass media is at the heart of these processes, for people take decisions for change once they have been motivated and empowered by information they have internalized and found relevant to themselves and their interests.

Even though communication for development came into being in the 1960s, and has clearly shown its usefulness and impact in change and development actions, its role is still not understood and appreciated to the point that it is routinely included in development planning. Through a brief account of how communication for development started, and a description of how it has itself changed and been refined over the years, we hope to make its potential contribution and importance clearer. The case studies that follow in Part Two will show some of its applications in practice and in different contexts.

Early Strategies for International Development Assistance

Assistance from the United Nations and from industrialized to developing countries began in the mid-1950s, shortly after the highly successful Marshall Plan had been concluded. Under that aid programme, the USA poured resources into Europe to rebuild its infrastructure and economy after the devastation of the Second

World War. Generous American financing for reconstruction, capital equipment, and technology helped Europe to recover much faster than it could have done if limited to its own resources.

The Marshall Plan established a model for early international assistance to developing countries. Its thrust was to provide inputs of technology and economic investment to help countries of the Third World to 'modernize'. The underlying assumption was that development should follow the pattern of Western industrial societies, and that the 'backwardness' of developing countries could be overcome, and 'progress' achieved by external inputs. This progress would be measurable in relation to factors such as gross national product, levels of literacy, urbanization, and growth in the industrial base. In effect, development would hinge on accelerating, and cramming into a short time span, a process that had taken centuries in the industrialized countries.

Essentially, the approach was linear, or 'top-down' from donors to recipients. Leaders in developing countries, often trained in industrialized countries, were generally unquestioning about this strategy. But the modernization approach overlooked some important differences between post-Second World War Europe and the developing countries. In Europe, the aim had been to *rebuild* – with improvements of course – infrastructures and economies that had existed before the war, whereas in most developing countries, the need was to build and create where there had been little before.

However, perhaps the most important difference was that Europe had highly trained and motivated people who were willing and able to put Marshall Plan funds and technology to immediate and good use, while in many developing countries, there were few people with the same attitudes, education and skills. This was especially so in countries that were emerging from long periods of colonial rule.

A final and important difference was that in the circumstances of post-war Europe, and with the cultural affinity between Americans and Europeans, it was legitimate to make assumptions about the inputs people required. In Third World countries, with different cultures and values, and at a different stage of development, making assumptions about what inputs people would see as important, and could and would use, was problematic. And in fact, the planners' assumptions often proved wrong. Consultation and dialogue to determine people's real needs and possibilities as the foundation for development programmes could have prevented the mistakes, but this did not occur under the modernization strategy.

The fault was not only on the side of aid agencies; governments in developing countries were sometimes even more high-handed in making assumptions about what poor peasants and other under-privileged people needed. In the minds of many officials they were, in any case, far too ignorant, conservative, fatalistic, and stubborn to have any worthwhile ideas.

As a result of these attitudes there were numerous development projects in the 1960s, which met with apathy from their so-called beneficiaries. In many cases, local populations never identified with the projects, nor did they ever become properly involved in them. Such projects usually received international assistance for a few years only, after which it was supposed that the government would take them over, but many collapsed soon after the international support terminated. Sometimes this was because the government had not been able, or willing, to assume full responsibility for the project with its own technicians, but just as often, the project collapsed because it had never developed any dynamic process of involvement with the local population. They did not see the project as relevant to their needs; it appeared to be something that belonged to the government and some foreign organization, whose staff were busily running around promoting strange ideas or building things for un-known purposes.

The situation common to many projects in those years is well illustrated by a case in Thailand. In the late 1960s, the Thai govern-ment wanted to increase fruit and vegetable production to meet the needs of the cities, and so a horticulture project was designed for the area near Kalasin in the north-east of the country. UNDP would finance the project and FAO would operate it.

The project took the form of a demonstration farm that would grow vegetables using irrigation, which had recently become available in the area. The FAO team, all Dutch horticulture specialists, did an excellent technical job, and quite soon had a flourishing demonstra-tion farm growing a variety of high-quality vegetables the whole year round. The assumption of the project planners had been that local people would come to visit the farm and, inspired by what they saw, would themselves want to grow vegetables. But in the event, almost no one even came to see the demonstration.

Faced with this lack of local interest, the project team began to make some enquiries. They found out that the tradition of the people was to work hard growing rice during the rainy season and to lead a more relaxed life or undertake some non-farming activities during the dry season. They had no particular interest in spending the whole year working in the fields to grow crops of which they had no experience. Furthermore, the economic incentive of growing vegetables was of limited interest because the farmers were increasing their rice yields by using the newly available irrigation water to supplement rainfall during their traditional cropping season. They were making more money than ever before, so why should they work in the fields the whole year round to grow vegetables?

This belated understanding of the human, social and economic environment caused years of time and effort to be lost before some local farmers could be induced to take an interest in vegetable growing. A prior communication and consultation process would have revealed the farmers' attitudes and helped to identify where the farmers' interests and those of the government overlapped. This area of overlapping interests would have been the starting point for negotiating an agreed horticultural development programme. If no common or overlapping interests could be identified during the dialogue, it would have been better to propose the project somewhere else.

There are many examples of projects that installed expensive infrastructure, especially for irrigation and drainage, only to find that the local people never used it or maintained it properly. In some cases it fell into total disrepair. One case of a grandiose infrastructure project that largely failed on the human front was Plan La Chontalpa in the State of Tabasco, Mexico, which is described in some detail in Chapter 4. There were many others like it, and we have seen an irrigation scheme in Tunisia where concrete flumes raised on stilts to carry water had collapsed. Nothing had been done to repair them, and many of the waterways were choked with mud. The irrigation scheme was in an area of traditional livestock production, where the people had no experience of irrigated agriculture, and no real interest in it.

There were also some cases of physical violence by local people to development projects. One occurred in the late 1960s in what was then Yugoslavia. It involved a drainage and land reclamation project in the delta of the Neretva River. The rationale for the project was that Yugoslavia was rapidly building a tourist industry on its spectacularly beautiful Dalmatian coast. The hotels and restaurants needed fresh horticultural produce, but the coast is cut off from the agricultural interior of the country by a range of mountains through which transport is difficult. The government therefore wanted to reclaim parts of the Neretva delta, which is close and easily accessible to the main tourist areas of the coast, and turn them into horticultural land. After much technical study, a UNDP-financed project began dredging operations and the construction of pumping stations.

For centuries, the people living near this beautiful area of marshland surrounded by limestone mountains had lived from fishing in the channels that meander through the reed beds, and from hunting the numerous aquatic birds. They were never consulted about the project, nor were they informed that they would have a chance to cultivate the newly reclaimed land. Not surprisingly, they saw drainage as a threat to their traditional livelihood. And so one night, a group of them protested by severely damaging one of the newly constructed pumping stations.

The Birth of Communication for Development

Evidently, development initiatives based on the modernization philosophy were often out of tune with people's interests and needs, and they did not take sufficiently into account the human behavioural aspects. It was against this background that the ideas of an Irishman called Erskine Childers began to take on importance.

Childers came from a prominent political family in Ireland. His father had been a cabinet minister in most of the development sectors in his country, and his mother was a social worker. From them, as Childers told us just a few months before he died in August 1996, aged only 68, he had 'acquired the distinct conviction that *people*, and *communicating* with them, were essential in any sustainable development process'. And he added: 'This seems so crashingly obvious that one can only shake one's head at how neglected it has been.'

In the 1950s and 1960s, Childers was a researcher and an author/broadcaster on international affairs, and also a periodic adviser to the UN. He studied communication in development processes, notably in India and Tanzania, and also in Egypt, where he made a detailed tracing of what he came to call the 'human communication aetiology of bilharziasis'.

Bilharziasis, an ancient scourge depicted even in Pharaonic tombs, is caused by a parasite carried by snails that breed in slow-moving rivers, lakes, and irrigation canals in most of the African continent. The larvae of the parasite penetrate people's skin, usually of the feet and legs, while they are working in the water, for example washing clothes or de-silting an irrigation channel. Once inside the body, the parasite lodges in one or more of the internal organs and multiplies. As mentioned in Chapter 1, in connection with rice growing in the Ivory Coast, bilharziasis is severely debilitating as it slowly but surely destroys the organs where it is lodged, especially the liver.

At the time of Childers' work in Egypt, about 47 per cent of the population, mainly in the area of the Nile delta, were affected by bilharziasis, and preventing infection was the only cure in those days. But the prevention, Childers discovered, would be riddled with human behaviour and communication problems. To begin with, since time immemorial, the Nile had been 'the gods' gift to Egypt'. Every child's blessing was to be exposed to its waters. As everywhere else, it was customary to wash clothes in the river and irrigation canals, exposing those doing so to penetration by the larvae.

Then, as Childers recounted, it seemed as if all possible behavioural problems were being assembled around a single scourge, for it was traditional to urinate and defecate into the river and canals, thereby returning larvae to the water to be picked up by the host-snail and renew the cycle. Any attempt to control the disease would call for enormous communication efforts to change entrenched behaviour patterns, in addition to building latrines, providing alternative sources of drinking water, and creating places for washing clothes.

Such experiences in the field increasingly convinced Childers of the importance of introducing communication into development, so he began to speak to senior UN staff during his frequent visits to New York. He badgered everyone he could with his ideas. He was particularly keen to convince the administrator of UNDP at the time, Paul Hoffman, and the executive director of UNICEF, Henry Labouisse, of the importance of communication. He was also able to speak to U Thant, the UN secretary-general.

Childers was a highly articulate and persuasive man, with a gentle demeanour and a soft Irish accent, and his messages finally struck home in 1966. U Thant told him the time had come to do something about his propositions, and Paul Hoffman told him that he had become more and more convinced that communicating with people was the key to the development process. Henry Labouisse was equally supportive because Childers' proposals could help UNICEF to reach parents with specific messages for improving the condition of children.

The outcome of Erskine Childers' propositions was that the UN, UNDP and UNICEF jointly sent him to Asia for further research, to organize some demonstrations of communication in development, and to produce a major policy paper on the subject. In Bangkok, he met a Thai sociologist, Mallica Vajrathon, who was UNICEF's regional information officer and later became his wife. They found that they had precisely the same ideas about development, and they jointly set up a project called the Development Support Communication Service (Asia) in Bangkok in 1967. This was financed by UNDP and UNICEF. In effect, its purpose was to serve other development projects throughout Asia by advising them on communication strategies, and by producing communication materials for them.

The policy paper that Childers had been asked to produce appeared in 1968, and is so perceptive and innovative about change and development that it is almost as important and relevant today as it was then. Childers' general proposition in those early days was to use communication to create wider and better understanding about projects, both among the local people and among society in general, and to apply audio-visual media to information and training. As he wrote in that paper:

> No innovation, however brilliantly designed and set down in a project Plan of Operations, becomes development until it has been communicated. No input or construction of material resources for development can be successful unless and until the innovations – the new techniques and surrounding changed attitudes which people will need to use those resources – have been communicated to them.

In his paper, Childers also described the way a community may react to projects that are parachuted in from above. A particular UN-assisted project he knew inspired him to write the following:

> From the moment a stranger appears in someone's field bearing government authority, a theodolite, and some stakes, and drives the stakes into that ground, a long chain-reaction of communication has been launched. It begins with the first villager who sees the stake, wonders about it, speculates with a neighbour, begins asking questions that ripple out to a rapidly increasing community of profoundly concerned people. Is 'Government' going to take their land? Will they get any compensation? Is it something to do with water? Will an ancestral burial ground be flooded? Is the new water for the landlord, or for us? When will 'it' happen? ... 'They' want us to build a new school house: will we be here, on our land, in five years' time; and if not, why put energy into a new school?

The engineers who drew up the design and specifications ... for this UN-assisted project were not asked – and should not have been asked – to contemplate such immediate consequences from the first act of construction. But was anyone else asked to contemplate, to draw up an accompanying information plan – a plan for purposive support communication both to explain 'the stakes' and all that would follow ... and to begin the diffusion of needed innovation among [the community] in time?

It will be evident from the passages just quoted that the focus of Childers' early communication thinking was in the framework of the then current modernization approach to development, with decisions being taken by governments and development agencies. His emphasis in those early days was principally to use communication to explain those decisions to the communities concerned, and to try to enlist their informed involvement in the development programme. He also saw communication as essential for telescoping the time-span of change – which would normally take generations – into just a few years by diffusing innovations among large numbers of ordinary people as fast as possible. In addition, communication, and especially audio-visual media, would help in the accelerated training of new cadres.

Development approaches have generally changed since those days, but governments even today, and even when democratically elected, may still behave as they did three decades ago, taking decisions that affect people deeply without informing them. They even do it with their own staff, as we saw when we were working in Argentina in 1994: a whole sub-section of a ministry was abolished overnight, and the first the staff heard about it was when they saw the news on television. They were sent to work in other parts of the ministry, but they were given no terms of reference and had to invent their own jobs.

Childers' influence was such that in 1969, UNDP sent a circular to all the UN agencies requesting that they give attention to communication inputs in projects they were operating with UNDP funding. As a result of this, and of Childers' work in Asia, the idea that communication and information could help in the implementation of development projects was quickly adopted by a number of international agencies. For example, FAO created its own Development Support Communication Branch in its Rome headquarters in 1969; UNICEF set up a unit in its headquarters in New York, and later began appointing communication specialists in its country offices; and when the UN Fund for Population Activities (UNFPA) began operations, also in 1969, it gave importance to communication and encompassed it in what it called 'Information, Education, and Communication', or IEC.

Most early communication work had to follow the top-down development approach of the time. Information was directed to people to make them understand a project's objectives and to try to enlist their participation, or to convince them of the benefits of a new health or agricultural technique. In FAO headquarters, for example, the technical staff and the extension specialists thought of communication as the use of mass media and audio-visual materials as a way of reaching more people, more effectively, and more persuasively with ideas and information generated by others who believed *they* knew best what people needed. 'Diffusion of innovations' and 'transfer of knowledge' were two phrases that summed up the underlying hypothesis of development work at the time.

However, some of the people working in communication for development soon began trying to promote wider functions beginning with communication processes at the village level before any development plans were laid. But most development technicians, with their top-down conditioning, did not accept this and continued in the belief that communicators were merely producers of materials to help them diffuse their messages more effectively. This often led to conflictual situations between, for example, traditional agricultural extension people and the new communication specialists, for the latter saw their main role as promoters of social processes, although the production of materials also played an important part in their work. And meanwhile, the development technicians continued to come along to the communicators and say, 'I want you to produce a film for my project on how to build latrines' – or on whatever the subject of their work was.

These requests for the production of some isolated piece of material, whether a radio programme, or a video, or a leaflet, usually resulted in stand-alone items. As such, they made little impact, for it is now proven that communication is most effective when it is based on qualitative research with the intended audiences, and on a strategy that uses different media and channels in a coordinated way.

In truth, development communicators in those early days often accepted their limited role as producers of materials, for they were still developing their own insights, strategic thinking, and experience. They had been given an empty canvas on which to start work, and it took some years before they developed the capacity to become involved in studying the whole human and behavioural situation faced by a development proposal and to come up with an integrated communication strategy and plan. Today, they see this as their mission.

Towards New Development Approaches

By the late 1960s, the first voices of dissent against the modernization approach to development were being raised, especially in Latin America. The first reason put forward was, quite simply, that it was not working. But Latin American intellectuals, predominantly with Marxist leanings, also advanced the notion that development in the industrialized countries went hand in hand with underdevelopment elsewhere; or in other words, that underdevelopment was really caused by global power and economic structures. The only solution that the proponents of this so-called dependency theory could suggest was that developing countries should withdraw from the world's market and economic structures and opt for self-reliance. This was hardly practical for all developing countries.

At about the same time, the Brazilian educationalist Paolo Freire provided some new insights about approaches to development. In his 1970 book *Pedagogy of the Oppressed*, he coined the word 'conscientization' as the educational process the poor needed to help them improve their condition and take charge of their own destinies. Conscientization resulted from a group communication and active education process during which people would be stimulated by a facilitator to discuss and analyse their reality, learning through this process and from each other. This was quite distinct from traditional education, which Freire termed the 'banking system', in which people remain passive while information is poured into their heads by a teacher or technician with superior knowledge.

By the mid-1970s, other development thinkers, mainly in northern Europe and Scandinavia, also began proposing new conceptual approaches and priorities. The Dag Hammarskjold Foundation in Sweden was a leading light in promoting this new development thinking, which is still generally in force in the late 1990s and which effectively opened the door for a much wider role for communication than it had under the modernization model.

The premise of the new thinking is that the first priority should be to satisfy the basic needs of the dominated and exploited. Those basic needs are considered to be material – food, shelter, clothing, education, health, and so on – and non-material – the need for expression, creativity, equality, conviviality, and the ability to understand and master one's own destiny.

This thinking also holds that there is no universal recipe for development, that it must be seen as an integrated, multi-dimensional and dialectic process that can differ from one society to another. However, even if the process may vary in different circumstances, it will have certain common criteria. Among these criteria is that, in addition to aiming to meet basic needs, development should be endogenous to a society, that is to say, it should originate from that society's values and its perceptions of its own future. It should be as self-reliant as possible, in that each society should draw on its own resources and strengths to the maximum practical extent before using external resources. It should make optimum use of natural resources, taking into account the potential of the local ecosystem, as well as the present and future limitations imposed by global considerations for the biosphere. Last but certainly not least, it should be based on participatory and truly democratic processes of decision-making at all levels of society.

This approach recognizes that the development process will often require changes in social relations, economic activities, and power structures before people can be enabled to participate in decisions that concern them and assume responsibility in self-management. Furthermore, this new approach does not limit itself to developing countries, for its proponents see its criteria as being equally valid for industrialized societies suffering from the negative effects of consumerism and social disintegration.

Almost all of the development criteria just outlined depend on communication for their practical application. For example, if a society is to take development actions rooted in its perception of its own future, it will need communication processes to achieve that common perception. Similarly, it cannot take decisions about its use of local natural resources, and the possible global implications, without full knowledge and understanding on which to base those decisions. Similarly again, communication is the basis for participatory and democratic decision-making. And finally, the changes in social relations, economic activities and power structures that this approach to development foresees will often lead to conflictual situations that can be resolved only through communication processes and negotiation.

In effect, the new thinking about development brought increased emphasis on its human and social dimensions. By the late 1970s, 'participation in development' had become a key phrase. But what is participation? For some years, the concept had different meanings for different people, usually according to their particular perspective on development work. Some of them, in rural and agricultural development, saw it as creating associations, cooperatives, and the like. In the health sector, 'participation' sometimes had the connotation of people paying part of the costs of their own health services. There were others, with leftist inclinations, who described 'participation' as the mass mobilization of people, as in Mao Tsetung's China, for building infrastructures, such as earth dams or irrigation systems.

However, there were also those who believed that 'participation' is achieved only when people become involved in the planning and decisions that affect their lives, and in putting those decisions into practice. A good example might be when, say, a group of people organize themselves for a joint horticultural project, negotiate for land with the village authorities, get advice from a horticultural specialist, and start to grow vegetables to raise funds for some community service, or to go into business for themselves.

A Global Seminar on Participatory Development held by UNICEF in Florence in 1990 agreed that only the last case is *true* participation. Today this would be generally accepted in development circles, for in the example, people are making decisions for themselves, creating new resources of vegetables and money, and, almost certainly, learning new skills. They are involved in an activity that will change and improve their lives and that of their families. The problem with the other types of participation mentioned above, even though they have positive aspects, is that if people do not gain a voice in planning and decision-making for an initiative that affects them, they may think that it is irrelevant. In addition, they will feel less ownership of the initiative and will be less likely to sustain it over time.

Talking about participation in development programmes is easier than actually achieving it. It was obvious, however, to more clear-sighted development specialists that prior consultation and dialogue with intended beneficiaries of such programmes should be a first step, in effect giving people a voice in decision-making. Thus, the concept of development from the bottom up, as opposed to the earlier top-down impositions, belatedly became part of development strategy, at least in theory.

Participation – constraints and opportunities

Although the new development thinking had opened the door for democratic and participatory development, in reality, the top-down focus remained for years, and still exists in many cases. Indeed, two decades or more after the human problems of the modernization approach began to become evident, there are still cases of project design based on assumptions about behaviour, rather than on communication and participation.

For example, in 1990, the Investment Centre of FAO, which prepares agricultural projects for the World Bank and similar lending institutions, carried out a review of 75 of the projects it had designed in various parts of the world in the 1970s and 1980s. The review states that 'problems attributed to poor project design ... have, since 1981, represented the highest proportion of all issues raised in the project post-evaluation reports'. It went on to say that 'design problems now represent by far the most important single reason for the unsatisfactory performance of World Bank-financed agricultural projects'.

The review identified several aspects of weak project design, and it also found that 54 per cent of the projects had failed to reach their production goals, mainly due to deficiencies in the technology being proposed and to slower adoption by farmers than had been assumed by the planners. It mentioned a project in India where farmers in a traditional livestock and rain-fed farming area were slow to pick up the appropriate water management practices when irrigation was provided. The project ran a year over time and terminated showing a negative economic rate of return. The review also singled out a case in Tanzania where 'drovers ... failed to use stock routes developed under a livestock project, largely because of justifiable concerns over the vulnerability of their stock to predators'.

These situations persist because, even if development people talk much about planning projects in participation with beneficiaries, in practice the process is not given the importance it deserves, with the result that the necessary time and resources are not made available. Furthermore, in the existing situation, projects usually have to be prepared to meet fixed schedules for their approval by the funding agency, whereas participatory planning cannot be so constrained.

Occasionally donor agencies do specify that time and resources must be spent on participatory planning, and even then it does not work out properly. This was the case in some FAO watershed management projects, funded by the government of Italy, in the early 1990s. Despite the commitment to participation, in the event the international project technicians seldom had the necessary attitudes or the patience to see the process through. When the participatory planning took longer than expected or ran into difficulties, they tended to take the easy way out by reverting to the old 'top-down' model of imposing their own solutions.

There are also strictly local reasons why participation in development may be difficult to achieve. One is that power structures and relationships, which are always present, will often be threatened when the people of a community are empowered to take decisions and implement development actions. In other words, the empowerment of some people will usually disempower someone else, at least when some sort of productive or economic activity is involved.

One real-life example of this, among many, took place some years ago in an FAO project in Rajasthan, India. The project introduced the grading and auctioning of wool along Australian lines. Wool had never been graded for quality in Rajasthan, and merchants had traditionally paid the same rock-bottom prices for all of it. In addition, they often cheated the simple herders, or offered extremely harsh credit terms to permit a man, for example, to marry off his daughter. It was hardly surprising that when the grading and auctioning of wool began, providing the herders for the first time in history with fair prices linked to the quality of their wool, the merchants reacted. They stopped two trucks carrying bales of graded wool to auction, tipped them off the roadside, and cut the bales open to scatter the wool to the winds.

At the political level too, participation may be difficult to tolerate, for it threatens the established order. As a high official in a UN agency said to us during an interview: 'If I were a politician, I would feel uneasy about participation. People should have a voice – but only up to a point!'

Yet another problem with participation is that development agencies lack flexibility in their procedures. For decades they have worked on the basis of projects that have predetermined and time-bound objectives, a schedule of activities, inputs and outputs, and a finite budget. Some agencies call this a logical framework, but it is illogical for participatory development, because when people truly become involved and can take decisions in a dynamic process as a project evolves, it may easily go in directions that were not foreseen – and in fact were impossible to foresee – during the planning process.

Participatory development needs more flexible systems for planning, managing, and financing projects, systems that can adapt to a process of evolution throughout a project's life. Development agencies could perhaps set broad budget provisions for a certain number of years, but allocate funds on a yearly basis, increasing them or decreasing them as a result of participatory monitoring and evaluation with the beneficiaries and other stake-holders. Projects that were making no progress could even be terminated and the funds transferred to more promising ones. The real possibility of closing down a project would also motivate communities to pull together to achieve success.

It is still early days in the efforts to bring about community participation at all stages of a development programme, and the obstacles are considerable. Most development agencies declare such participation as an objective, but also admit that they have not progressed as far as they would like. But on the positive side, some worldwide tendencies of recent years now favour participation. One is the collapse of authoritarian regimes almost everywhere, but equally important are the rapid processes of decentralization in many countries. Governments are passing the responsibility to local authorities for most of the functions that were previously conducted from the centre. This brings the planning of development down to a more local level where people's voices have a better chance of being heard, and where the local authorities are more in tune with the circumstances. Even so, there is often a need to democratize the attitudes of local authorities to make them better disposed to enter into dialogue with people.

The Evolution of Communication for Development

After starting out in a rather unstructured and piecemeal fashion, communication for development gradually became more ordered and professional, and more strategic in its application. This was at least in part because it began to draw on some of the precepts of marketing. The usual definition of marketing is 'identifying a need and satisfying that need, with a profit'. Its relevance to development lies precisely in that principle of identifying needs and satisfying them.

In the minds of many people, marketing, promotion, and advertising have negative connotations linked to selling, and so they are often thought to be vulgar and commercial. It is often forgotten that marketing theory and practice draw on a mix of elements borrowed from the respected fields of anthropology, social psychology, behavioural science, and communication theory. These are then linked to skilful use of communication media. *True* marketing sets out to discover unfulfilled demand, not to create demand, and its theoretical basis has nothing whatsoever to do with selling soap and cigarettes.

It was logical that some marketing specialists began to promote the idea that their methods could help to achieve social objectives. They could provide valuable insights into group behaviour, people's motivations, target audiences and their characteristics, and into the design of media strategies and messages. Marketing specialists were particularly interested in the areas of health and nutrition, where they believed that their concepts and practices could be powerful allies in helping people to change their attitudes and behaviour. The essence of their logic was that if useful commercial products could be promoted by marketing techniques, why could the same techniques not be applied to social aims and behaviours? This concept came to be known as 'social marketing'. It could be defined as 'identifying a socio-economic need and helping people to satisfy it, for their own profit'.

The main proponent of social marketing was Richard Manoff, the head of a successful New York marketing agency. He first became involved in public health and nutrition in 1965, when he was part of a US delegation to FAO. A few years later he began to apply marketing techniques to promote changes in health practices, nutrition, and family planning in a number of developing countries. Manoff's proposals and his expanding experience in social marketing caught the attention of several important development agencies, including WHO, UNICEF, and USAID. Since then, USAID's numerous programmes in communication for health and for population have been based almost entirely on social marketing strategies.

The health sector, in fact, has used social marketing more than others, but communication for various development sectors has now borrowed many social marketing principles and techniques, without necessarily using the whole package.

The first of these principles is *audience segmentation*, which is the practical recognition of the fact that people's beliefs, attitudes, aspirations, and behaviour are conditioned by their circumstances. These include education, occupation, gender, social status, income, and so on. It follows that under a broad generic title, such as 'rural women' or 'fishermen', there will almost always be several distinct audience segments that need to be identified and worked with, in line with the specific communication and development objective.

Qualitative research is another marketing principle that has also been increasingly adopted by communication for development. It is used to determine audiences' perceptions, attitudes, and motivations about a particular issue and what they consider to be obstacles and resistance points to any necessary changes in their practices. Another function is to find out how they express themselves, what terminology they use, what information channels they prefer, and the importance and credibility each one has. This provides guidance on how to formulate messages to achieve maximum comprehension and acceptability by the audiences and on what media channels would best reach them.

Such research often reveals authoritative information sources that are not media *per se*, but other sectors within the community, especially opinion leaders. These sectors then become relay audiences who can be reached with appropriate information that they will pass on to the primary audiences. Furthermore, it is often found that behaviour patterns are being influenced by opinion leaders and unless they change, there will be no change by the main target audience.

In practice, audience segmentation and qualitative research might work in the following way for promoting, say, family planning in rural areas in a Muslim country, and where the health sector is offering the necessary services. One might begin by singling out women who already had at least three children under the age of 6 as the primary target audience. Qualitative research with such women might show that they are interested in spacing their children and limiting their numbers. They want to be able to bring up their children properly and are concerned about specific aspects of their own health related to frequent childbearing. They want more information about the various family planning services and methods available. They use some particular phrases when talking about different aspects of family planning and health. They listen to the radio most days while they are preparing the evening meal, and this is the only media channel they use.

The women might also say that many of their husbands are resistant to family planning, or even hostile towards it, mainly because the religious authorities in the community are against it. The women might make it clear that they need their husbands' approval before they can go to a family planning clinic. Furthermore, it might emerge that for traditional reasons many of the women's elderly mothers are also against family planning.

In such circumstances, it would be a waste of effort mounting communication activities aimed only at women with at least three children under the age of 6. Communication would also have to reach husbands, religious authorities, and elderly women. Therefore, further qualitative research would be needed with these other audiences to determine the most suitable content of messages and the best channels for delivering them. For mothers who already had three children under 6, it would already be known that the message content should be the various family planning services and methods available, health aspects should be stressed as motivation, and a suitable channel would be radio programmes when they were preparing the evening meal.

Focus Group Discussions (FGDs) are a classic technique for doing qualitative research. In brief, an FGD sets out to create a situation in which a small group of 8–12 people of the same social, economic, and educational level, and who share similar lifestyles and problems, discuss a particular issue of concern. An FGD has a facilitator and an observer, both playing a low-profile role. The facilitator gets the process started and guides it gently with some predetermined, open-ended questions, usually beginning with factual matters, but gradually going into increasing depth and analysis. The key to the process is to get the group participants to discuss among themselves and not with the facilitator. The observer listens, watches the body language in the group, and takes notes of what is said.

The FGD technique may be informal and loosely structured, but with a skilful facilitator, it can generate a group interaction that is uniquely effective in penetrating deep-seated attitudes, and finding out how people's minds work about some specific issue. The process usually takes on aspects that are similar to group therapy.

FGDs have been used for several years for participatory analysis with people concerned with health issues. The agricultural sector has lagged behind, but we have used them in a variety of agricultural situations, from large-scale farmers in Argentina to bare subsistence farmers in Zambia, Uganda and Bolivia. In all cases, they have provided a wealth of useful information that can be used to help farmers to help themselves and to plan what outside assistance is needed.

Another feature of social marketing is careful *message design* to appeal to the concerns and perspectives of the specific audience segments. In the Muslim country of our earlier example, strategic message design for the religious leaders resisting family planning might involve selecting passages from the Koran relating to the moral obligation to preserve life, and setting these against the mortality of mothers and babies during childbirth. One might also use the passages that refer to proper child-care, set against the difficulties of caring for large numbers of children. This material, when woven into messages for the religious authorities, could provide legitimacy for family planning and help persuade them to support it. Real examples of communication with religious leaders will be found in Chapters 3 and 6.

Pre-testing of communication materials with groups that are representative of the target audience before putting them in final form for broadcasting or distribution is another social marketing principle. It helps to ensure that the materials are comprehensible and that their messages are appropriate for the specific audience.

Other key principles of social marketing are *monitoring, feedback*, and *adjustment*. Even after good qualitative research and pre-testing of materials, one needs to confirm that the communication activities are on course. So, continuous monitoring and feedback are conducted to check that the messages are being received, understood and accepted by the intended audience. Any misunderstandings or undesired effects being caused by the messages and materials are corrected.

A good example of this process took place in Honduras some years ago when a USAID-supported programme for oral rehydration therapy (ORT) for infants was under way. The rehydration solution was called Litrosol and it was intensely promoted by communication media. However, ongoing monitoring with mothers revealed that most of them thought there were two different types of diarrhoea that affected their children. They had local names for each, and they were only giving their children Litrosol for what they perceived as one of these types of diarrhoea. The communicators wanted to adjust their media messages and use both the local diarrhoea names, but the doctors refused to let them, on the grounds that to do so would reinforce unfounded, traditional beliefs. The compromise solution was to recast the messages to say that Litrosol was good for *all* sorts of diarrhoea attack.

Even if marketing has provided communicators for development with better organized and systematic approaches, there are many who abhor social marketing. They consider it to be top-down and manipulative, for they say that it uses refined social science skills and powerful mass media to try to change people's behaviour patterns to conform to criteria established by outsiders with superior knowledge. On the other hand, those who defend social marketing point out that few development interventions, even those based on community participation, do not involve manipulation of some groups by others. There may also be manipulation within peer groups. Furthermore, even in socially advanced and democratic countries, such as Denmark or Sweden, governments are constantly issuing manipulatory exhortations to their people to use car seat-belts, to eat more bread and less fat, or not to drink and drive.

Those in favour of social marketing also argue that the themes to which it is applied are usually of undoubted health or social benefit, and seen in this light, some of its protagonists jokingly call it 'ethical manipulation'. They consider that it is morally defensible to use all the skills – and even wiles – available to us to induce behavioural change when it concerns, for example, reducing infant mortality, curbing teenage pregnancies, or preventing the spread of infectious diseases such as AIDS.

The truth about the merits or otherwise of social marketing surely lies somewhere between the extreme positions for and against it. Those who state that there are certain behaviour patterns that should be changed, in the interests of people themselves and of society in general, certainly have a point. Most of these desirable changes lie in the areas of health, nutrition, and safety. AIDS is a good example. Limiting the spread of HIV is undoubtedly of vital importance to individuals and to society, and this must surely justify any form of communication, manipulatory or not, to try to change behaviour. The real ethical problem with social marketing would be evident if it were used to manipulate people towards a behavioural change, or the adoption of an innovation, without the *total certainty* that it was in their interests, and in the interests of society to do so.

As an illustration, taken from UNICEF's area of work, one can hardly object to social marketing to promote the use of ORT to save infants from death. However, to use it to persuade a group of women to adopt a particular income-generating activity would be an unjustifiable imposition; and it would be dangerous too because it might fail, with long-term negative consequences. In such circumstances, a communication process without a predetermined behavioural objective should be used to help the women analyse the alternatives and make their own decision about what they want to do, and can do.

Overall, marketing has provided communication for development with a number of valuable strategies and techniques, and they can be used without relation to top-down approaches or the persuasive inducing of behavioural change. Qualitative research, audience segmentation, proper message design, pre-testing of communication materials, and ongoing feedback are valuable tools in any communication activity.

Communication in Today's Development Strategies

Marketing certainly provided a number of approaches and techniques, but it was the notion of 'bottom-up' development and the aim of achieving participation that caused the greatest evolution in the conceptual aspects of communication and its potential role. Many of the early practitioners of communication soon propounded the view that there is a direct connection between communication and true participation – in effect that they are two sides of the same coin. Indeed, before people of a community can participate, they must have appropriate information, and they must follow a communication process to reach a collective perception of the local situation and of the options for improvement.

However, people often have difficulty in conceptualizing and articulating their view of their problems, needs, and possibilities, especially in poor communities of low educational levels. Nor do they have access to the information they need to form rational opinions and to take coherent decisions. Hence the usefulness of communication inputs, which may use media such as video recording and playback, or local radio broadcasts, or just group communication work with simple aids such as flip-charts. In reality, when communication processes are used to inform people, enable them to contribute their points of view, reach consensus, and carry out an agreed change or development action together, it can be said that communication *is* participation.

The need for people to acquire new knowledge and skills is as important as ever in development programmes, but information and training activities should be based on people's interests and needs, as identified in consultation with them. The traditional role of audio-visual media to improve the effectiveness of information and training programmes is obviously still as valid as ever. Great progress has been made, and experience gained, in using what were once considered delicate and sophisticated media, such as video, with local populations in harsh technical environments, as described in Chapter 4. Much has also been learned about how to structure and present information to make it accessible to people of low educational levels.

Bottom-up and participatory development approaches have introduced changes in the way mass media should be used. Bombarding people with messages has gone out, at least in principle. Greater access to the media by ordinary people, and participation in programming, have become the aim. For example, in the area of broadcasting, more emphasis is now placed on community media, with much participation from the audience in the programming, as described in Chapter 7.

Similarly, improving interpersonal communication between development workers in the field and their client populations has become necessary. This is in the sense of making field workers more effective facilitators of change, listening more than they talk, and helping people to help themselves, as opposed to making them better preachers of some development sermon.

Qualitative research techniques, such as Focus Group Discussions, used originally just to investigate people's perceptions and attitudes, have been found to be a perfect technique for participatory diagnosis of problems, planning, and evaluation with communities.

In general terms, for today's change and development strategies, the communication aims are to stimulate debate and 'conscientization' for participatory decision-making and action, and second, to help people acquire the new knowledge and skills they need. A third aim is to use communication to promote better teamwork, cooperation and coordination between various governmental, or non-governmental, organizations involved in multidisciplinary development programmes.

Is Communication for Change and Development Utopian?

Some people may think that communication strategies for democratic decision-making, change, and development, are too idealistic to be put into practice, and that they have little relevance in the reality of today's world. Fortunately, however, there have been a number of experiences to prove that these concepts can be made to work.

The first of these noteworthy experiences took place in Canada, which has always been a leader in communication for development. As long ago as the 1930s, Canada pioneered radio programming for farmers and organized group listening, or Radio Farm Forums as they were called. These later became the model for numerous rural broadcasting projects in developing countries. Equally innovative was the setting up of a unit in the mid-1960s called Challenge for Change, as part of the Canadian National Film Board. The objective of this unit was to use film – and video when it became available later – for social development purposes. When Challenge for Change became involved in a place called Fogo Island, off the east coast of Newfoundland, the experience proved so important that it set a precedent for much communication for development in the future.

In the late 1960s, Fogo Island was in serious economic and social decline. Its people lived mainly from fishing, but their boats were small and their markets on the island were limited. Mainland-based fleets were able to roam further and had assured markets for their catch when they returned to port. This and other factors had led to such a decline in Fogo that the provincial government began working on a proposal to help the inhabitants evacuate to the mainland. At that point, the Extension Department of Memorial University of Newfoundland, in St Johns, and Challenge for Change stepped in and asked if they could carry out an experiment in the island.

On arriving in Fogo, the team told the islanders that they would like to make some films with them and show them to the community. They assured the people that no films would be taken away from the island without their permission, and that anyone interviewed on camera would have a chance to see the resulting film first and have changes made before it was shown to anybody else.

They began to shoot films in pairs, usually to show both sides of an argument concerning the future of the island. For example, they made one film with a young man who explained why he was convinced that the only hope he had of making good in life was to leave for the mainland. They made the opposing film with another young man who had managed to build a long-lining fishing boat, was content with his life, and had no desire to leave.

These and many other films, and later videos, were shown to the community during evening meetings to spark off a debate. The results were striking. People argued and became emotional, but they also became involved in a serious analysis of the situation affecting their community. In addition, the filmed interviews drew attention to excellent insights and ideas held by people who would normally not have the chance or the inclination to express them in public.

Over the months, what communicators have come to call the 'Fogo Process' took hold. The people began to see themselves and their situation more clearly. The films were providing a mirror image, and the discussions that followed were opening their minds to problems and their causes and to possible courses of action. In effect, this was the same sort of process as 'conscientization', invented by Paolo Freire at about the same time.

The culmination on Fogo was that the people were able to develop a well-articulated proposal to stay on the island, but with help from the provincial government to provide certain key things to make it possible. For example, they required training facilities for young fishermen, credit to build fishing boats, and so on. The authorities were able to meet the requests, and the people decided not to leave the island.

The imaginative way communication media were used to stimulate this process of participatory problem diagnosis and development planning remains a shining example of what can be done. Other examples will be described in the rest of this book, but one must raise one's hat to the team who worked in Fogo, and equally to the Canadian authorities who were willing to listen to the people and help them with development as they, the people, wanted it.

This and similar experiences in development are important because they illustrate that the essence of involving and mobilizing people is the sharing of knowledge and ideas between them, and between them and development workers, through communication processes. Such sharing of knowledge implies an exchange between communication equals: on the one hand, technical specialists and the authorities learn about people's needs and possibilities, as they see them, and on the other, people learn of the ideas of the specialists and the authorities. The ultimate purpose of knowledge-sharing is to help people develop the capacity to take increasing control over their environment, agriculture, health, habitat, family size, and the other factors that so critically impinge on their quality of life.

The Functions of Communication for Development

In practical terms, communication for development has three separate but related components: *social communication*, *educational communication*, and *institutional communication*.

Social communication

In the community promotes dialogue, reflection, participatory situation analysis, consensus building, decision-making, and planning of actions for change and development. In essence, it is the process of mobilizing people and communities, and helping them to gain the insights and confidence needed to tackle their problems. It is also used for participatory monitoring and evaluation. It may employ audio-visual media to stimulate the process of group discussion and to record the outcome, but it may also be conducted using aids such as simple flip-charts to help people visualize and keep track of the points of the discussion as they go along. Mass media services may support the process, and even become involved in it, especially when they are locally based. Traditional media, such as theatre, music and dance, can also be successfully used.

Educational communication

Is used to help people acquire the knowledge and skills they need to be able to put change and development decisions into action. It takes educational content from specialists and presents it in various media forms, particularly using audio-visual technology, to help people understand, learn, and remember. It is an essential element in training programmes at all levels.

Institutional communication

Creates the flows of information inside and between all the partners involved in a development action, including government departments, parastatal organizations, NGOs, and the communities. The aim is to improve coordination and management by creating a common understanding among the various partners of the project's objectives, activities and progress. Such common understanding is the basis for good teamwork.

The point needs to be made that despite the increasing use of the word 'communication' in many countries to cover the press and public relations functions of a corporation or institution, the concepts of communication that we present in this book have nothing whatsoever to do with institutional image building. That said, we might sum up with a definition:

Communication for development is the use of communication processes, techniques and media to help people towards a full awareness of their situation and their options for change, to resolve conflicts, to work towards consensus, to help people plan actions for change and sustainable development, to help people acquire the knowledge and skills they need to improve their condition and that of society, and to improve the effectiveness of institutions.

Communication for Development at Work

Part Two will present a series of case studies showing how communication has been used to promote development and change. Some of the examples are global in scope, while others are national, or local within a single country.

The case studies show how well-planned and well-executed communication has been a powerful force in helping societies achieve social aims and adapt to changing circumstances. They cover communication for health, for agriculture and rural development, and for population.

The case studies have been chosen to show a variety of different strategies and media at work. The common thread running through them all is that the objective was to facilitate change and development through providing information and communication processes of the right kind, at the right time, and in the right form. In all the cases, the result was better awareness and understanding of the problems and needs, and the enabling of people to take the necessary actions to improve the situation.

CHAPTER 3

A Process without Precedent: Societies Mobilized for Immunization

Six years is but an instant in human history – too brief, it would seem, to bring any fundamental improvement in the human condition. Yet the six years between 1984 and 1990 saw a process take place that was without precedent for its magnitude and global scope. Before 1984, the number of the world's children who were immunized against the principal childhood diseases was about 20 per cent, and not increasing much. Then, a worldwide movement was launched that increased the coverage to 80 per cent in just those six years. Much of the increase was in countries so poor, with so little infrastructure, and such a long history of high infant mortality, that there had seemed to be little hope of bringing radical improvements in child health. The stunning achievement of raising immunization coverage in this way was the result of what is called 'social mobilization'.

UNICEF was the driving force behind the social mobilization that led to the vast increase in vaccination coverage and also to the widespread adoption of other measures that would reduce infant mortality. As the late James P. Grant, the executive director of UNICEF at the time, wrote:

Social development is linked to concerted public action. No matter how valid and worthy the cause, little progress is made in achieving it until a ground swell of public support is built up and diverse sectors of society become actively involved in the process of change.

An unprecedented gap now exists between what could be done and what is being done to overcome the worst aspects of poverty that claim the lives of 35,000 children a day. The gaps between what is and what could be ... are not likely to be closed by any automatic or inevitable process of social development; they are closed most often by the commitment and action of large and growing numbers of people who begin to exert pressure for change ... Communication [is] an essential part of this process. Serious advances [can] only be made when large numbers of people begin to know more, care more, and do more. Fortunately, we live in a communication epoch in which mass media are constantly expanding their outreach and influence.

It was such thinking that led UNICEF into promoting social mobilization, which is a practical recognition and operational strategy that takes into account the essentially human nature of development. Furthermore, it implicitly recognizes that social progress can take place only as a result of attitudinal and behavioural change across broad sectors of society.

The UNICEF leadership took into account past experience with great movements, such as those already mentioned for the abolition of slavery, colonialism, apartheid, and so on. Thus social mobilization for child survival and development has its philosophical origins in these great movements, but it did not suddenly appear on the UNICEF scene. On the contrary, it grew over time, building on some enlightened and yet pragmatic experiences in the field, and as various types of communication activity were dovetailed into a cohesive whole.

The first major building block in social mobilization was the Child Survival and Development Revolution (CSDR), launched in 1982. Its four main elements were growth monitoring, oral rehydration therapy, breastfeeding, and immunization. UNICEF's premise was that dramatic reductions in infant mortality could be achieved if parents could be persuaded and helped to apply these four relatively cheap and simple measures routinely. They were measures that could be promoted through communication processes and media, and particularly through social marketing, which UNICEF embraced for some years.

Other building blocks in the process that led to social mobilization were 'advocacy' and 'forming strategic alliances'. Advocacy in a country context is pleading the cause of children, or of specific actions in their favour, in order to generate moral and substantive support, mainly from decision-makers and the influential. Advocacy has always been inherent in UNICEF's work.

Strategic alliances for UNICEF's objectives began to assume identity and prominence in the early 1980s because, with its limited resources, UNICEF could never be more than a catalyst within a country. There was little, if any, chance of making a major impact without the support, and preferably active involvement, of as many allies as possible. Then, over a few years in the early 1980s, and in a few countries, these separate elements began to coalesce for child survival, and a new and better integrated pattern began to emerge: advocacy, alliance building, mobilizing resources, and communication to create demand for services and to impart information became part of a single continuum known as social mobilization.

Social mobilization can be defined as a planned process that enlists the support and active involvement of any and all sectors within a society that can play a role in achieving an agreed social objective, converging the interest and actions of institutions, groups, and communities towards that objective, thereby mobilizing the human and material resources to reach it, and rooting it in society's conscience, particularly in the community, to ensure its sustainability.

In UNICEF's work, social mobilization is the base for achieving large-scale delivery and acceptance of services that will benefit children and families. In practice, UNICEF's objectives depend upon changing aspects of people's behaviour. These changes may include parents having their infants fully immunized, or boiling drinking water, or giving oral rehydration salts to children with diarrhoea, or allowing their daughters to attend school.

In addition, the changes needed may also include modifying government policy, or persuading national or provincial planners to give greater priority and budget resources to child survival and development, or improving the social skills of health workers, or changing the way journalists and media producers perceive and report on social issues, or changing a community's perception of its problems and its ability to solve them.

When planning social mobilization, a first consideration is whom to mobilize. In the main this depends on who has the moral or political authority, or the power or influence, to tackle the specific problem, or to help achieve a particular goal. In most countries, the targets for social mobilization related to child survival and development issues begin with political leaders, decision-makers, and opinion leaders. Obviously, ministries and institutions dealing with social affairs, health, education, and information need to be mobilized, but in addition, other less obvious bodies such as those concerned with defence, planning, and finance may well have a potential role to play. Programme managers and service providers, such as health workers, teachers, and extension and cooperative agents form another target.

In the non-governmental sector, targets for mobilization are usually voluntary organizations, private-sector media producers and advertisers, and local, traditional, and religious leaders. The industrial and commercial sector may also be usefully mobilized.

Finally, and in every case of course, the users of services, or beneficiaries, must be mobilized. In UNICEF's sphere of interest, these include women, parents, and others providing care to children.

The planning for social mobilization begins with a situation analysis, set in the context of the social problem and the action or behavioural change required from different sectors of society to resolve it. The analysis examines the characteristics of major target audiences (including their media habits) and maps societal information flow. It identifies potential allies and points of resistance, ways to improve the knowledge and motivation of beneficiaries, constraints on attitudinal and behavioural change and how to overcome them, effective media channels (mass and traditional), the potential for community participation, and ways to improve service provision.

Clearly, research will be needed to obtain quantitative and qualitative information for the analysis. This research uses techniques, including some current in marketing, such as Focus Group Discussions.

The results of the social mobilization analysis lay the foundation for a communication strategy and plan to reach and influence each of the audiences. The plan may include lobbying and individual contacts, orientation and training workshops, or mass media campaigns, according to the specific audience. The overall social mobilization plan is made up of a series of interlocking and complementary communication and promotional activities.

Social Mobilization for Child Immunization

Social mobilization first came into prominence in connection with the Expanded Programme of Immunization (EPI) and Universal Child Immunization (UCI). EPI was an initiative of the World Health Organization (WHO). It was formally launched in 1974, and in 1977, WHO declared its aim of immunizing all children against the six principal and preventable childhood diseases by 1990. This was to be achieved through a steady improvement of health services. However, by the early 1980s, it had become clear that the target of immunization for all children by 1990 could not possibly be met at the existing rate of progress, and this was brought to the attention of the 1982 session of the World Health Assembly.

Faced with this situation, UNICEF proposed launching a massive drive to immunize at least 80 per cent of the world's children by 1990. This fitted into its recently launched Child Survival and

Development Revolution, and 80 per cent coverage would be enough, in a first instance, to block the transmission of the main childhood diseases and make a major impact on their prevalence.

The UNICEF proposal initially met with misgivings in WHO, which not so long before had seen the collapse of its campaign to eliminate malaria from the world. That setback caused many in WHO to doubt the wisdom of such single-strategy, vertical campaigns. They still felt that it was more important to build up primary health care services, and through them, gradually achieve immunization for all children and other health inputs. The critics also maintained that to achieve UCI would require extraordinary efforts that might work against routine activities, and prove unsustainable in the long run.

The same misgivings were also present in the health services of some countries. However, there were also many health officials, such as a key one in Colombia, who summed up the opinion in favour of a massive immunization drive when he said: 'There were millions of children that needed to be immunized then and there. We could not wait for the health services to build their capacity to reach all children on a regular basis. We had to begin a national drive to try to reach every child that was unprotected.'

Similar thinking had been inspiring UNICEF: if one waited for the services to be in place, UCI would simply take too long to achieve. Urgent action, based on provisional structures and temporary measures if necessary, should begin. UCI could be the catalyst for a chain reaction that would, in a very few years, result in expanded and improved health services.

A number of international development agencies became involved in the discussions about UCI, including the World Bank, UNDP, and the Rockefeller Foundation. Finally, in 1984, the objective of fully immunizing 80 per cent of the world's children by 1990 was agreed as a joint UNICEF and WHO programme under the title Universal Child Immunization–1990. It would be based on UNICEF's proposal of a massive drive.

The challenges of UCI–1990

To achieve UCI would mean overcoming a wide range of obstacles. First, health service staff would have to be motivated to accept the goal of UCI–1990, and resistance could be expected in some quarters. Then they would need to be trained for their part in achieving it. Other problems were organizational and logistical. For example, vaccines must be kept cool to retain their potency. Cold-chain facilities would need to be created to keep them cool from the moment they were unloaded from the aircraft bringing them from overseas, through their journey to a refrigerated store, from there to outlying health centres, and from these to be carried by foot or bicycle for use in some remote community, often without electricity. Everyone handling the vaccines, from those unloading the aircraft to the vaccinators, would need orientation and training, and so would technicians to maintain and repair the cold-chain equipment. Transport would be needed, and information and monitoring systems would have to be set up to keep track of progress.

Last but by no means least, parents would have to be persuaded to bring their children for vaccination, and to return the number of times necessary to provide them with full immunity. And this would have to be done despite the difficulty of explaining a concept such as immunization to illiterate or poorly educated parents, and despite the mother's concern when her child reacts to a vaccination by running a slight fever and being generally miserable for a few hours.

Individual countries would have to work out the best strategy and plan for reaching UCI in their particular circumstances. In many, creating the necessary conditions would mean starting virtually from nothing, and the dimension of the challenge was enormous. In 1981, the average immunization coverage in all developing countries for children under one year old was about 20 per cent. There were some countries with much lower rates; for example, Bangladesh had only 2 per cent coverage, even though immunization services were readily available to about 20 per cent of the population. Yet by 1990, worldwide coverage had been multiplied fourfold to about 80 per cent. Taking into account population increase in the intervening years, this actually represented a fivefold increase in the numbers of children immunized.

The rapid acceleration in vaccination coverage that made this achievement possible began with the launching of social mobilization initiatives. In the following pages, the social mobilization process for UCI–1990 is described by the sectors that were mobilized. However, where social mobilization was successfully carried out, all, or almost all, of the sectors described separately here were mobilized in an interlocking and mutually reinforcing way, thus concentrating them around the immunization goal.

Creating the Political Will at the Top

More than thirty heads of state lent their personal prestige and political support to UCI–1990. This was rarely a spontaneous commitment, and UNICEF played a key role in obtaining it. James Grant, UNICEF's executive director, had worked in Turkey during the Green Revolution, and from that experience he had learned that political will in favour of a social development action is instrumental in conducting the action to a successful conclusion. He therefore took an active role in obtaining political commitment for immunization. His interventions were primarily of three types: direct meetings with heads of state; opening doors at very high level for UNICEF representatives who could subsequently, with access assured, sustain the advocacy effort; and, finally, encouraging UNICEF representatives themselves to push for a higher level of political commitment than they might have otherwise attempted.

Spouses of heads of state also played an important role. In Egypt, Suzanne Mubarak, the wife of the president, had a long-standing involvement with an NGO concerned with children. Her interest was such that when the Child Survival and Development Revolution got under way in the mid-1980s, she was a natural and committed ally. And later President Mubarak also put his full weight behind child survival, declaring a decade for the Protection and Development of the Egyptian Child (1989–99). That pithy declaration, which included precise, demanding, and measurable objectives – such as the eradication of new outbreaks of polio by 1994 and decreasing infant mortality to fewer than 50 per thousand live births – has been providing the framework and legitimacy for those promoting, persuading, and organizing the necessary actions. It is constantly used as part of advocacy and in media work. Mainly as a result of this political will for child survival, Egypt was the first country in the world to reach full coverage with immunization, and also, with ORT to prevent children dying from dehydration during diarrhoea attacks.

In India, James Grant had met Prime Minister Mrs Indira Gandhi in 1984, not long before her assassination, and gained her commitment to UCI–1990. However, it was her son, Rajiv, who launched the Universal Immunization Programme – as it was known in India – and he created a Technology Mission on Immunization attached directly to his office. The prime minister's commitment and involvement were instrumental in giving the programme the prestige and momentum it needed to succeed as well as it did.

In numerous countries, the head of state opened immunization campaigns by personally immunizing a child. In the case of Colombia, the first country to carry out integrated social mobilization for UCI beginning in 1984, President Belisario Betancur administered a dose of oral polio vaccine to an infant in front of television cameras.

With the highest levels in the state committed to UCI, government structures were naturally motivated to work towards the nationally set goal. Where the political will was insufficient, progress towards UCI was hampered. For example, in Senegal, where the political will at the top was inconstant, immunization campaigns were launched in a spasmodic fashion, with the result that the widespread and continuing commitment necessary from those responsible for service delivery was never created. Immunization therefore tended to go by fits and starts, and much of what was achieved was the result of the personal commitment of a relatively small number of health sector staff, often working in isolation, rather than as part of a motivated and enthusiastic national team.

UNICEF's successful attempt to generate the political will for UCI in many countries, though often spearheaded by James Grant, was usually a combined effort in which the UNICEF representatives in the countries, officials from headquarters, and UNICEF's goodwill ambassadors all played an important role. When these goodwill ambassadors, who included international celebrities such as the late Audrey Hepburn, Liv Ullman, and Imran Khan, visited a country, they had contacts and influence at the highest level. This, and the publicity and media exposure that surrounded their visits, were major elements in generating political support and public interest.

Local Elections as a Springboard

Generating political will at the *local* level was not left out. In Colombia in 1986, a law had been passed decentralizing the nation's administration, politics, and finance. As part of this process, the first popular elections of mayors for the 1,009 municipalities were planned for 1988. Under the new law, the mayors would take over the management of services, such as health and education, which had previously been run by central government.

The UNICEF Country Office took the intellectual lead in mounting a campaign in favour of children's issues that would run parallel with the election campaigns of mayoral candidates. The aim was to induce these candidates to include programmes in favour of children in their political platforms. The campaign was conducted in partnership with the National Federation of Coffee Growers, and with a newly created NGO known as the Procomun, set up to promote good local government following the introduction of the decentralized administration system.

One of us (S.R.-E.), who was UNICEF information officer in Colombia at the time, played the central role in conceiving and implementing the campaign. It consisted of a series of integrated communication activities and materials. The prime element in the campaign was a TV spot broadcast on all the main TV channels several times a day during the weeks that the mayoral candidates were electioneering. This spot showed an 8-year-old girl, Juanita, coming out of school and talking to her companions about the mayoral elections, with Juanita saying that when she grew up, she wanted to be mayor so that she could improve the situation for children. Then, turning to camera, looking straight into the lens, and raising her index finger in a gesture of discovery, she exclaimed, 'I have an idea!'

Juanita's idea was to write a letter to mayoral candidates. The resulting text was written on a page torn from a school notebook, and in Juanita's clear but still unformed hand, with the punctuation errors and faulty syntax of an 8-year-old left uncorrected:

Mayor,

I am Juanita, you do not know me, but I know you. I know you are a very important person. Who is going to be in charge here. Who is liked and respected by people. My mother says that you are going to do a lot for us, because now there is money to do things in this community, and that you will do them. For this, you must think about me and the other children like me. I would like you to know that we are lacking schools, clean water, food, health ... Our problems are many but there are easy solutions, that don't need much money, only that you want to do them. I cannot vote because I am a child. I cannot give you my support yet, but you, yes, you can give me yours.

Excuse me and thank you!!! Juanita.

A recording of the text of this letter read by Juanita was broadcast repeatedly over the radio, and posters appeared all over the country showing Juanita's face and the punchline of her letter in her handwriting: 'I cannot give you my support yet, but you, yes, you can give me yours.' At the same time, a pamphlet, again with Juanita's photograph and her punchline, was sent to each of the 3,500 mayoral candidates. Inside were reproduced the full text of Juanita's letter, shown on the page torn from her school notebook, and a charming child's drawing of a model community with a school, community hall, clinic, children's playground, and sweetshop. The other side of the pamphlet presented information about the state of children in Colombia. In simple language, it provided data on child mortality, malnutrition, lack of access to primary education, school drop-out rates, street children, uncared for and abandoned children, and so on. To stimulate the mayoral candidates to reflection, the text asked them whether they knew the situation concerning these issues in their own communities.

Under the heading, 'As mayor, what could you do?' it suggested actions they might take at the municipal level to improve the situation, and described the positive results that could be obtained.

As a result of the Juanita campaign, many mayoral candidates wrote letters to pledge their support for the betterment of the condition of children, to ask for more details, and for advice. The election of the mayor of Bogotá, the capital, was given special attention because that office carries great prestige and importance in the country. After the mayoral candidates had received their pack of information materials about children's issues in Colombia, the main radio network in the country, Caracol, invited them all to a round-table discussion, during which children's issues were raised. The one who was best able to address these issues in a knowledgeable and positive way was later elected mayor. In that role, he launched a Basic Social Service project in the poor quarters of Bogotá, with UNICEF support.

Mayors under pressure

About a year after the Juanita campaign, which had aimed to sensitize mayors to the general needs of children, I (S.R.-E.) began to develop an idea of how one might involve mayors more directly and actively in achieving the objectives set by UCI–1990. A special communication strategy would be needed because many of the mayors were not very well educated, and generalized information about the children of Colombia might not be easy for them to relate to the particular circumstances of the children in their own municipalities.

Furthermore, national targets, such as that of immunizing 80 per cent of the country's children, mean little at the local level, and the natural reaction of local authorities could be to consider such a target as being the responsibility of the central Ministry of Health. The solution I had in mind was to interpret national targets in a local framework, and at the same time urge mayors to fulfil their responsibilities.

I took my idea to the Ministry of Health and to various potential allies, and with their support, and using the production services of a professional advertising agency, we launched a campaign linked to the 1989 national vaccination days and targeted at incumbent mayors. We designed and printed customized posters for each of the 1,009 communities in the country. At the top was Juanita's punchline to make the thematic link with the Juanita campaign, and the phrase 'This is the reality in ... ' followed by the name of the community in large red letters. This was followed by a list of the three vaccines needed to prevent the main childhood diseases, and the number of children in the community who had *not* received full coverage was printed against each.

We realized that the numbers alone might mean little to the mayor, so the poster included a rating of the immunization coverage as either 'good', 'average', or 'poor'. After this, the poster stated how many children under one year old there were in the community in 1989, and ended with an exhortation to the mayor: 'Mayor, let no child remain without immunization at the end of your term of office.'

These posters needed to be prominently displayed in each municipality. For obvious reasons, this might not happen if they were sent only to the mayor. So we also arranged for them to be sent to the telecommunications office, schoolteachers, priests, agricultural credit bank, and so on. They went with a covering letter from the management of the different entities, asking them to support children's concerns and, in particular, to display the posters. There were about seven separate dispatches of the material for each municipality, some 70,000 dispatches in all. We were able to persuade the postal services to provide totally free distribution in return for the post office logo on the packaging of the materials.

This pressure on mayors produced varied responses. The mayors with good coverage were, of course, delighted that the whole of their community could see and appreciate the results of their efforts. For those with poor coverage, a first reaction was quite frequently to complain to the Ministry of Health that the figures were wrong, but they soon accepted the challenge and got to work.

... and presidential candidates too

Building on the success of the advocacy work with mayors, we similarly exploited the 1990 Colombian presidential elections in the interests of children. UNICEF again played a catalytic role, supported this time by the Presidential Council for Human Rights. A folder was sent to each of the main presidential candidates who had party representation in Congress. It contained a short paper emphasizing the rights of children and describing their general situation in Colombia. There were even shorter papers on specific issues such as child health, education, street children, child abuse, and so on. Each of these issue-specific papers ended with a series of questions to the presidential candidate, asking specifically what he would do to tackle the issues, if elected, and giving him a deadline by which to reply. Identical folders were distributed to the press and electronic media.

Each candidate was effectively obliged to put his party machinery to work formulating a political platform concerning children's issues. Once all of the replies had been received, we called in the media. The main newspaper, *El Tiempo*, carried a full-page spread describing the political platform for children of each of the presidential candidates. This was in addition to the large amount of mass media interest and coverage that had already been stimulated by sending the folder to them at the same time as it was sent to the presidential candidates.

Galvanizing the Deliverers of Services

In the 1980s, health services in a majority of developing countries were working on increasingly tight budgets because of structural adjustment programmes imposed by the World Bank and the International Monetary Fund. With few prospects for improvement, with scarce resources, and with low salaries, staff could hardly be expected to be enthusiastic and motivated about their work. In addition, the policies and the way resources were allocated in many countries militated strongly against primary health care services. Unless these factors could be changed, UCI–1990 would never be achieved.

Nigeria provides an interesting example of how things stood in the early 1980s. At that time, as mentioned in Chapter 1, four children out of ten were dying before reaching five years of age, which represented 2,000 child deaths *per day*. Only 2 per cent of the national budget was being devoted to health, and primary health care hardly existed.

UNICEF staff in the country believed that governments, if approached correctly, could be made to change their policies, and galvanized into activity. To do this, however, UNICEF staff would have to come up with solutions as opposed to problems – solutions that could be a monument to the national regime. Another factor that they could play on was that governments have an insatiable need to be loved by their people.

In analysing the different approaches that could be used to change policies and galvanize service deliverers, the UNICEF staff in Nigeria identified the following twelve angles for appealing to their government audiences:

- Alarm and shame: with 2,000 children a day dying, it should not be difficult to create a sense of alarm and shame among officials.
- Facts and information: providing insights into the real situation, for example by taking officials to the field to see it for themselves and telling them what *could* be done about it.
- Giving credit: making officials feel good, feel warm inside, about something they had done, or ostensibly done, or something worthwhile they were going to do. This could make them into allies.
- Endorsement from the eminent: bringing in people eminent in the sphere of child health and development and having them comment favourably on what they saw being done.
- Local and national pride: praising the success of a local or national endeavour outside its immediate environment.
- Intermediate achievement: calling attention to the fact that a programme was well on the way to success and that its objectives could certainly be achieved, if the effort were made.
- Praise: praising directly, or better still indirectly, the efforts of national individuals concerned with a programme.
- Fear of not performing: pointing out that the highest authorities in the land were supporting the programme and expected results.
- The bandwagon effect: exploiting the competitive spirit in a society to persuade all departments of an administration to work together, with each anxious to have a share in the action.
- Legitimacy and authority: exploiting the policy commitments or legislative provisions to make service providers pay attention.
- Ownership: telling people that the programme belonged to them, and that what was being accomplished was due to them.
- Hijack: taking advantage of contacts with eminent persons to associate them with what needed to be done, and in such a way that they could not wriggle out.

In the early 1980s, there were 480 Nigerian children dying each day of measles alone, and of these, 50 a day were dying in the main children's hospital. It was clear that the immunization programme itself needed a shot in the arm. The first step was to convince the health authorities that the existing immunization services were not functioning. A short video that showed 80,000 doses of vaccine languishing against the *outside* wall of a cold store was a good beginning. Fact-finding trips to the field were not common for Ministry of Health officials, for the institutional culture did not perceive them as essential. So UNICEF arranged and paid for a series of field visits for national staff as the only way for them to see the realities of their health service with their own eyes.

Typically, in most countries, once the top management of the delivery services were committed, the mobilizing of staff began with a series of meetings or workshops. The purpose of these workshops was to reach consensus on what had to be done, on the problems that would have to be resolved, and to start formulating a strategy for doing so.

In Colombia, the health directors from the provinces were called together for a preliminary discussion about an intensified immunization drive. The director from the Atlantic Department had, of his own initiative, been carrying out some mobilization in his area, and he therefore had some practical experience.

A first question raised by a health director, and a perfectly normal one before social mobilization came on the scene, was: 'Who's going to give us the vehicles to transport our vaccination teams?' 'We don't need vehicles,' replied the colleague from the Atlantic Department. Amid the general scepticism of his colleagues, he went on, 'The army and the police have plenty of vehicles. If we go about it right, we can get them to provide the transport.' Such lateral thinking, and the implication of calling on allies to help, was a revolutionary step for staff of the Ministry of Health. Yet it became commonplace as the immunization drive went on and as problems arose and were resolved by staff who came up with imaginative solutions.

In this connection, there is the anecdote of the light aircraft that was to deliver vaccine to a remote area in Colombia. It was delayed by bad weather, and when it was finally able to take off, it would arrive after nightfall at the airstrip, which had neither lights nor navigational aids. After some frantic telephone consultations, the local health staff mobilized as many of the local population with vehicles as they could; they all drove out to the airstrip, where they parked strategically and turned on their headlights so that the pilot could locate the field and make his landing safely.

The role of management and training

Traditionally, health services had never, or almost never, been managed by objectives. Programmes launched under the Child Survival and Development Revolution, such as promotion of ORT, or accelerated programmes of immunization, set precise national and local objectives for the first time in many countries. This provided the framework and the motivation for improving the management of the health delivery system.

A first step in creating the preconditions for good management in most countries was the setting up of an interdisciplinary management group, which brought together people from a range of government sectors such as health, education, information, social affairs, and defence, as well as representatives from NGOs. This management group became the focal point from which coordination and teamwork among the various partners could be promoted and managed. The best of these management groups were led by remarkable people. They had to combine good technical knowledge with excellent management capabilities, and also with the social skills that would make it possible for them to promote cooperation and teamwork among the diverse partners.

The work schedules these special management groups set themselves were often gruelling. For example, the group set up in Colombia for the immunization crusade would meet every day at 7.30 a.m. and the meeting would last most of the morning. This went on for several months each year as preparations were being made for the annual vaccination days. However, they were not meetings in the normal sense of the word. They were more akin to the proceedings in an operations room. There were continual incoming and outgoing telephone calls to the 33 regional health services in the country. Each of these had to prepare a monthly work plan and timetable, and this was monitored every second day by the management group.

In addition, during the initial stages of the UCI drive, norms and instructions had to be drawn up for the more than 10,000 vaccination posts in Colombia, covering everything from the handling of vaccines and cold-chain management to the child age range and the techniques of administering each vaccine. Staff training had to be planned and put into operation, and so on. It was a mammoth task and most of the members of the management group were carrying it out in addition to much of their routine work.

Orientation and training of health staff were essential in all countries. Training of trainers was a first priority, but after that, training was provided for a wide spectrum of people who ranged from physicians to nurses, schoolteachers, pharmacists, social workers, laboratory technicians, statisticians, and cold-chain maintenance staff. To give an idea of the dimension of the training operation in some countries, it involved about 70,000 people in Egypt, while in India, the very successful immunization programme required the retraining of the entire 150,000 medical and paramedical staff of the national health system. In addition, the training was extended to NGOs and private practitioners.

Training in social skills was often required to improve the way medical and paramedical staff related to their patients. For example, in Algeria, one of us (C.F.) trained and supervised a local team to do research into the reasons for mothers dropping out before the immunization cycle of their infants was complete. Our initial results in one area showed that mothers were deeply resentful of the authoritarian and superior behaviour of the paramedical staff towards them during their first or early visits, and so they refused to return. We had a prickly meeting with the health managers, who flatly rejected this research finding. It was only after continued research in other areas of the country confirmed that the problem was general that they agreed to training in social skills for their field staff.

In Bangladesh there was a similar situation. There, the BCG vaccine against tuberculosis is given in the first days of a baby's life, and by the late 1980s, over 90 per cent of parents in most of the country were bringing in their children spontaneously for this first shot, only to drop out later in the immunization cycle. Behavioural research showed that the reason for drop out was that health workers were not taking the trouble to talk to parents about the immunization cycle and the need to return for further vaccinations on certain dates. This led to an in-depth analysis of the training needs of field-level health workers in Bangladesh and to a programme of training workshops in interpersonal communication skills. The curriculum for this training was developed with typical health workers, so as best to meet their needs as they saw them.

Also in Bangladesh, efforts were made to break down the hier-archical attitudes in government service, inspire an openness towards participatory planning, and induce more democratic procedures. This was done in workshops, usually under a UNICEF umbrella, which brought together people from different institutions and different levels to discuss a problem and to plan a strategy for tackling it. Modern methods for participatory meetings were used, ensuring that all present could speak their minds in a democratic environment, rather than the traditional meetings in which the hierarchically superior dominate the proceedings. The result was that all levels of staff worked as a team with each respecting the knowledge and opinions of the others. Managers were often surprised by the perceptions and ideas brought to the proceedings by the 'simple' fieldworkers. Such discussions leading to an agreed plan gave everyone a sense of ownership, thereby ensuring their commitment to seeing their plan put successfully into practice.

Enlisting the Media

Integrated communication, based on mass media, group media, traditional and folk media, and interpersonal channels, is the usual tool of social mobilization. Some countries that were working towards UCI–1990 successfully developed such integrated communication activities. However, others used a single mass media channel almost exclusively – usually television – but also backed it with interpersonal channels. Others still used interpersonal channels intensively, and hardly any mass media at all.

Of these different strategies, the integrated communication approach was generally the most successful, and it is cheaper to reach large numbers of people through mass media and interpersonal channels than it is to reach them through interpersonal channels only. However, there were specific factors that favoured one approach or another in a given country. One of these was the way the mass media were organized, which varies in different parts of the world. For example, in Latin America, the US model of commercial media has been generally followed, with thousands of radio and television stations scattered all over the continent.

In other parts of the world, notably in Africa, the Middle East, and Asia, where there was a European colonial influence, the usual pattern is one of state-owned radio and TV. State-owned systems invariably have central production and broadcasting of programmes and, unless the country is very small and flat, relay stations to boost the signal into the remoter areas. In some countries, the state-owned systems also have regional stations, which may produce and broadcast their own programmes locally, as well as relaying central programmes for part of the day.

There were implications for UCI in these distinct media arrangements. In countries where the strategy for UCI was to accelerate on a region-by-region basis, increasing the number of regions each year, and where the media were state-owned and broadcasting to the whole nation, it was not possible to use radio and television in support until the acceleration process had covered the whole country. This was the case in Bangladesh, which started its drive for UCI by concentrating on 8 *upazilas* (sub-districts) in the first year, multiplied to 64 the next, and so on until the whole country was being covered in four years.

Examples of countries that were able to develop a truly integrated communication strategy, using all the mass media and numerous interpersonal channels, were Colombia, the Congo, Syria, and Turkey. Of these Colombia was the forerunner and probably provides the best example of what was done.

Colombia was able to rely on an excellent mass media infrastructure. Its 520 radio stations reach everywhere, and in 1987, television was reaching about 70 per cent of the population. The written press was read by only about 20 per cent. The largest radio network is Caracol, which owns some 125 stations. Its director at the time was concerned with social issues, for earlier, while working in a provincial city, he had seen children with bellies swollen from the effects of waterborne parasites, and had launched a radio campaign about the need to boil drinking water.

Given this social awareness, it was not difficult to persuade Caracol to put its resources into promoting immunization. In effect, Caracol became totally committed to promoting it. Initially, Caracol worked alone, but then in the final years leading up to 1990, it took the initiative of approaching the other radio networks in the country and inviting them to participate in an endeavour it called 'United Radio for Colombia's Children'.

With regard to television, apart from the Juanita TV spot mentioned earlier, there were a number of other TV spots that were creatively produced by some of the best commercial talent in the country. Much of this talent was provided free of charge or in return only for out-of-pocket expenses. Air time was also free.

The main involvement of the written press in Colombia was through *El Tiempo*, one of the most important and respected papers, and one that threw its weight behind the immunization drive. Given the relatively small distribution of newspapers in Colombia, its audience was primarily the urban elite. However, as part of social mobilization, it was also very important to reach this sector, for their interest and moral support were very influential in creating a favourable climate of public opinion. The written press also helped unify opinion in favour of UCI among the medical profession, and at the same time it was motivating for them to see their efforts being given public prominence.

Contrary to the integrated media use in Colombia, Egypt relied primarily on the single channel of television, but backed by intense interpersonal communication. It achieved remarkable results in promoting immunization, and this may be surprising to communication professionals who normally prefer multi-media approaches. It can perhaps be explained by the fact that prior research had shown that television was by far the most influential and preferred medium among about 70 per cent of the population. Furthermore, Egypt's numerous health workers were available to follow up, through personal contacts, on the awareness created by television spots.

Printed materials such as leaflets, stickers, posters, banners, and so on played an enormous role almost everywhere. Some of the materials were to motivate parents to bring their children for vaccination on specific vaccination days; others were of a more general informational nature, explaining, for example, the various doses and their timing to achieve full coverage; still others were in the nature of a reminder about immunization. In the last category, an innovative step in India was to produce millions of 'posters' on tin sheet to give them a longer life and provide a semi-permanent reminder about immunization.

In many countries, an identity for the UCI programme was created through a logo that appeared on all the materials produced, and was also displayed on hoardings and banners. Perhaps the most famous was the *moni* logo in Bangladesh. *Moni* is a term of endearment used for children in that country, and the logo was a drawing of a child crawling towards the viewer, with six arrows pointing in towards it to symbolize the six main diseases. Separating the arrows from the child, there was a bright red ring to symbolize the protective effect of immunization.

The *moni* logo was carefully pre-tested before being finalized, and it was later evaluated. These evaluations showed that it was recognized correctly by 100 per cent of the population in Bangladesh. It appeared on the 20 million matchboxes produced and sold in the country each month. A shoe company put it on its boxes, and it was also displayed by several commercial companies which, when putting up large hoardings to promote their own wares, also included the *moni* logo prominently on them. Most of the 130 or so national and local newspapers in Bangladesh printed the *moni* logo on their masthead for a year or more. Banners and flags with the logo were used to identify vaccination sites.

The remarkable thing about the *moni* logo was not the logo itself but rather its widespread display. This was the result of some intensive advocacy, even if commercial companies realized that associating themselves with UCI would be good for their image, and thus the relationship would be symbiotic.

In Colombia, a comic-strip child, Pitin, was developed and tested for the UCI effort. Pitin, portrayed as a 3- to 4-year old, figured in many of the TV spots and as a logo on the other materials. The name 'Pitin' was pre-tested, with the objective of appealing to children, for he was part of a child-to-child communication strategy; the idea was that children, attracted by Pitin, would talk to their parents about having themselves and their siblings immunized. Pitin costumes that an adult could wear were made, like the Father Christmas garb seen in stores in Western countries in December. During the run-up to vaccination days, Pitins on fire-trucks went around with the reminder that infants must be vaccinated. Later, Pitin was regionalized and given an ethnic identity and clothing that suited him to the different situations in the country.

Traditional media

Bangladesh made particularly good use of traditional media. The country has a heritage of poetry, and today there is a handful of popular poets who write epic works that are produced as very cheap booklets in print runs of 50,000 copies at a time. UNICEF managed to interest these poets in including health and other social material in their work. By the late 1980s, about 8 million booklets a year, which included such information woven into their narratives, were being printed and sold. The hawkers of these booklets read the poems aloud in public places, including the river launch harbour in Dhaka through which 400,000 people pass daily. Those who buy the booklets take them home as treasured possessions to be read aloud by a literate member of the family.

The use of local theatre groups and other traditional art forms was also important in many countries. Again in Bangladesh, there is the Gram Theatre, which was founded in 1981 with the social aim of starting village fairs and forming theatre groups at village level all over the country. It has 167 theatre groups, with some 7,000 amateur actors and theatre workers, and it has played, and is still playing, an important role in social action. With UNICEF, the Gram Theatre has staged hundreds of performances on immunization and other social themes.

Drawing on advertising and marketing skills

The Child Survival and Development Revolution, and particularly UCI, called for high-quality promotion and information materials in many countries. But information units of ministries could never attract and keep the creativity needed to produce them. Even if those government information people did have the talent, they seldom had the resources to do the audience research and pre-testing that would have enabled them to improve their work. It was for these reasons that, for decades, typical broadcasts for health, agriculture and the like had been boring and repetitive. The promotion of UCI and other child survival measures showed that television spots, and other mass media materials for health, must not be any less attractive than materials for promoting commercial products if they are to hold people's attention and make an impact.

Indonesia was a forerunner in using professionally made media spots, for breastfeeding, in the late 1970s, but later, many countries decided to adopt that strategy. Another early experience, also to promote breastfeeding, was in Brazil in the early and mid-1980s. This used professional media spots intensively and had great impact. An evaluation carried out in 1990 showed that in Greater São Paulo, the median duration of breastfeeding had increased from 84 to 146 days.

Brazil's breastfeeding campaign was followed by a series of other mobilization actions in favour of children in the following years, including UCI and street children. El Globo, the mighty media empire, committed itself to the crusade for children, but equally important was that talent from the advertising and promotion industry to conduct behavioural science research, and to plan, design, and produce materials, was also enrolled.

In many countries, involving marketing professionals resulted in

TV spots and other materials which, because they incorporated all the scientific methods, the skills and the art of the marketing industry, made an impact that no materials from a government information unit had ever made before.

In India too, professional market research expertise was called in to conduct a Knowledge, Attitudes, and Practice (KAP) study in 1984 on immunization. Sponsored by UNICEF, this study by an Indian company laid the groundwork for the communication strategy used. A further series of KAP studies in subsequent years provided the information needed to fine-tune the communication work in order to influence families who had been left out, who had dropped out, or who were hard to reach.

For the most part, the mass media, whether commercial or state-owned, were eager and willing to participate in social mobilization for UCI and other CSDR actions. Some international development agencies have historically been willing to pay for air time for social development programmes, but UNICEF has always preferred to work on the assumption that support from the media can be mobilized quite easily and without payment for social programmes concerning children.

This hypothesis has generally proven correct, even where the media are private. The Brazilian experience shows the extent to which the private communication sector is prepared to become involved. In addition to the air time given free by El Globo, the talents of the advertising and marketing industry were usually made available free, with only the costs of materials being paid for by UNICEF or other outside resources. In the five years from 1985 to 1990, the Brazilian media and advertising industry made available US$30 million worth of services and resources for mobilization in favour of children's issues.

Enrolling the Allies

Before the advent of social mobilization, health issues were usually the almost exclusive domain of a country's ministry of health. But social mobilization introduced the notion that health issues should involve all possible allies, whether as moral supporters, as mobilizers of others, or as service providers to complement the efforts of the ministry of health.

With this general principle in mind, UCI was the focus for some remarkable experiences in the involvement of a wide variety of allies; it was the first time in history that the health sector had been able to enlist such broad-based support for its work. In countries all over the world, ministries and services that normally had few if any contacts with the ministry of health, and certainly no regular operational links, became involved. Ministries of information, education, defence, religious affairs, post and telegraph were some examples, as were departments of statistics, police and other security forces.

In the non-governmental sector, a wide range of allies were enlisted. Among those that became involved in UCI were religious leaders, thousands of NGOs working in development, trade unions, university staff, Scout movements, theatre, other entertainment and cultural groups, and volunteers of all types, as well as industrial and commercial firms.

Without the dedicated involvement of NGOs in many countries, UCI would not have been achieved. However, there were many difficulties at the beginning, for UCI required close cooperation between the non-governmental and governmental sectors, whereas traditionally, NGOs bypass government services. As one NGO spokesman said: 'Governments usually thought that NGOs were insignificant and lightweight meddlers, while NGOs thought that government services were useless. Both sides were wrong! The government is good at supplying resources, but it is lousy at mobilizing people, which is what the NGOs are very good at.'

At the community level, much of the mobilization work, and in many cases support for service delivery too, was carried out by NGOs. It is well known that Rotary International raised US$226 million for their Polio Plus programme, under which they provided polio vaccines as part of UCI. What is perhaps less well known is that *local* Rotary Clubs were also involved, taking on a variety of tasks from providing sandwich lunches for vaccination staff during campaigns in Turkey to working with local authorities and helping in mobilization efforts in Bangladeshi communities.

In fact, in Bangladesh most of the mobilization work was carried out by NGOs, particularly by the Bangladesh Rural Advancement Committee, which has a field staff of 5,000 people. The mobilization work by NGOs in Bangladesh was crucial because, as already explained, the centralized mass media could not be used to any extent until the expanding immunization services were available nationally. And in India too, all manner of NGOs became involved, including a coalminers' union in Madhya Pradesh, which assumed responsibility for the immunization of entire communities.

At the community level in many countries, the village leader, the schoolteacher, and the religious leader formed the trio of influential people who, once convinced, were the most effective promoters of UCI, and indeed of any other social action related to child survival and development. In Turkey, the 220,000 primary schoolteachers returned to duty early after their summer break to help prepare the immunization campaign.

The religious authorities and leaders proved a major resource everywhere. In most countries, whatever the dominant religion, it was possible to reach the religious leaders in the communities through their central organizations. In Turkey, in addition to asking for the general support of the local *imams* for immunization, a sermon was prepared that was preached simultaneously from each of the country's 54,000 mosques on the Friday evening before the campaign was launched. Mosques also served as vaccination points in Turkey, as they did in Jordan and Iran.

Throughout the Islamic world, obtaining the active involvement of the religious leaders was made easier by a publication called *Child Care in Islam*. UNICEF supported the publication of this booklet by the Al Azhar University and Mosque in Egypt, the leading centre of Islamic thought. The publication put child care in the context of Islamic teaching, and gave the arguments that would convince the religious leaders to support child survival measures. For example, immunization was promoted within the context of the Islamic duty to preserve life.

For Catholic countries, the Vatican itself became involved following a meeting between the Pope and James Grant in 1983. During Grant's discussions in the Vatican, an interesting question came up: how long did it take for an order or a policy issued by the Vatican to become operational everywhere in the far-flung areas of its influence? In the opinion of the Vatican spokesman, it would take eight to ten years, at least. In the event, however, the Catholic Church was mobilized for UCI very quickly. The Vatican exerted pressure from above and provided legitimacy, while concurrently the Church was mobilized through local interventions in country after country.

Many countries involved schoolchildren in the task of promoting UCI, but Colombia pulled off the biggest and most sustainable coup. Through the Ministry of Education, material on health was introduced into the school curriculum for 16- and 17-year-olds, with related practical work in their communities. These young people, called *vigías de la salud* (health monitors) tracked down left-outs and drop-outs from the immunization programme, or provided information about clean water and sanitation, and so on. This health monitor system, first set up for UCI, still exists. Thus, in any one year, Colombia now has more than 330,000 young people active in health issues in their communities. In addition, the country will have future generations of better informed and more health-conscious citizens.

Commerce and industry were important partners. In addition to the sort of cooperation they gave in exposing logos and other materials, such as the *moni* logo in Bangladesh, they also provided much logistical and practical help. Just one example was the Fish and Meat Corporation in Turkey, which provided refrigerated space for the 41 million doses of vaccine required for the first campaign.

Individuals were also of great importance as allies. In particular, many actors, entertainers and famous people played a central role by making available their time at no cost, or at a small percentage of their normal rates, to appear in television spots or short skits. In almost every country, some of these people offered their services with a minimum of persuasion. Many were well-known soap-opera stars.

In summary, the mobilizing of so many allies for UCI, of such a wide diversity, in country after country, was the first time in history that such a concerted global action had been achieved. It was calculated that in many countries more people were mobilized to action on a vaccination day than were normally mobilized for national elections, with the results being followed through the media with similar interest and excitement.

Motivating New Actions and Creating New Values among Parents

The final and instrumental link in the process of reaching UCI was, of course, the parents of the children to be immunized. They had to be convinced of the need, and motivated to actually bring their children to a vaccination point. At the same time, they needed to internalize the value of immunizing children so that, over time, immunization would become part of the popular culture, thereby ensuring its sustainability.

In most countries, the mass media offered the quickest and easiest way to reach families with information that could create awareness on the necessary scale. However, actual behavioural change almost always requires a personal contact – with a development worker, an influential member of the community, or someone who has experience of the new behaviour being proposed. The media will still be playing a supporting and reinforcing role, however, facilitating the interpersonal communication work, and giving it legitimacy and credibility. For example, there is a widespread belief in many societies with a low level of education that 'if the TV (or radio) said it, it must be true'. When a health worker says much the same thing a few days later during a personal contact, his or her credibility is immediate. Mass media can also be used very cheaply and effectively as a continuing reminder to people.

The message content used for parents in most countries was based on a positive approach. The notion of protecting children, and of having parents gain peace of mind for their children's health, were commonly used themes. It was found to be generally more effective to take a positive approach that appealed to parents' sense of responsibility, rather than to create fear in parents' minds about what might happen if their children were not immunized.

Polio, however, was often treated differently. Compared to the other immunizable diseases, the effects of polio are more visible, as well as being horribly permanent. Many campaigns played on this. One example was a series of television spots made in Egypt. Among them was one showing a small crippled girl with steel leg-braces watching while her friends run and play together in a park. The expression of sorrow on her face, and the tears running down her cheeks as the spot closes, were heart-wrenching. Equally moving were other spots showing children with wasted and distorted legs struggling to drag themselves by their arms along a rail fixed to a wall in a rehabilitation centre. The day after these spots appeared on television, parents with their children arrived in droves at health centres to have them immunized against polio.

In Algeria, on the other hand, the polio spots were positive, apart from the opening logo showing the silhouette of a crippled person. After that logo, one spot cut to a pair of feet in football boots manoeuvring a ball with great agility. The camera then moved up the legs and body until the face of a national football star came into view. 'If you want your children to have legs like mine,' he said on camera, 'vaccinate them against polio!' This Algerian spot was also highly effective, and it is difficult to reach a conclusion regarding the positive versus the negative approach, but the use of well-known stars of sport and entertainment was a successful strategy everywhere.

Although media and contacts by health staff achieved most of the advance towards UCI, there were many countries where pockets of low coverage remained as 1990 approached. To reach the hardcore left-outs and drop-outs, some innovative tactics were used. For example, a channel created in Bangladesh was the 'mothers of fully immunized children', given the quaint acronym of MOFICS. They were enlisted to mobilize women whose children remain unprotected. And who could be better than the women in the community to reach and convince their peers?

However, merely reaching parents with information was not always enough to ensure action, for there were sometimes social constraints to be overcome. One such critical constraint in some societies was how far women could move alone to take their children for immunization. For example, in Bangladesh, the general rule is that a woman is confined to a small area around her home, the area in which the rest of her family's social group live. The vaccination point was often outside that area. Since the male opinion leaders are the guardians of such traditions, it was first necessary to reach them and convince them that immunization was important and that it was morally correct for mothers to take their children to the vaccination points outside their normal area of movement. It is interesting that in Bangladesh it was later said that this extra freedom for women to move, brought about by UCI, had become a feature of the society.

The experience worldwide with creating new actions and values among parents shows that there was no one model of a communication strategy that could be applied. Every country had to examine its own situation and come up with its own strategy. However, certain common factors of success do emerge. These include: good qualitative research among intended audiences; truly creative use of media, integrated with and in support of interpersonal communication; training in social skills for field workers; and the identification of intermediate audiences who could influence the primary audience of parents.

Social Mobilization under a Spotlight

Despite its evident effectiveness for UCI, social mobilization has its critics. Some people, who are not fully informed, associate social mobilization with campaigns only, and say that campaigns lead to unsustainable actions. In fact, even if social mobilization does use campaigns, they are usually only a part of a broader strategy.

It is true, however, that some countries did base their mobilization strategies for UCI almost exclusively on campaigns that were time-bound and with little activity between them. These same countries often tended to overlook the other elements, such as management, training, and the ongoing dissemination of information between campaigns that would build sustained participation by all concerned. For example, the campaign conducted in Turkey in 1985 was a model of organization and effectiveness, mobilizing every conceivable sector of the population that could play a useful role. However, vaccination coverage dropped in subsequent years and climbed only slowly back to the levels reached in 1985. In fact, there had been a sort of one-big-effort-for-all-time feeling about the 1985 campaign, and it was difficult to maintain the momentum.

Burkina Faso suffered a similar experience after its very successful 'Operation Commando' in 1984, the first such operation in Africa. Over one million children were immunized in a single three-week period, but thereafter, the impetus declined. In this case, however, political changes were partly to blame. Other countries that used campaigns as part of social mobilization for UCI did not fall into this trap; they were able to piggyback on repeated campaigns, maintain a level of interest and commitment in non-campaign periods, and gradually build their regular health services to the point where routine vaccination could be promoted.

The lesson learned from UCI is that social mobilization should be a process planned and implemented in stages, and not thought of as a one-shot effort, for changes in society take time. An additional factor is that officials in many governments are rotated at quite short intervals. They are therefore a fleeting target and mobilizing one 'generation' of officials may not lead to sustained interest among those who succeed them in their institutions.

A criticism from health professionals is that social mobilization may create so much demand on unprepared health services that they will become uncooperative and their users become frustrated. This opens the discussion about matching mobilization of demand to the ability of the services to respond. On the one extreme, the cautious say that all the health services must be in place before any mobilization can begin, while at the other extreme are those who say that demand must be mobilized to the point where the pressure forces health services to respond. In most cases, the correct strategy lies somewhere between the two extremes: keep mobilization and delivery capacity more or less in balance, but if anything, keep mobilization slightly ahead to put the services on their mettle.

Social mobilization is considered by some people to be top-down in nature, and the word 'mobilization' has military connotations that may help them to believe this. In fact, good social mobilization is top-down and bottom-up at the same time, since it works at all levels of society. It may be true that it is top-down if one wants to take the extreme view that mobilization for immunization was decided without consulting the community. On the other hand, the active involvement and participation at community level in UCI has led in many countries to the creation of groups and structures that will be able to set their own agendas in future.

Overall, there can be no doubt that UCI–1990 would never have been achieved without social mobilization. In concrete terms, that achievement saved more than 12 million children's lives after mobilization began in 1984. On an annual basis, more than 3 million lives continue to be saved. It also means that over 100 million infants during the first year of their lives are being reached four or five times with vaccines each year, which adds up to 500 million contacts between children and organized delivery systems, sometimes in areas so remote that not even the postal services reach them. More children are fully immunized in Nepal, India, Nigeria, and El Salvador at age one than are children in London, New York, and Washington, DC at age two. Furthermore, in many of the countries that achieved UCI–1990, immunization has taken root in the conscience of society, creating an 'immunization culture'.

At the country level in Bangladesh, for example, social mobilization for UCI led to the creation of 108,000 outreach posts for immunization, most of them in private houses lent regularly for the purpose. These outreach posts are now being used for family planning services too, so they have become a resource on to which other primary health care inputs are being grafted.

Almost everywhere, the mobilization of allies and the creation of inter-ministerial cooperation and broad-based teamwork for UCI set new patterns for future social action. The shared satisfaction in the achievement was evident when talking to the partners in the effort, and the memory of this satisfaction remained as a stimulus for other joint efforts in the future.

The attitudes of the media changed in many countries. They became more interested in social and health issues than they were before becoming involved in supporting UCI, and today they give them much more coverage. In turn, this has led to a push-pull effect of the public taking a greater interest in health topics in the media. One readership survey in Colombia showed that, after national news, the next most appreciated subject was health.

Management of health services improved immeasurably. Naturally, during UCI itself, good planning, management, and monitoring through improved information systems were crucial to success, and they have generally remained in place. Furthermore, as explained to us by a WHO official, the good management for UCI pointed the way towards the use of those same management approaches and criteria in other health sectors. Today, WHO staff can tell officials of a ministry of health that their management of UCI was out-standing, and suggest that they try to apply the same techniques and criteria to other health services. In fact, the success of UCI was a precedent for setting new standards for health management.

Perhaps the most important consequence of social mobilization for UCI was that for the first time in history, and on a massive scale, action for health became the concern and the property of large sectors of the population, and not the sole responsibility of ministries of health. Equally important was the increased community-level involvement in practical health actions, for which the people themselves have assumed responsibility. This results from the realization among even the poorest, the illiterate, and the most marginalized by society, that better health for their children – even survival – lies to a large extent in their hands.

CHAPTER 4

Communication for Rural Development in Mexico: in Good Times and in Bad

Mexico has a glorious history. Its great civilizations have left spectacular pyramids and archaeological sites all over the country. The Spanish conquerors systematically stamped out the culture they found when they arrived, but much of Mexico's glorious past is still reflected in the way Mexicans think and are today. They show a talent for grand plans and designs, manifested in many large modern buildings, some of them of great originality and beauty. Mexican aspirations for a return to greatness also show in imaginative and large-scale development programmes. In the context of one of these, and over the last two decades, Mexico has created a unique and highly successful system of communication for rural development that has attracted worldwide attention. This system has endured through Mexico's enormous economic difficulties and crises, with related ups and downs, adapting as necessary to changing circumstances. It has helped peasants to improve their quality of life, to participate in decisions that affect them, and to develop social cohesion.

Mexico's Rural Scene

The Mexican Revolution was instrumental in setting the country's rural scene. Beginning in 1910, with the relatively simple objective of ousting President Porfirio Díaz, the revolution then turned into Latin America's first popular uprising against the domination and oppression by the vast landowners and others of enormous wealth. It only finished in the 1940s when its objectives were institutionalized as the basis of future national policy.

Land reform was a main thrust of the revolution, and the peasantry took an active part under famous leaders such as Emiliano

Zapata and Pancho Villa. Beginning in the 1920s, land confiscated from the oligarchy was distributed to peasants under the *ejido* tenure system, which goes back to pre-Colombian times; it provides for common ownership of land but grants individuals usufruct rights on plots assigned to them. Until recently, these rights could not legally be divided, ceded, or leased to others, but they could be passed on through inheritance. Normally, a member of an *ejido* has a plot of 10 hectares of irrigated land, or 20 hectares of rain-fed land. There are some 27,000 *ejidos* in Mexico grouping about 3.5 million farm families. An *ejido*, in effect, is a community of farming families, with its own social structure, administration, and a series of committees to deal with community matters.

A group of *ejidos* may join together to form a second-level association known as a Union de Ejidos. A union will often provide services to its member *ejidos*, such as storing and marketing of grain, supply of farm inputs, and the like.

In general, the *ejido* system embraces subsistence peasants in the poorer areas. The richer areas with irrigation are mainly in the hands of individual commercial farmers, often operating on a much larger scale.

Since the revolution, peasants have enjoyed a special place in Mexican society. For many decades, government intervention in markets kept farm prices favourably high. In 1982, subsidies represented about 22 per cent of the value of agricultural produce. Then, owing to economic crises, and to structural adjustment programmes that began to open the Mexican economy, the agricultural sector came under serious pressure. In real terms, prices of farm produce dropped by about 35 per cent between 1980 and 1988, a situation aggravated by an increase of almost 15 per cent in the costs of farm inputs in the same period. This pressure on the agricultural sector has continued since 1988. Faced with high inflation, very high interest rates on their loans, and soaring input costs, many farmers have been bankrupted.

The agro-ecological scene and agricultural production

Almost half of Mexico lies in the great desert belt of the earth and receives under 600 millimetres of rainfall a year. At the other extreme, much of the rest of the country, especially in the tropical areas near the coasts, receives excessive rainfall, averaging 1,700 millimetres but exceeding 2,000 in many places.

Traditionally, Mexico's agricultural development hinged on increasing and improving irrigated farming in the dry areas. Vast investment went into this sector, and today the country has about 6 million hectares under irrigation. But by the mid-1960s, population growth was overtaking increases in food production and the government began to plan development in the rain-fed areas, which make up about 75 per cent of all cultivated land. In particular, the tropical wetlands of the coastal plains seemed to offer unique opportunities for a new agricultural frontier. They had been ignored for decades and as a result were almost totally lacking in infrastructure, particularly roads and drainage systems. They were given over mainly to extensive and inefficient ranching.

It was in the context of a new policy to develop the tropical wetlands that an enormous agro-industrial project known as Plan la Chontalpa, in the state of Tabasco, was born in the mid-1960s. The objectives were to improve an area of 83,000 hectares by installing 1,200 kilometres of drains, by building 600 kilometres of roads and 70 bridges, and by drilling more than 80 deep wells. Some 4,400 rural families were to be settled in 22 new villages. As part of the plan, 60,000 hectares of land were to be deforested and expropriated to create new *ejidos* and to reorganize the existing ones under a collective farming system.

The project achieved notable success in the creation of the infrastructure, but it fell seriously short on the human level. In effect, Plan la Chontalpa was a massive 'top-down' intervention for which there was no prior consultation or agreement with its beneficiaries. All the decisions were taken by the authorities, and the local population never identified with the project.

The project staff were aware of the population's apathy, and even antipathy. As one Mexican described the situation to us: 'To try to involve the peasants more, government officials were constantly telling them that the new infrastructure belonged to them. So a peasant, looking at a house built by the project, would ask if it was really his. He would be assured that it was, and so the next night he would remove the roofing material and take it back to improve his old house!' A more formal description of the situation appeared in a government report:

> The extensive infrastructure of the project ... shows serious levels of under-utilization, failure to maintain the works, failure to install drainage in individual plots, and inadequate use of wells, irrigation equipment,

and soils. The lack of effective mechanisms for participation of the beneficiaries has been an important cause of this situation.

By the mid-1970s, and despite the negative experience of Plan La Chontalpa, government attention was again focused on the tropical wetlands, for they cover almost a quarter of Mexico's total area and many of their soils are of medium to high potential. They could no longer be left out of the nation's development, especially taking into account that the country's food needs had grown to the point where it had to begin importing grain for the first time in its history.

However, the development problems in the tropical wetlands were enormous, beginning with the excessive and violent rainfall, which causes erosion of unprotected land, flooding, saturation and compaction of the soils. Good drainage systems were therefore a first requirement. Another problem was that so much of the area was being used for livestock production that the pressure of population on what remained for agriculture had caused the onset of serious land degradation. The agricultural communities living in the area had been undergoing a continuing process of impoverishment. By the early 1980s, almost all of the economically active population in the rural areas was earning less than the country's legal minimum salary, and over half of the farming families were operating at below subsistence level. Less than half of the rural houses had piped drinking water; only 30 per cent were connected to a drainage system; 44 per cent had no electricity; and malnutrition and disease were endemic.

The people in the area are characterized by ethnic, cultural, and linguistic diversity. In effect, 60 per cent of the indigenous people of Mexico live in these areas, and not all of them speak Spanish. And finally, the illiteracy level was among the highest in the country, reaching 32 per cent of the adult population.

After the expensive lesson of Plan la Chontalpa, the Secretariat for Agriculture and Water Resources (SARH) decided that future development in the tropical wetlands would be planned and executed with the participation of the local people. To achieve this, the identification of the physical, technical, and socio-economic problems would need to be followed by proposals for their solution that were fully appropriate for the communities, and agreed to by them. Furthermore, it would be fundamental to promote better social organization among the population as a means of overcoming conflictual situations and to promote development through participatory actions. None of this could be achieved without a communication process, or a dialogue, with the peasants at all stages.

The Genesis of a Development Programme for the Tropical Wetlands and its Rural Communication System

In accordance with the then current concept of integrated rural development, the staff of SARH and their FAO advisers decided that the development programme should cover all of the factors that determine, or influence, the living and working conditions of rural families. However, the planners had also learned through their field research that peasants do not usually see their problems in terms of separate components; rather, they see their reality as a single continuum in which the elements are all interrelated and integrated.

For this reason, any development programme should be a complete and integrated response to the peasants' situation, even if the development technicians saw it as being made up of different components – for example, infrastructure, technical assistance, credit, research, and training. However, an integrated development programme could not be put into practice without the participation of the peasants in the process of identifying and analysing their problems, planning and implementing actions to resolve them, and monitoring and evaluating the results. In effect, the peasants would need to become the protagonists in their own development, with appropriate assistance and support from outside.

These insights into how a development programme should be were the result of much research with peasants themselves. One day in 1977, when this research process was under way, one of the professionals involved had an important idea: why not try video recording and playback, with the peasants' prior agreement, to promote discussion among them and to help them analyse their situation? At the same time, the researchers might gain a clearer understanding of how the peasants saw things. There happened to be an FAO project to support farmer training in Mexico at that time, and it had some old black-and-white, open-reel video equipment that it lent to the researchers in the tropical wetlands.

As it turned out, video recording and playback with peasants gave remarkable results. It stimulated a process of reflection and helped them to analyse the reality in which they lived and what might be done about it. These same recordings were used by the planners as audio-visual testimonials about the attitudes and ways of thinking of the peasants. Those early videos were taken into account in the planning for development in the tropical wetlands, and they also set an important trend for the future.

In 1978, the result of the research and planning culminated in the Programme of Integrated Rural Development in the Tropical Wetlands, known under its Spanish acronym as PRODERITH. This programme had two phases, the first from 1978 to 1984, and the second from 1986 to 1995. There was a break in World Bank support between the two phases, but the programme continued to function on a reduced scale.

The first phase, PRODERITH I, was based on three overall strategies. First, it was to be a *learning process*. It would try to generate field experiences that were small enough to be 'test benches' but big enough to be replicated on a larger scale. Second, it would aim to achieve the *participation* of all involved, whether they were peasants, PRODERITH staff, or staff of cooperating institutions. And third, to bring an integrated approach to rural development, PRODERITH would need first-rate *coordination* between the various institutions involved.

PRODERITH's overall objectives were to increase the agricultural production and productivity in the tropics, improve the living and working conditions of peasants and their families, and conserve natural resources. Its immediate objectives were to work intensely, as a pilot operation, with 3,500 peasant families on 54,000 hectares of land, in three separate Project Areas of the tropical wetlands. The aim was to quadruple the income of peasant families over the level obtained in 1977. At the same time, the programme would provide technical assistance to farmers occupying 500,000 hectares in expansion zones around the programme's intensive zones, increasing their incomes by 50 per cent over the 1977 levels.

From its very beginning PRODERITH would have a Rural Communication System that would play an integral part in its work. The other PRODERITH components would be: technical assistance; credit; organization and social participation of peasants; research into agricultural and livestock production in the tropics; the building of infrastructure for drainage and soil conservation; and opening access roads.

Mexico had solid experience in many aspects of agricultural development and in the building of infrastructure, but it was relatively weak in the area of communication. The government therefore asked FAO to provide technical assistance for this component of

PRODERITH, and FAO duly assigned an Argentinean, Santiago Funes, as a communication adviser.

Funes played a central role in building the Rural Communication System. Now in his mid-fifties, he is an intense, thoughtful man, of enormous intellectual capacity. He can be as clear-minded and articulate about economic and social issues of development in a ministerial-level meeting as he can be jocular and teasing when sitting chewing the fat with a group of peasants. In fact, he was able to contribute enormously to PRODERITH's overall approach and methodology because of his empathy with peasants and his understanding of their world. Most people who have such understanding gain it through being born in the peasant world or through spending much of their life in it, but Funes came to it quite differently. He was from a modest urban home in Córdoba, but through intelligence and hard work, he obtained scholarships that earned him a first-class education, including a degree in modern literature.

As a young man he had strong leftist leanings, and he co-authored a book on mass communication and social revolution. Indeed, he was set on a career as a writer when he went to Chile in the early 1970s for research on another book. There he met up with a small team of people working on an FAO-supported project for agrarian reform. Its special emphasis was on capacity building and training among peasant farmers to enable them to take proper advantage of the opportunity offered to them by land distribution. The team, which was beginning to conduct the first experiences anywhere with video for training in rural areas, also needed someone to prepare printed materials for peasants, and Funes joined them.

Up to that time, it had never occurred to Funes that almost three-quarters of the world's people were peasants, and he had never had anything to do with them. The leader of the FAO team in Chile told Funes that communication was going to become more and more important for genuine rural development in which the peasants actively participated. He added that communication in a rural context was quite different from communication in an urban one, and that if Funes was going to produce the right sort of materials, he needed to know and understand rural communities and their economy.

So Funes spent many months getting to know peasant life and economy in Chile, and the experience changed him. He realized that the potential for communication was enormous in a setting where it was almost non-existent between rural communities and the outside world, but where it was essential if the communities were to advance. He recalls one meeting in a small town south of Santiago de Chile where one of the project's training team held forth at length to a group of peasants. He was followed by total silence. Funes realized that communicating with peasants was a special challenge, involving style and method as much as content. He had discovered 'three-quarters of the world's people' and how he could direct his skills to working with them, with the results we shall describe here.

Overview of the PRODERITH methodology

PRODERITH took a novel approach from the start in its field work. Before beginning any intervention whatsoever, it sent *promotores*[1] to live with the communities. They were specially trained and, if necessary, spoke the local language. Their role was to get to know the people, win their confidence, and start to discuss possible development actions that PRODERITH could support.

The next step was the creation of Field Units in the Project Areas. These were small, multi-disciplinary teams of development specialists, which normally included an agronomist, a veterinarian or livestock specialist, a civil engineer, and a social worker. They had been trained by the programme in three-month courses that covered the technical, economic, and social aspects of rural development.

The first task of the Field Units was to present and explain PRODERITH in detail. They then worked with the communities in a diagnosis of their situation, of their options for development, and of specific actions that could be taken by the community. Once development work was actually in progress, the Field Units were also responsible for orientation and training in the community. These processes were facilitated by intense use of video and supporting printed materials.

The Field Units were supported by Methodology Groups. There was one such group for each four Field Units, and it provided the communication services – primarily the video recording and playback and printed materials.

As proposed from the beginning, the participation of all concerned – peasants, technicians, and institutional staff – remained a

---

1. This word cannot be satisfactorily translated. They are development workers with good interpersonal and group dynamic skills whose task is to promote discussion and analysis and generally prepare the ground for development actions.

basic tenet of the PRODERITH methodology, and it was fostered through communication. Yet another cornerstone of PRODERITH methodology was the in-depth initial training, and subsequent refresher training, of its field staff. Especially important was to give technical people a social focus for their work. The programme ultimately trained more than four hundred field technicians.

The Rural Communication System

The Communication System worked in three main areas: it promoted the objective of generating 'informed and conscious participation of the peasants at all stages of the development process'; it provided orientation and training of peasants and staff; and it improved institutional coordination and management.

Communication for situation analysis, motivation and participation

Peasants often have difficulty in articulating their view of their reality, and they seldom declare their 'truth' to outsiders in a normal interview situation. And as Santiago Funes says, although each peasant certainly has his or her *individual* perceptions, development work cannot be sustained on the basis of these. What is required is a *collective* perception within the community of the local situation and of the options for improving it. This can only be reached through an internal debate within that community about its situation and possible future.

The Communication System began by using information and testimonials on video during PRODERITH's early contacts with communities to explain the programme and its development focus. Once a community had expressed its interest in participating in PRODERITH – and not all did because they said that the government had misled them in the past – the next objective was to help the community generate what was called an *Internal Development Project.* Basically, this was a consensus that actions could and should be taken to improve the situation. Video recording and playback were used to stimulate and deepen the debate within the community about its past, present, and possible future. For the communities, video recordings made with them were somewhat like looking into a mirror; they provided new perspectives.

Concurrently, a classical socio-economic and technical study was under way to identify the feasibility in technical and economic terms of a range of possible development initiatives. With these options available, the communication team began what was termed the *Information Cycle*. They worked with a small group of between ten and twenty community members who had been chosen by the community to represent it during the process. The purpose of the Information Cycle was to discuss the results of the study and its proposals and to establish the feasibility *in human and social* terms of each one.

The output from this work was a *Local Development Plan* (LDP). A documentary video was made to describe this LDP, both to help the community – especially the illiterate – understand it properly, and also to provide a record of the agreements reached. Although this participatory planning process could take several months, the investment of time and resources was worthwhile for two reasons: first, the LDP truly reflected local needs and possibilities; and second, the peasants' involvement in drawing it up made it much more likely that they would also participate in putting it into effect.

There was a particularly ingenious use of video for situation analysis and motivation in Yucatan. PRODERITH was trying to establish an entry point in the area around the small town of Tizimin, but there was much local resistance to outside interventions. This was because a 10,000-hectare irrigation scheme installed a few years earlier by a rural credit bank had failed dramatically: after the farmers had provided the land and the irrigation scheme had been built, it was found that the water was too saline to grow crops. Serious damage was done to the land, and the peasants were left with a debt to the bank, which was waived only after several years of protest and struggle.

An assessment by PRODERITH of the situation in the Tizimin area had revealed a number of problems, and one of the most serious concerned malnutrition and food security. PRODERITH staff thought the local population should discuss this issue, but they had little idea of how to spark a dialogue among and with the indigenous, Mayan-speaking people.

The ingenious solution proved to be video recordings with Don Clotilde Cob, an 82-year-old man who could talk about the problems in a historical context. He was a proud ex-revolutionary, who had learned Spanish and taught himself to read and write as an adult. He was articulate and lucid in both Mayan and Spanish.

This charismatic old man, with his white hair and neat beard, sat cross-legged in front of a video camera for hours on end. He held forth about the past, about the revolution, about the greatness of Mayan culture, and about life today. He deplored the decline of such Mayan traditions as the family vegetable plot, explained how he cultivated his own maize, and complained that today's young people did not even know how to do that properly. He accused the young of abandoning all that had been good in Mayan culture; they would sell eggs to buy cigarettes and soft drinks, and so it was no wonder that diets today were worse than they were in his youth.

Scores of people sat in attentive silence in the villages as these tapes were played. In the evening, under a tree, the words in Mayan flowed from the screen, and the old man's eloquent voice and emphatic gestures spread their spell. For many, it was the first time they had ever heard anyone talk about the practical values of their culture. It was also the first time they had seen a peasant like themselves on 'television', and talking their own language. They frequently asked that the tapes be played again and again. The desired effect was achieved: the people began to take stock of their situation and think seriously about their values, and so the ground was prepared for when PRODERITH began to discuss development proposals.

There is also a good example of the Communication System helping to create participation. In one Project Area, the technicians had proposed a drainage scheme to cure the regular flooding that occurred in a particular place. A peasant thought that the scheme would not work because the technicians were wrong in their analysis of the cause of the flooding. The peasant was video-recorded as he explained his reasons, scratching a diagram in the soil with a stick to illustrate his points.

After the technicians had seen the tape, they studied the situation on the ground again, and found that the peasant had been right. Members of the community had been standing by when the recording was being made with the peasant, and the fact that technicians took his opinions into account, and changed their plans, created a sense of self-esteem and participation in decision-making.

Communication for training and education

The Local Development Plans invariably identified training and education needs in the community. To meet them, the Rural Communication System adopted a methodology based on video with supporting printed materials, the whole forming so-called 'peda-gogical packages'.[2]

A package covers a subject, say apiculture or child nutrition, broken down into a series of videos each of 10–15 minutes' duration and constituting a single lesson of the course. Typically, there would be from three to ten video lessons in a course, depending upon the breadth and complexity of the subject. The trainees each receive a printed manual, with many illustrations, to consult during the course and to take home as a reference for the future. A printed guide for the technicians who will be using the material provides them with additional information on how best to use the package.

During PRODERITH I, these training packages were used only in the presence of a subject-matter specialist from a Field Unit. He would lead the discussion after the presentation of the video and conduct a session of practical work whenever possible. As one of PRODERITH's field staff said:

> The sessions in which we present the training materials are certainly important. We see the videos, we discuss the information, we read the printed material, and we conduct the practical work. But what is really important is what happens after the session, when the peasants are walking home in small groups, talking. That is when the information is analysed and discussed among equals, and when the real decisions are taken.

Thus the educational philosophy of PRODERITH was to introduce information for discussion as an active learning process, rather than to convey it for passive assimilation. A vast range of subjects was covered by the video-based training packages. Naturally, many were on agricultural production techniques, but many were for more general education linked to the needs of rural development. To give an idea of the variety, some of the programmes covered: basic arithmetic to help peasants manage their affairs better, soils and climate, purification of drinking water, food and nutrition, children's diseases, latrines, the role of women and their organization for rural development, and so on.

The same methodology was used for training and orientation of PRODERITH's own staff. Some of these packages covered concepts

---

2. This methodology, first tried in Chile by the FAO team working in agrarian reform but curtailed by the overthrow of the Allende government, was fully developed by a member of the same team in Peru in the mid-1970s. It has spread from there to a number of countries of Latin America, Asia, and Africa.

of rural development, but others were on specific technical subjects, such as the traditional cultivation of maize, principles of immunization, pests and diseases of grain, and so on.

In the very early days of PRODERITH, there had been some field technicians who said they would have nothing to do with video, referring to the playback units as 'idiot boxes', but it did not take long to convince them of their value. Many among PRODERITH's staff came to praise the role of video and the fact that the training packages helped greatly to standardize the information they wished to present to farmers, putting it into a form in which it was readily accessible, even to the illiterate.

Communication for coordination and management

PRODERITH's multi-faceted approach to rural development required understanding and coordination among the various parts of the organization, as well as with and within other institutions. The Communication System provided the flow of information necessary for this improved coordination and management. For example, reports in video form were made on the progress and service requirements in a particular Project Area so that the various institutions could play their part as necessary.

The Communication System was also used to feed back negative information from Project Areas so that the central management could take appropriate remedial action. On one occasion, peasants were complaining about the delays in building a promised drainage scheme and were openly critical of PRODERITH. The communication team recorded these complaints on video and edited them into a single programme, obliquely called *Material for Discussion*. This was played to the top management of PRODERITH.

One might have expected an explosion about ignorant peasants daring to criticize the programme and its management. On the contrary, the management welcomed the video and recommended its widespread use in the Project Area as a way of pressuring those responsible to speed up construction. The video was also used in other areas to stimulate discussions as to whether the responsibility for building infrastructure should be decentralized, with peasants assuming a greater role.

Operational Aspects of the Communication System

Under PRODERITH I, and until 1985, the Communication System was run from a Central Unit in Mexico City where most of the communication staff were based, even if small teams of two to three people were also outposted in the Project Areas. This Central Unit, and the whole of the PRODERITH headquarters, was transferred to Cuernavaca after the disastrous 1985 earthquake in the capital and has remained there ever since.

The Central Unit took overall responsibility for all programmes produced by the System. The research, scripting and shooting could be done either by staff of the Central Unit or by staff outposted in the Project Areas, who were equipped with cameras and recorders. The outposted staff sent their recorded cassettes to the Central Unit, with an outline script, and all editing was done there.

The staff of the Rural Communication System initially came from a variety of backgrounds. The majority had a technical education and some experience in agriculture or social work. PRODERITH provided them with intensive training lasting several months in concepts of rural development and in the production and use of video and their supporting printed materials.

Later, some recruits to the Communication System were media specialists, especially graduates from film schools. This was the case when there was emphasis on videos for institutional audiences, for it was thought that they would be best able to produce materials in tune with the visual culture of the government staff. Later still, people were also recruited from schools of social communication.

At its peak of productivity in 1981, the Communication System was able to produce about one hundred videos a year. Then the economic situation in Mexico began to limit public expenditure, and by 1985, its staff had been reduced from about forty to about twenty, with a concomitant reduction in production capacity.

Until the late 1980s, the Communication System used three-quarter-inch Umatic equipment for the production of programmes and copied them on to half-inch Betamax cassettes for playback in the communities. Then the Video 8 format was introduced, and this cheap, compact, and agile equipment proved excellent in the field. It became the standard for most production and playback. The video equipment proved remarkably durable. Much of it worked satisfactorily for 12–15 years, and units were replaced more because new and more appropriate models were available than because they had broken down beyond repair.

Playback units for use in the field gave more trouble than the production equipment, mainly because plugging and unplugging of the cables between the various components damaged the connections. To overcome this, the communication team designed and built special wooden carrying cases. The inside was divided into compartments for each of the components, which remained permanently connected to each other. These carrying cases could be loaded into any vehicle, and on arrival at the community, simply unloaded, opened up and set to operate, using a vehicle battery.

The Rural Communication System under PRODERITH I aroused worldwide interest, and the World Bank praised it in a number of its documents. One staff member of the World Bank with responsibility for Mexico stated that the Communication System had been 'central to the success of PRODERITH I', which in fact, achieved all of its major objectives.

PRODERITH II and a Change of Context

The first years of PRODERITH I were, relatively speaking, years of the fat cows, but in the last years, up to its formal close in 1984, Mexico was in economic crisis. This was because the country had borrowed heavily during the glut of 'petro-dollars' following the creation of OPEC, and its external debt had grown from US$15,000 million in 1975 to US$70,000 million by 1981.

The discovery of oil in the Gulf of Mexico brought a bonanza in the years 1978–81, and the government relied mainly on that revenue to finance its internal and external debts. This proved disastrous because, in 1982, oil prices dropped sharply, and at about the same time there was also a steep increase in global interest rates, which increased the cost of debt servicing. The economic crisis that resulted was aggravated by the 1985 earthquake in Mexico City, which is estimated to have cost 2 per cent of GDP.

However, the success of PRODERITH I had been such that there was pressure to continue and expand it. Ideally, the second phase, PRODERITH II, would have run on directly from the first, but the economic difficulties and organizational delays before the World Bank's second loan was approved produced a financial hiatus before PRODERITH II could begin. When it did, in 1986, it was expanded to cover intensive work with 90,000 families – compared to fewer than 5,000 under the first phase – on 1.2 million hectares, in eight Project Areas. (This was later expanded again to 1.4 million hectares and nine Project Areas.) There were more than 650,000 people in the Project Areas, living in more than 500 *ejidos* and communities, most of them made up of less than a hundred families.

Because of the economic crisis, international lending agencies were pressing Mexico to decentralize and reduce government spending under a structural adjustment programme. This, and the enormous increase in size of the second phase compared to the first, meant that the programme would have to operate in quite different circumstances. In the prevailing economic and political climate, the direct and intense work with rural families under PRODERITH I could not be scaled up to meet the expanded needs. In addition, the structural adjustment programmes under way set an imperative: the control and management of infrastructures and services must be transferred to their users, particularly to farmers' associations.

In discussing their future work, PRODERITH staff identified what they termed the 'social base' as the springboard for development. During Phase I, the social base had been certain groups of rural people who were willing to enter into an institutional relationship with PRODERITH and obtain services and investment support through it. But PRODERITH II would need more than a 'clientele'. It would need a social base of groups of people with mechanisms and instruments for taking control of their own development affairs and managing them. Clearly, the precept of Phase I, that the peasant should be the protagonist of his own development, needed to be taken much further under the second phase, especially in the context of the new national policy of transferring hitherto centrally held responsibilities and functions to the rural population.

Important in planning the strategy and actions for PRODERITH II were the new circumstances of the technical assistance services. In the transitional years of 1984–86 between the two phases of PRODERITH, some 60–70 per cent of the well-trained field technicians who had worked in the multidisciplinary Field Units had been lost. In addition there were organizational changes: PRODERITH had originally been launched as a special programme within SARH, but with considerable resources and independence of action. For various bureaucratic reasons, SARH decided to reduce PRODERITH's autonomy as a special programme and bring it into its normal operations. The main step in this process, taken towards the end of Phase I, was to make the PRODERITH field staff responsible to the local state office of SARH. The multidisciplinary Field Units of PRODERITH disappeared under the new arrangements, and SARH created new Centres of Support for Rural Development (CADRIs) in their place.

In addition to the crippling blow of having lost so much of its trained field staff, there was less motivation and commitment to PRODERITH in the CADRIs; and there was also a dilution within SARH of the funds that previously had been used exclusively for technical assistance for PRODERITH. Yet another factor in diminishing PRODERITH's field work was a return, in many CADRIs, to old styles of extension work.

Faced with this situation, the PRODERITH management tried to create a new technical assistance system. This was based on private groups of technicians who were contracted to provide support in the field. But finance continued to be a problem and this system also declined over the years. Thus, while PRODERITH I had achieved intense technical support in the field, under PRODERITH II this virtually disappeared. In effect, there was a severe decline in technical assistance capacity when it was sorely needed for the expansion under PRODERITH II.

Similarly, the key input of farm credit, of great importance under PRODERITH I, was reduced almost to nothing because of the country's economic plight. In 1986, oil prices had plunged again just as the country was still trying to recover from the earthquake of the previous year. A measure of the size of the problems is that GDP dropped by 3.8 per cent in 1986.

It was evident that with all the above changes in context, the Rural Communication System would also need to change; it could not continue as an essentially centralized operation, as it had been under PRODERITH I, and meet the vastly expanded needs of the second phase while the country was also in economic crisis.

The Communication System in these Changing Circumstances

Beginning in mid-1987, Santiago Funes and the staff of the Communication System began a long period of internal debate and discussion about their work in the new circumstances of PRODERITH II. A first general conclusion was that, although the system developed under PRODERITH I was democratic in nature, the way it was run was centralized. It was also centred on the medium of video. The new demands under PRODERITH II would call for a decentralized system, and the use of any media that might be appropriate in a given situation. Another important consideration was that, in line with government policy, the Communication System would have to be planned so that it could be transferred to the farmers, in the same way as other services.

Many aspects of the communication work under Phase I would still be valid, even if they needed to be expanded or organized differently. A special new area of work would be to support and strengthen organizations and associations of agricultural producers, whether in the *ejido* system or not. In the longer term, they would be expected to take over many of the services previously provided by the state. Only through a communication process leading to consensus would they be able to strengthen their capacity for action and management to the point where they could assume such a role.

During their discussions, the communication staff paid special attention to the social aspects of their work. In part, this attention was stimulated by a consultant who was called in to help advise on future policies. In his contacts with the communication staff, he repeatedly asked them the same question: 'Are you producing images, or are you producing social effects?' From the beginning, the purpose of the Rural Communication System had been to influence social situations by using media. However, the consultant's question was highly provocative and it caused new reflections among the staff about their work.

In addition, an FAO Development Communication Case Study about the Grameen Bank in Bangladesh provoked thought. This study emphasized that *shared interests* are the force that bring networks and formations into being, hold them together, and cause them to evolve. The case study described how the Grameen Bank had set communication processes in train which helped the poorest-of-the-poor out of their state of social discontinuity and distrust into a new state of self-confidence and mutual trust, thereby creating a new social and economic environment for themselves. The communication processes were achieved through interpersonal channels and group dynamics, rather than through media.

The Grameen Bank experience led the PRODERITH communication staff to consider the information and communication networks that build up between certain individuals or social groups when there are shared interests. PRODERITH could perhaps select and strengthen those communication networks, thereby facilitating the transfer of appropriate knowledge, increasing the decision and management capacities of rural communities, and accelerating the process of adaptation and change.

The communication staff also wanted to reduce the emphasis on the exclusive use of video and printed material, for they realized that other media might be more effective in certain aspects of strengthening and feeding networks. They therefore identified how interpersonal, group, and mass media might fit into a typical network situation.

Decentralizing the Communication System would hinge on creating Regional Communication Units that would be in a position to independently carry out communication planning and the production and dissemination of materials. And peasants would need to become much more closely involved in actions of the Communication System in their communities.

In order to transfer Regional Communication Units to peasants, the plan was to work with the various levels of producer organizations, and in particular with Uniones de Ejidos. By involving them from the start, it was hoped to build their interest and capacity to the point where they could assume full and autonomous responsibility for managing the Regional Units.

The New Communication Strategy – the Reality in the Field

Looking back, it is now clear that the severity of the economic situation that afflicted Mexico, and the effects of the structural adjustment programmes, were greater than anyone foresaw, or perhaps could have foreseen. And some people now say that the expansion planned for PRODERITH II was too large for the economic conditions that developed in the country.

The first step towards decentralizing the Rural Communication System was the decision to establish a Regional Communication Unit in a Project Area known as Pujal Coy, inland from Tampico on the Gulf of Mexico. The unit would be in a small town called Tamuín, and from the beginning, it was conceived and run with a view to transferring it to a peasant organization.

The work began in 1988 with the renovation of a small white-washed house with a palm-thatched roof in a dusty back street of this sleepy rural town. The building belonged to SARH and had been a meteorological station. It recorded the vagaries of the climate in the area, from incandescent temperatures to occasional bone-chilling cold air from Canada, from extreme droughts to devastating floods. A two-year time frame was established for setting up the Regional Communication Unit, Tamuín (RCUT) and for transferring it to a peasant organization. It had a steering committee made up of peasant organizations and of local and central institutions to review progress from time to time, and to decide on priorities and work plans.

An old but restored three-quarter-inch video editing suite from the Central Unit in Cuernavaca was installed. New Video 8 camcorders for production and 16 playback units of the same format were purchased and put into their wooden carrying cases. The staff for the RCUT, nine in number, were drawn partly from peasant communities and partly from CADRIs in the area. The peasants were in the 18- to 23-year-old range. All had secondary education and one had a technical qualification in agriculture. The CADRI staff had experience of working with PRODERITH, but no experience in the production of communication materials. There were almost even numbers of men and women in the team.

The first training they received was a one-month course in the presentation and use of communication materials in rural communities. The course covered much more than how to set up and use the video playback units: it included an overview of communication as a process and part of rural development, as well as aspects of rural society and economy, the means of agricultural production, and the marketing of produce, and how all of these relate to development. The course was both theoretical and practical in that, towards the end, the trainees were expected to use the video playback modules in their own communities, but under the supervision of their instructors until they felt at ease with the task.

The next training was in how to produce materials. An intensive three-month production course was organized in late 1988 for participants selected from those who had completed the earlier course for presenters. The mix of CADRI staff and peasants in that course caused some tensions initially, but as time passed and the intensity of the work gripped them, the differences of level were smoothed out and mutual respect developed.

One feature of the training was that producers should be able to handle all aspects of the process, through researching the topic, scriptwriting, shooting, editing, and testing of the materials with peasant audiences. This overall grasp would lead to generally more successful materials and to better use of time and resources, even if some specific technical aspect, say editing, were less skilfully executed.

The decentralized communication unit set up in Tamuín was the model for other PRODERITH Project Areas. However, not all of the other Regional Communication Units that followed it were carbon copies. The model was varied according to local needs. By 1995, a total of five Regional Units in different parts of the country were fully operational.

Creating communication capacity in the communities

Communication capacity within the communities was built up using courses for presenters of videos as the spearhead. Regular presenters' courses were organized over the years for peasants nominated by their community. Initially, these were nearly always men, but the Regional Communication Units ultimately convinced the communities to nominate women as well.

When the trained presenters went home, they became a Communication Committee. Their tasks were to identify communication needs in their community and arrange video presentations and other activities accordingly. They were also to formulate requests for assistance to the Regional Communication Units, especially for the production of materials they needed but which were not already in PRODERITH's collection.

Communities in the tropical wetlands vary from small and homogeneous to large and heterogeneous. Examples of the latter can be found in the Pujal Coy area around Tamuín. It has only been settled in recent decades, and land-hungry people have come from all over Mexico to create new settlements and *ejidos*. The result is that many new and large villages of up to 5,000 people have been built. Frequently, one such population centre contains a number of *ejidos* which are, in effect, sub-communities within the larger one. These *ejidos* are often ethnically mixed, with local indigenous people such as *Huastecos*, who have their own language, and Spanish-speaking *Mestizos*.

One such community is Santa Martha, a settlement 85 kilometres from Tamuín along a dirt road. In 1989, Santa Martha grouped 14 *ejidos*, 600 families, and several different ethnic groups. It was a sprawling, miscellaneous collection of houses and dusty roads squatting under the fierce sun, without shade trees or anything else to redeem its shabby character. Health levels were poor, and outbreaks of diarrhoea among the infants in the summer months caused many deaths through dehydration. The *Mestizos* tended to look down on the *Huastecos* and other indigenous people, and there was little interaction between them. This lack of social integration was evidently an obstacle to development.

The RCUT opened a dialogue with Santa Martha in 1989 and began to train people as presenters of video programmes. They went back to their *ejidos* after their training, formed Communication Committees, and organized video playback sessions. But since each *ejido* was a sub-community within Santa Martha, this involved moving the playback unit between sessions, and other logistical problems.

Then, one day, the head of a Communication Committee had no battery to power the playback unit because the one he had planned to use belonged to a vehicle that had left urgently to take someone to hospital. No other battery was available, so the peasant mounted his bicycle at 4 a.m. to ride the 85 kilometres of unpaved road to Tamuín to borrow a battery from the RCUT. He was going to hold his playback session that evening at all costs.

This incident helped the staff of the Communication System to put into action a strategy that they had been planning for some time to foster social integration in communities like Santa Martha, and to create the basis for community actions. A first step would be to have a single place which all the Communication Committees could use for their video sessions, where there would be a power supply and where the equipment could be stored. This would overcome the existing logistical problems, but at the same time it would be a focal point in the community.

The idea was discussed between RCUT staff and the community of Santa Martha and a decision was taken to put up a small one-room building, in a central location, in which to keep the video playback unit. While in use, it would be set on a large window ledge facing outwards. The audience would be seated outside to watch the programmes. The land, labour and materials were provided by the community and the building was finished within a week. The people also erected a makeshift shelter for those sitting outside to watch the videos. Further discussions with the community led to the proposal of installing a sound system that would enable them to call people together, without having to walk house to house. The system was duly installed with four loudspeakers high on a mast above the small building. The sound reaches the whole community.

The new building and its sheltered area outside immediately

assumed a place in the life of the community. It provided a physical space for gatherings that had been lacking, and it was not long before the community asked for help to construct a proper covered area next to the building to replace the makeshift shelter. With only the roofing timbers provided by the RCUT, they erected a large structure with open sides and a palm-thatched roof. The community called this covered meeting area the *palapa*,[3] and with pride refer to it today as the *palapa cultural.*

This was the birth of the first Local Communication Unit (LCU), which grouped several Communication Committees in the community under one roof. That first Santa Martha LCU was the model which was replicated in a number of other communities in the Pujal Coy area. Groups of peasants who had seen the Santa Martha LCU, or heard about it, came to request similar units. In the following years, LCUs were also set up in other PRODERITH Project Areas.

The LCUs played an important part in promoting the social dynamics and energizing force that the communication staff hoped for. Beginning in Santa Martha, the *palapa* became an integrating factor in the often disparate communities. Without this integration, there could be little community identification and spirit, and little social organization to resolve community problems. Many development initiatives were decided under those palm-thatched *palapas*. The videos watched there and discussed, and the sound system, provided the community with information that helped to improve its standard of living.

By 1995, there were 13 LCUs operating in PRODERITH Project Areas around the country, and there were 76 Communication Committees. They have played an important role, especially in the area of health and community development following the aforementioned decline in technical assistance and credit under PRODERITH II. This effectively reduced the demand for training videos on agriculture, because as several farmers told us, they could not apply what they saw in the videos, for they had no resources to do so, and no technical services were available. Artificial insemination was specifically mentioned in this connection.

On the other hand, rural development actions that depend on applying new knowledge that costs little or nothing have been successfully promoted by the LCUs. For example, in Santa Martha,

---

3. This is a local word to describe an open-sided building with a palm-thatched roof.

infant deaths from dehydration during attacks of diarrhoea were completely eliminated after the use of a video programme, printed materials and group discussions to explain the value and practice of oral rehydration therapy.

Cholera prevention was also an area of significant communication success. There were numerous cholera cases in the broad Pujal Coy area during the epidemic that affected so much of South and Central America in the early 1990s. However, there was not a single case in a community that had an LCU working with video and its sound system.

The *palapas* of the LCUs have often been the scene for lengthy communication processes that led to important decisions for development in the community. In Santa Martha, for example, among the activities that resulted was a tree planting programme which has transformed the appearance of the community, and given it the comfort of shade. And traditional medical services were also organized as the result of discussions in the *palapa*.

Perhaps the most important achievement promoted by communication in the Pujal Coy area concerned the drinking water system. The system, built under PRODERITH I, was supposed to supply water to a series of communities. Owing to a design fault, the system never functioned properly and some communities were left almost without piped water. A video was made with one of the peasant leaders in the area who explained the problem. This documentary was taken to the central authorities, who agreed to look into the matter. Communication work in the communities resulted in the women creating Drinking Water Committees. Engineers from the central authorities came to the *palapa* for discussions with the women, and finally, after many years, the necessary redesign and construction were carried out. At the same time, the Drinking Water Committees in the various communities negotiated agreements that those first on the supply line would not abuse their privileged situation, guaranteeing that even the last community on the line would receive its share of water.

In other communities too, the LCU has often triggered action by women. The head of the Communication Committee in Samaria, a village near Tizimin in Yucatan, visited a nearby community and saw that they had installed a mill for grinding maize. Back in his own community, he organized discussions in the *palapa*. The result was that 12 women formed a group, obtained credit, and bought a mill to provide services to others. They were so successful that they were able to pay off the debt after nine months instead of the year agreed with the bank.

The effect of the sound systems

The sound systems in the LCUs have become fully integrated into the communities. PRODERITH provided equipment at a cost of about US$2,500 for each set, but the Communication Committees assumed responsibility for running it. In most communities, it is used for about two hours in the early morning and the same in the evening, always 'broadcasting' in local languages. Music and announcements make up most of the programmes, but on occasion, the Regional Communication Units produced and distributed so-called 'information capsules', which were also 'broadcast'. These capsules, similar to micro-programmes for radio, usually covered health topics and were very effective.

All announcements of a social or of a development nature are free, whereas commercial messages (for instance, from someone who has something to sell) are paid for. A typical charge is the equivalent of about US$1.50 for five repetitions of the same message. The revenue goes mainly for repair and maintenance and to buy cassettes, although some of it may go as a small compensation to the announcers who, by agreement, must be volunteers.

The sound systems have considerable value for the communities, who have appropriated them as their own, even if formal ownership rests with PRODERITH. The communities now pay for repairs when needed, but events in a community in Yucatan illustrate even better the question of effective ownership. In that case, the Communication Committee had come to an agreement with the local doctor to install the sound equipment in the compound of the village health centre. It was plugged into the centre's power supply and it worked successfully for many months from that base. A new doctor then replaced the previous one. She claimed that the LCU belonged to the health centre and that she would control it. No amount of discussion could convince her otherwise, so the people simply proved their ownership by forcibly removing the equipment and installing it in another location.

The LCUs and the sound systems have sometimes been at the centre of community struggles for influence and power. In the early days of an LCU in one community, the local schoolmaster tried to oust the *Huasteco* who was the head of the Communication Committee, saying in disparaging tones that his Spanish was bad and that he should not be allowed to speak over the sound system. Furthermore, the man was illiterate.

Fortunately, the arrogant schoolmaster failed to make his case: the *Huasteco* learned to read and write, went on to become highly respected, and was ultimately elected as *juez*, or head of the community. Indeed, an important general achievement of the LCUs is the improved sense of integration and community identity they have brought about. Many of the old tensions that existed between different ethnic and linguistic groups have disappeared. It would have been unthinkable a few years ago for a *Huasteco* to become the *juez* in an ethnically mixed community.

Certainly the communities have assimilated the LCUs into their lives, but so far, it seems that the potential of the sound systems for stimulating community action has not been fully realized. During a group discussion with the heads of the Communication Committees in the Tamuín area, we found that they considered the main benefit of the sound systems to be the saving of time and effort when calling meetings, and the 'broadcasting' of the information capsules about health. But the group showed little awareness of the possibility of using the sound systems to discuss common problems that could perhaps be resolved by common action.

One interesting example occurred in Santa Martha. When trying to provide an illustration of this possible use of the sound system, we asked whether the community faced any particular problem at that moment. The head of the Communication Committee replied that there was indeed a problem, but that solving it would need a lot of money. On being pressed for more details, he said that the toilets in the school had been out of order for several weeks. We then proposed trying to provoke a public debate over the sound system about this problem, leading perhaps to group action by parents through contributions in cash or kind to repair the toilets. Our proposal met with initial surprise, but on further discussion, those present said it was a good idea and worth trying.

However, when we discussed such social dynamics and energizing with other Mexicans, they said that processes of this sort are in severe decline because the problems of the rural sector in recent years have left people disconcerted and demotivated. They are like people who have barely survived an accident and who are wandering about, dazed and aimless.

New videos for new needs

The collection of training videos produced under PRODERITH I was enormous, so there was little need to produce more under PRODERITH II, especially with the decline in technical assistance. But other demands were placed on the Communication System, and it had to be flexible and adapt its content and style accordingly.

Many of the new communication needs concerned policy and legislative measures introduced by the government in recent years. For example, as part of its plan to transform agriculture, the government took a radical and controversial policy step in 1992: it modified Article 27 of the National Constitution concerning land tenure. Under the new provisions, *ejido* members are being given formal title to their plots and are then permitted to sell them. Essentially, this opens the door for the replacement of the *ejido* system by much larger farms, even by agribusinesses. In this way, a sort of agrarian reform in reverse can be achieved, but probably at high social cost, for some 28 per cent of Mexico's people still live in rural areas, and the number of poor in these areas is increasing. The situation could worsen as *ejido* members and other smallholders are forced off their land in the coming years.

The amended Article 27 was a momentous change in the rural sector. Land tenure had been an emotional issue for centuries in Mexico, leading to revolution, land reform, and the introduction of the *ejido* system. To reverse the changes that had cost so much blood, and had become enshrined in the social and political conscience of Mexican peasantry, was a convulsion of the ground rules that had governed peasant life for almost eight decades. It needed a great deal of explanation, and also justification.

In addition, there were practical aspects of selling their rights that peasants needed to understand. In some cases, they sold them without realizing that they also covered the land on which their house was built. So without knowing what they were doing, they sometimes sold their land and also their home, leading to such domestic conflict that their families broke up. Videos and printed materials were therefore produced about the new Article 27.

The decentralization of the Rural Communication System, and the passing of the responsibility to Communication Committees to conduct video presentations, brought important changes. For example, many of the video programmes in the PRODERITH collection are designed to provoke a discussion among the audience about some aspect of their situation or their production systems. To lead such a group discussion properly calls for special skills, and under PRODERITH I there was always a well-trained field technician present for this task. In recent years, however, the Communication Committees have assumed the responsibility, but it is perhaps unrealistic to expect that group discussion skills can be effectively and quickly acquired by a member of a peasant community after only limited training.

We saw an example of the problem one evening in Yucatan, when a community had asked to see a video about irrigation systems in the northern part of the state. The documentary showed that much of the irrigation infrastructure was poorly used and maintained. It was a programme that could be very useful to peasants if the presenter were able to provide a good verbal introduction before the video, and promote a discussion afterwards, about how the experiences shown related to those of the audience. This would be a first step towards agreed actions to improve the use and maintenance of their own irrigation system. Instead of this, the presenter made a very general statement about the need to grow more vegetables under irrigation, and there was no analysis or discussion.

The network notion in practice

Following the 1987 discussions among the staff, which identified the idea of a communication approach based on networks, the notion was refined in the field with the help of social scientists. It was confirmed that naturally occurring networks were created by social groupings who had common interests. In addition, any sort of production or development initiative would call for an induced network that would involve others outside the community – for example, producers' organizations, input providers, middlemen, development institutions, local authorities, and the like.

Early attempts to apply the network approach failed, mainly because the actors in the networks were not properly identified. This was the case for an African Bee Control Programme in the late 1980s. The aggressive African bee had escaped from a research centre in Brazil and was making its way north year by year. When its arrival in Mexico was imminent, the government and PRODERITH wanted to reach beekeepers, many of whom were small and independent, with information about what to do when it arrived. The network identified by the communication staff was made up of institutions and beekeepers' associations. They all had their own agendas, which did not necessarily involve the small and independent beekeepers, who in the event, were hardly reached. In sum, the common interests that should be the feature of a true network did not exist.

Nevertheless, the network idea went on to become a feature of the communication methodology under PRODERITH II, but only after much experimental work in the field. In practice, it proved rather difficult for outsiders, such as development technicians, to identify the actors in a network. However, once the idea was explained to peasants, they quickly grasped the concept. With respect to any given topic, they proved able to define efficiently and clearly the internal relationships within the community or organization, and also the relationships with outside groups or sectors of society.

The use of the network approach was always linked directly to some concrete problem or programme. A first step was to analyse the problem or programme and delimit those aspects that had, or should have, communication actions. Then, all those who were involved in it – whether individuals, groups, organizations, or institutions – could be identified. Their position within that network determined the type of communication relationship that was to be established.

The network methodology proved very useful. The identification of a network became the first step in PRODERITH's design of a communication strategy for a given initiative or problem. In addition, the people who were trained to become the local Communication Committees were taught about it and encouraged to use it in their own communities.

Attempts to transfer regional communication units to farmers

During the work of PRODERITH I in the Pujal Coy area, close contacts had been built up with the Union de Ejidos Camino a la Liberación del Campesino. The title 'Path to Peasant Liberation' was in the sense of liberating peasants from rapacious middlemen who frequently cheated peasants when purchasing their harvests. In fact, the Union marketed its members' crops for a commission of only 1 per cent and made bulk purchases of inputs for them to get the best deals. The Union had 17 member *ejidos* with about 960 farmers, cultivating some 30,000 hectares.

When the RCUT was to be established, the management of the

Union, which also had a committee for social action, was enthusiastic about becoming involved, for it was clear that communication was potentially important for strengthening peasant organizations. For example, the Union needed to expand its number of members and convince them all to sell their produce through it, thereby increasing its bargaining power with buyers. In fact, it was implicit from the start of the RCUT that the Union would one day assume responsibility for it, thereby completing the transfer to a peasant organization as planned. The Union created a rural communication committee and was a member of the steering committee of the RCUT.

However, the transfer of the RCUT to the Union never took place. The increasingly desperate economic situation surrounding agriculture in Mexico in recent years, and especially the opening of markets to foreign competition from the mid-1980s onwards, never gave the small farmers or the Union a chance to create any resources beyond those required for sheer survival.

An anecdote will illustrate the problems. When one of us was visiting PRODERITH, in late 1989, the Union had 800 tons of soya beans in its store. They had just been harvested and the Union was trying to sell them. The industry had agreed a more or less fair price some weeks before, but at the moment the Union was ready to sell, there was a massive import of soya beans from the United States. The market price dropped sharply, but the Union could not wait for a recovery because the soya beans had been harvested in rainy conditions and were spoiling rapidly in its store.

For similar reasons, none of the five Regional Communication Units was transferred to local farmer organizations. As the only apparent alternative, all of the Regional Communication Units became enterprises that were expected to become self-supporting through selling their services. By the end of 1995, none had been able to generate the contracts that would make this possible. One cause of this may be that the staff, while well trained in methodology and in the production of materials, received no training in management and running of their Units. Thus, they may lack capacity in preparing good proposals and in negotiating them with potential clients.

Rural Communication in Mexico: Successes, Problems, Prospects

The Rural Communication System has been highly successful, despite Mexico's economic circumstances of the 1980s. Unfortunately, this decade has so far not brought economic relief: just as Mexicans were beginning to forget the crises of the 1980s, their newly found and growing confidence was shattered on 24 December 1994, when the Mexican peso was suddenly devalued to less than half of its previous value against the US dollar.

This triggered the greatest crisis of the last 60 years. One Mexican summed up the national feeling when he told us, 'The whole issue of the North American Free Trade Agreement and the government's pronouncements had led us to believe that our country was entering the First World, on a par with its new free-trade partners, Canada and the United States. And just when we were confident that all was well, that new horizons of opportunity and prosperity finally lay ahead, the sky fell in!'

As its staff say, the simple fact that the Rural Communication System has survived at all, in such circumstances, is remarkable. In addition, however, its achievements are unequalled by any other development programme anywhere. For example, by the end of 1995, it had produced more than 900 video programmes, an average of more than 50 titles a year, and provided video-based information and training sessions for a total of more than 540,000 people. It had also built a core of highly competent specialists in communication for development and a rich infrastructure of production facilities.

Even if it did not prove possible to transfer the Communication System to peasant organizations, it was successfully decentralized in the sense that active Regional and Local Communication Units were established. Furthermore, creating capacity within rural communities to identify communication networks and needs, and to make use of video materials and sound systems, was a pioneering and unprecedented initiative.

Finally, and perhaps most important of all, the Rural Communication System showed how to make the peasant the protagonist in his own development, an aim that is now widely recognized as essential, but seldom realized.

And all this was achieved at a cost of less than 1.5 per cent of the investment in the two phases of PRODERITH. But set against these successes, there is a serious institutional problem as we write. It is often said that Mexico is reinvented every six years as each new president makes institutional changes. The future of the Rural Communication System now depends on a restructuring of secretariats – the equivalent of ministries – by the present government of Ernesto Zedillo: the powerful National Water Commission, which is the institutional home of the Communication System, was moved from the Secretariat for Agriculture and Water Resources to a newly created Secretariat for the Environment, Natural Resources, and Fisheries.

This reorganization effectively left the Communication System in a secretariat that has little to do with agricultural and rural development. One is forced to the conclusion that, despite all its successes, the Communication System has still not been institutionalized as part of national rural development policy and operations. If it had been, it would not have been transferred to a secretariat where it is divorced from its special area of experience and competence.

Another question of concern for the future of communication is to what extent the participatory attitudes and working concepts originally applied during PRODERITH have survived more widely in Mexico's agricultural and rural development sector.

After bad experiences such as Plan la Chontalpa, the successes under PRODERITH in involving rural people led the director-general of the National Water Commission in the late 1980s to state in a video interview that *nothing would be built in the future without consulting the proposed beneficiaries.*[4] Such a statement, from someone so important, seemed to represent a breakthrough in official thinking. However, in Yucatan in September 1995, we were involved in a discussion with farmers about a new irrigation system that was being installed by the National Water Commission in their *ejido*. The work was proceeding in those very days.

The farmers told us that they had been pleading with the National Water Commission for many years to install the small irrigation scheme, but after finally agreeing, the engineer in charge never discussed his plans for the scheme with the community. When the construction work began, the farmers soon saw that it could not function as a gravity system. This was because an existing road would bisect it, and there were also problems with land levelling. In all probability, the farmers would have to irrigate with hosepipes, a time-consuming and expensive operation.

Perhaps there was no economically viable alternative for constructing the scheme, but the point for concern is that there was no dialogue with its future users. It seems that the old superior attitudes of many technical people towards peasants die very hard; give them the slightest chance to resurge and they come slinking in through the back door again.

---

4. Emphasis added by the authors.

The issue of participatory approaches with peasants assumes particular importance in the crisis now affecting them. The infrastructure installed under PRODERITH increased the area of land in Mexico's tropics that *could* be cultivated successfully by more than 50 per cent. But as we have seen, the human resource development, and the other inputs for integrated rural development, were relatively weak under PRODERITH II. A possible PRODERITH III is being considered and its central function would be to build human and organizational capacity among peasants so that they could make optimum use of that new infrastructure and lands. Participatory approaches would be essential to achieve that.

Whatever happens in the future, it can be fairly claimed that there has never been a more imaginative communication programme on such a large scale in the rural sector. Despite all the problems, the conceptual and technical aspects of communication for development were handled with great insight, and extremely valuable experience in rural development was gained. Santiago Funes played a central role in this, but he built a team of highly qualified Mexicans too before leaving the job. Funes has a powerful personality, and today he wonders whether his presence and his way of operating were obstacles in creating the conditions in which the Mexican authorities would fully appropriate and institutionalize communication as part of rural development policy and practice.

It remains to be seen how the future of communication for rural development in Mexico will work out, but it would be sad indeed if policy and administrative decisions were to cause the loss of the communication experience, expertise, and capacity generated under PRODERITH.

CHAPTER 5

The Quick and the Dead: a Tale of Two Educational Radio Programmes

In this chapter, we will describe two very early uses of radio for information and education in rural areas, in quite different conditions of development, thousands of miles apart. The concepts they used were also entirely different, but both of them were successful. They began more or less at the same time, and one is still going strong today, but the other one died after 40 years, or to be more precise was killed for interesting reasons related to power relations, religion, and politics. We will begin with the one that is still alive.

The One that Lived: Entertainment and Education for British Farmers

Some people have an instinctive understanding of communication for development. One of these was Godfrey Baseley, who was the rural programme organizer of the British Broadcasting Corporation (BBC) from 1942 to 1965. Baseley was the mastermind behind the invention, and the production for many years, of *The Archers – An Everyday Story of Countryfolk*. This dramatized series was launched in January 1951 and is still running today, the longest radio series in history, anywhere in the world. It was launched at a critical time for British agriculture, and it became immensely popular with rural and urban people alike. At its high point, before the introduction of television in Britain, two out of every three adults listened to the 15-minute instalments of the series every evening. The series had an enormous impact on agriculture, while at the same time providing a way for urban people to understand rural issues and problems.

One of us (C.F.) came to know Baseley personally, but long after he had retired from the BBC. He was in his early eighties, and still very active; his main means of transport around the Gloucestershire village where he lived was a Honda motorized tricycle. I had the idea of inviting Godfrey Baseley to a workshop on communication for development that FAO was organizing in Tunis for several countries of North Africa, so that he could talk about his experience and the thinking behind *The Archers*. I was in Tunis several days before he arrived, and I had warned our hosts that Monsieur Baseley was an elderly gentleman, over 80 years of age, and that we had to look after him carefully. So an official from the Ministry of Agriculture and I went to the airport in an official car to collect him.

It was the month of June, and hot. There was a dust-laden wind blowing out of the desert, and a rainstorm hit the airport as Baseley's flight landed. The Tunisian official was terrified that Monsieur Baseley would catch cold, and told our driver to fetch the car and bring it to the door of the terminal.

Godfrey Baseley came out of customs, hale and hearty, and obviously uncomfortable wearing his jacket and tie in what, by then, had become a Turkish bath. I introduced him to the Tunisian official, and we stood around waiting until Baseley said, in his marvellously warm and resonant voice, with an accent that was redolent of Britain's rural west country, 'What are we waiting for then?' I explained that we were waiting for the car to collect us at the door because our host was worried he might catch cold. Baseley guffawed. 'Tell him not to worry, lad. And tell him I went to London Airport on my Honda this morning,' he said, with a mischievous grin, stripping off his jacket and tie and mopping his brow. I translated his comment in all seriousness, and the expression on the face of our Tunisian official was a study in astonishment. He must have believed Baseley's story, and that the British are all mad, because he never asked how Baseley had got his suitcase to the airport.

Baseley, with his down-to-earth approach to communication for development, linked to inimitable talent and imagination, was a great success during the workshop, and I had the chance and the privilege of learning more about *The Archers* during many hours of talking with him. As we were revising this book for publication, in February 1997, we were saddened to hear that Godfrey Baseley had died at the age of 92.

The rural scene in Britain during and after the Second World War

There are parallels between rural England in the 1940s and many areas of developing countries today. Farms were small, about half of them under 20 hectares, and most were family holdings handed down from father to son. Except in certain specialized agricultural areas, farming generally followed a mixed pattern: cattle for milk and meat, with farmers rearing their own replacements; sheep, pigs, and a variety of poultry to help provide ready cash; and a small area of arable land to provide some of the basic cereals required for feeding the livestock through the winter months. The main source of farm power was still the horse.

This pattern of farming had remained unchanged for many years until the Second World War, when German submarines in the Atlantic began sinking ship after ship bringing food and other supplies to Great Britain. With its imports of food threatened, the British government could no longer allow farmers to continue in their traditional manner; drastic and rapid changes needed to be forced through to produce more food domestically.

The government issued production orders, and each county had a War Agricultural Executive Committee to ensure compliance with those orders. There were Field Officers, usually men and women with specialized technical qualifications, to enforce the rules and regulations and to give help and advice when new techniques were required. To many of the smaller farmers who had valued their independence, these officers were unpopular and were looked upon as 'enforcement officials' rather than advisers. This feeling persisted after the war, because the same stringent rules and regulations for agricultural production remained in force for some time. In fact, Great Britain was still short of food, and rationing persisted for several years after the end of the war.

Radio programmes for farmers were nothing new in those years. A senior 'talks' producer in the BBC's London complex had made farm programmes his speciality. Over the years, he had discovered a number of very capable broadcasters from among the higher echelons in the farming community, and from universities and research stations. Since increasing agricultural productivity was the priority, the radio programmes had become increasingly technical, spending much of their time covering the latest findings of the research institutions in the country.

Godfrey Baseley and the genesis of an idea

Baseley, to quote his own words, 'was born and bred a countryman with a long line of ancestors who had lived and farmed in the area to the south and west of Birmingham'. His father was a farmer and a butcher, and Baseley worked with him as a young man. However, he had ambitions in the area of entertainment, so he became involved in amateur theatre in his spare time. Later, he worked in radio and accumulated several years of experience as an actor, story reader, and occasionally as a singer in musical comedy.

With the advent of the Second World War, Baseley joined the Ministry of Information as a 'staff speaker' (he was medically unfit for military service). Then, after about two years of speaking to varied audiences on topics connected with the war effort, he joined the BBC's Outside Broadcasting Unit in Birmingham.

At the end of the war, Baseley was entrusted with the task of running farm radio programming for the Midlands region of Britain. In this new job, he initially followed the established pattern of farming programmes based on technical talks and interviews involving agricultural researchers, advisory staff, and progressive farmers. However, like any skilled communicator, Baseley was constantly seeking feedback in response to his efforts, and when talking to farmers, he discovered that they 'didn't listen to such talks'. They had had 'enough of that during the war' when they 'were ordered about by the same sort of people from the War Ag.', as they called the War Agricultural Executive Committee. Some farmers, and particularly the small ones who actually needed the advice most, would often add, 'And what do they know about *practical farming*? All they know is what they've read in books.'

Baseley's experience in entertainment, in trying to hold the attention of audiences as a public speaker – particularly when the topic was an unpopular government wartime order – came to his rescue as he sought ways of attracting farmers to listen. He began to incorporate topics for farmers' wives and children in the hope that the radio would at least be turned on, and that the farmers themselves might hear some ideas of interest to them. He also began to have more actual farmers speaking on the programme.

Increasingly, letters began to come in from farmers with questions about some topic that had been raised in a programme, but the interest could hardly be described as enthusiastic. However, and somewhat to Baseley's surprise, letters also began to arrive from people living in the towns who wanted to know more about an item they had heard mentioned, or who wanted more information about the countryside. But Baseley's main objective was the farming population, and the weekly 15-minute farm programme was not arousing the interest and response he wanted.

Baseley began to reflect on possible new approaches to farm broadcasts. When travelling around in the countryside and talking to farmers, he had often asked them how they discovered and first put into practice the many new techniques and procedures that were appearing in the more advanced farming areas. The most frequent response was: 'I look over the neighbour's hedge, and if what I see looks good, and likely to be more profitable than what I'm doing, I follow suit. If what I see doesn't look right, I'll have nothing to do with it.'

Baseley became intrigued by this notion of imitation as a force for change, and he launched a new series of radio programmes called *Over a Neighbour's Hedge*. For these, Baseley found a well-known, respected, and successful farmer, a person with a keen eye for changes that were taking place in market and customer requirements. Together, they visited farmers and their families each week, looked at their operations, and discussed what was going on. Later, in the studio, Baseley and the farming personality would talk about what they had seen and heard. Baseley's role was to ask pertinent questions and ensure that the more technical issues were explained in simple terms.

The formula was an almost instant success, and the previous weekly and more traditional 15-minute farm programme was dropped. But within a year, *Over a Neighbour's Hedge* ran into a serious problem: the respected farmer, the linchpin of the operation, became so involved with matters concerning the National Farmers' Union that he no longer had time to make the programme.

Reflecting on his experience with *Over a Neighbour's Hedge*, Baseley came to the conclusion that it should be possible to create programmes that would attract rural people through telling a story, but at the same time, this story would be used as a vehicle for conveying information and education. It could also meet the interest expressed from the urban sector in having information about the countryside. There were several radio serials that were attracting large audiences in Britain at the time. One was about a medical doctor and his patients in an urban area; another was about crime and the work of the police called *Dick Barton – Special Agent*. This recounted the adventures of a 'super-cop' and had an enormous following.

Baseley mulled over the idea of *inventing* a rural setting and a farming family as a basis for a dramatized series, and he tried the idea out on a number of people, including during a meeting of farmers called in 1948 to discuss Britain's overall needs for farm radio programmes. Baseley's idea was supported, with one farmer saying, 'What we need is a sort of farming Dick Barton!'

Baseley began to promote his idea of a dramatized series about rural life, but it was only after two years of cajoling and negotiating with BBC programming chiefs that he managed to obtain approval and funds for a pilot run of five episodes of 15 minutes' duration each. These went on air in the early summer of 1950, in the BBC's Midland Region service only.

Audience research showed favourable reactions to the pilot programmes, so Baseley spent much of the rest of the year campaigning for approval to go ahead with the series on a daily basis and to have it broadcast on a nationally heard network – the BBC Light Programme. He succeeded, and finally, on 1 January 1951, *The Archers – An Everyday Story of Countryfolk* came into being. There is still no sign of its end 46 years later.

The concepts behind The Archers

Baseley was particularly fortunate in that the BBC assigned to him the two highly competent writers of radio drama who had been responsible for *Dick Barton – Special Agent*, a series that had been discontinued mainly because it was thought to be a bad influence on the morals of the young. These writers, Edward Mason and Geoffrey Webb, had a remarkable gift for dramatic story-telling, but they knew nothing in particular about agriculture or rural life. Baseley's first task was to create the characters, and an environment for them, which would provide proper scope for a story-line, and at the same time a vehicle for information and education in appropriate doses. He decided that he would need the following characters, eight in number, as his core cast:

Lead character This person, the farmer, should be knowledgeable without being too clever, that is to say half a step ahead of the average farmer, rather than a farming star. He should be a person always ready to help others, well informed in a general way, and with sound judgement. He should not have problems of excessive drinking, drugs, gambling, illicit sexual relations, or the like. He should be involved in the events of the community so that his sound common sense and judgement could play a useful part in any situation, especially of a controversial nature – and there should be plenty of controversy to keep the story alive.

Mother figure This should be a person whom the listeners would trust and come to depend upon; a kind, warm and understanding person, and fair in her judgements. She should be knowledgeable in family and home matters. She would not always appear in her home environment but would mix with others so that her influence could be brought to bear in a variety of situations. For example, she might visit a young mother with her first baby who would benefit – as would listeners – from any advice she might provide about the welfare of the child.

Girl/boy They should represent the romantic element of the story-line. Young, impetuous, joyful, jealous, sporting, and so on; they should also be opposites in some ways. They could be rich/poor, town/country, or come from opposing religious backgrounds. In effect, something like a Romeo and Juliet situation was needed.

Mature lovers These should be two people who were very much in love but who were facing numerous problems, such as pending divorce, difference in age, family objections, or financial difficulties. One of the characters could have been married previously, or if strongly emotional or aggressive situations were required, could still be married but estranged. With these characters, unlike the young lovers, there would be strong implications of a sexual relationship, but since the series was aimed at family listening (and given the prevailing moral standards of those years) no scene would ever depict a situation that positively affirmed the existence of such a relationship.

Comedy element A character would be created to introduce comic relief, especially if it had been necessary to place serious emphasis on a particular message, instruction, or event concerned with farming. Apart from the humour that this character would provide, he would also be traditional in his attitudes, a 'slow adopter' of agricultural innovations, in today's parlance.

Irritant element An essential character, not only for the audience to hate, but also to use as a means of inspiring even more love, sympathy and understanding for the rest of the characters. There is an 'irritant element' in almost every community. The person would be a middle-aged woman, a spinster or a widow with very positive views and rules, entirely of her own making, about morals, behaviour, religion, and so on. She would be a gossip, always prying into other people's affairs and coming to premature and wrong conclusions.

She would also be a useful character for presenting the views and ideas of the more prudish listeners. She would have much to say about the 'mature lovers', and be the cause of trouble in the community in many other ways. As Baseley remarked to me, 'Trouble is the bread and butter of a daily serial!'

In putting flesh and bone on these elements, Baseley invented Dan Archer, 55 years old, his wife Doris, 54 years old, and their three children, Jack, Philip and Christine. The eldest son, Jack, was married to a girl from London called Peggy, whom he had met while they were both in the armed forces during the war. Peggy knew nothing about country life and explaining things to her would provide a natural way of introducing general farming information and education into the series. Phil, the second son, was at agricultural college, and this created a way of introducing technical information into the programmes. The daughter, Chris, with a similar technical education, would be a collector of milk samples for the Ministry of Agriculture. Her visits to farms all over the area provided a way of introducing practical information about what other farmers were doing.

The 'irritant' was Jack's mother-in-law. She was 'a sharp-faced, black-coated woman who always moaned when she was feeling happy'!

The comic figure was a neighbouring farmer, Walter Gabriel. He was a widower, semi-literate, out of date in all his farming methods, and a likeable old rascal who was always asking for advice and help in running his smallholding.

These basic characters formed the core of the story. Any other characters introduced were no more than props and scenery within the structure of the programme. They were added to provide atmosphere and to assist in the development of any particular story-line.

Baseley realized that unless the characters were totally authentic, and therefore credible, the series could never succeed. He therefore built up a physical description of each one, and a historical background of Dan and Doris Archer that went back several generations. This was the basic briefing for the two writers, Mason and Webb, but of course, they also needed to know about the characters' emotions and reactions to other people and events. Were they passionate in their loving? Were they of a jealous nature, quick to quarrel or hate? Impatient or tolerant? Kind, cruel, spiteful, quick-tempered, emotional, sensual? Did they laugh or cry easily? Were they forgiving, or did they hold grievances for short or long periods? It was through such characteristics that exciting and dramatic situations could be created, for as Baseley said, human relationships are of infinite variety and the raw material for inventive writing. But he applied a basic rule to ensure authenticity: since the characters were fictional, the writers could attribute any characteristics to them they wanted as the series got under way, but once established, these attributes must not be changed.

No less effort went into creating an authentic location. It had to be a village with sufficient population to support a school, church, chapel, village stores, and a pub, all of which would provide venues for talk and discussion. And the farm itself had to be a typical farm of that time in Great Britain.

The whole environment was carefully created, named, and even mapped. It was somewhere in the Midlands; the village was called Ambridge; the Archers' farm was called Brookfield; the neighbouring farms were also given names; and the nearest market town was called Borchester. Baseley, the writers, and the programme producer travelled extensively around mixed farming areas in the Midlands for information on which to model the Archers' farm, for which Baseley created a detailed cropping and stocking pattern.

There was to be a major difference between *The Archers* and any other radio serial that had been broadcast in Britain up to that time: it would deliberately set out to include informational and educational material in an entertaining story. And so some principles had to be established from the start. A prime consideration was the need to attract and maintain an audience. As Baseley stated in his down-to-earth way, 'Unless people listen to your programme, and regularly at that, you'll get nowhere!'

This led to the question of the proper proportions between entertainment, information, and education. It was decided that the guideline for the mix would be 60 per cent entertainment, 30 per cent information, and 10 per cent education. And to keep interest alive, no scene should last more than 6 minutes and there would be no more than three scenes within each 15-minute episode. Furthermore, each episode would end with a 'cliff-hanger', that is to say, it would leave unfinished some exciting or vital event, and by so doing ensure that the audience would be motivated to tune in the next day to discover the answer or result.

Music would play an important part in *The Archers*. There would be a distinctive musical introduction, and mood music would be used to enhance the emotional effect, to help the transition between time and location within an episode, and to provide a tidy end to each episode. The signature tune chosen was *Barwick Green*, by Arthur Woods, a melody quite similar in general character to the signature tune that announces the BBC World Service News. Woods' catchy tune now signifies *The Archers* to tens of millions of Britons.

Producing The Archers

The writers and Baseley planned everything together, but the actual writing of the scripts was the responsibility of one of the two writers at a time. Each writer would prepare 20 scripts, to cover one month of programmes, and then hand over to the other. The one who was not writing had sufficient time to prepare for his session well in advance, would be available for consultation, or could go on location to brief himself in respect of technical issues that were likely to arise during his next stint.

Baseley, the overall editor, had the responsibility of providing the brief to the writers. These briefs set the themes to be covered; they pertained to the farming scene, and also to the lives of the characters. Baseley, checking with subject matter specialists as necessary, also provided background information of a technical nature to the writers.

Topicality was always looked for as a means of adding authenticity to the series. For this reason, some hot news item from the actual day an episode went on air was often built into that episode. The item might concern an important government announcement, for example a farm price review or some legislation concerning agriculture, the result of a major sporting event, or just some up-to-date facts on an issue that was receiving coverage in the press. To do this, the writers always included 30–90 seconds of material in each episode that was not essential to the story-line. This material could be dropped at the last moment, if required, and something topical inserted in its place.

Also in the interests of authenticity, Baseley was a stickler about sound effects. For example, different makes and models of tractors make different sounds, so once established, the recording was not changed unless it had been specifically mentioned in the script that Archer or another farmer had bought a new tractor.

Authenticity was such a feature of the series that it was something of a sport for listeners to try to find errors in it, and a constant stream of comments arrived through the mail, year in year out. Occasionally, Baseley found that he could not win in this struggle for authenticity. On one occasion, in a scene in the village hall, the people were to sing the famous piece by Elgar, *Land of Hope and Glory*. The only recording that Baseley could find was made by a choir in the Albert Hall, London. After the episode had been broadcast, derisive letters poured in to say that no community singing could ever sound as good as that. Chastened, Baseley made an actual recording in a village hall, complete with creaking floorboards and shuffling feet. Some time later, he used it in an episode, but even more derisive letters poured in to say that no group, even in the most backward village, could ever sing as badly as that, and with all that background noise.

The success of The Archers

It was clear almost at once that Baseley and his team had the right formula for the series, and that all the careful preparation had been worthwhile. Within weeks of going on air, it had built a regular audience of 2 million people. After a so-called trial period of three months, the series was given prime listening time, from 6.45 p.m. to 7 p.m. each weekday evening, with an omnibus edition on Saturday morning for those who had missed any of the instalments during the week. The audience swelled quickly to 4 million; and as has already been mentioned, it is estimated that at its height, that is to say in 1955 and before television became a dominant medium, two out of three adults in Great Britain (more than 20 million people) were listening to *The Archers* on a regular basis.

The success of *The Archers* with listeners lay in its professionalism in telling a good story, in an utterly convincing manner, about a rural family and other people close to it. Its enormous following gave it two main areas of social usefulness. First, it was a vehicle for transmission of information and education to the farming community; second, it provided an information bridge between the urban population and rural people. Via this bridge, millions of town-dwellers were kept informed of what was happening in the countryside, and of the problems affecting farmers and farming. As a general result, agriculture gained prestige and recognition.

The authorities in Britain were quick to recognize the potential of the series for improving agriculture and rural life, and Baseley soon had an abundance of requests from many sources asking that he introduce their messages into the series. One example, when *The Archers* was already well established, was a request from the Ministry of Agriculture for Baseley to help in influencing farmers to change from multi-purpose breeds of cattle – such as the Shorthorns that Dan Archer owned – to more specialized milk-producing breeds, particularly Friesians. A remarkable testimonial to the influence of the series is that the Shorthorn Society heard about this request and pleaded with Baseley not to have Dan Archer get rid of his Shorthorns, because if he did, so would every other farmer keeping the breed.

In this same period, however, the Ministry of Agriculture was concerned that farmers should know the symptoms of foot-and-mouth disease and understand fully why all cloven-hoofed animals on a farm had to be slaughtered where there was an outbreak of it, or whenever animals had been in contact with a source of infection. Baseley and his team decided that they could marry the two requirements, and not upset Shorthorn owners too much, by having an outbreak of foot-and-mouth disease on Brookfield Farm. And this is what they did, in 1956.

The potential of the drama serial shows itself to the full in such circumstances. First, there were conversations about one of the Archers' cows, which seemed to be ailing, about its symptoms, and conjecture that it might be foot-and-mouth disease. Suspense built up until a veterinarian confirmed their worst fears and the Ministry of Agriculture's machinery went into operation to contain the outbreak.

The Archer family was forced to watch their years of effort to build a good herd brought to nothing as their animals were led to slaughter and the carcasses burned. Listeners shared the emotions and the tragedy at the loss of favourite animals. In fact, it was a tear-jerking scene as Dan and Doris Archer watched the slaughter of animals that had been in their possession for many years, most of them the high-quality result of their ability to upgrade their stock through selective breeding.

Having hooked the audience emotionally, the conversations in the series explored every possible cause of the outbreak. Through this, there emerged a natural explanation of how the disease spreads, what the first symptoms of the disease are, why all livestock markets within a considerable distance had to be closed, why such rigid discipline in movements between farms was necessary, and so on.

After discussing every aspect of the situation, and extracting every possible human emotion from it, the series went on to follow the Archers as they discussed among themselves, and with others, the rebuilding of their dairy enterprise. In due course, they introduced Friesian cattle, in line with the Ministry of Agriculture's policy to improve the efficiency of milk production.

The Archers *causes a national uproar*

Another example of the use of *The Archers* as a vehicle for information concerned a message from the fire-fighting services. They had been promoting the idea of farm ponds for both fire-fighting and irrigation, but with little success. Baseley was asked to intervene and the result was a stable fire on Brookfield Farm in which Dan's daughter-in-law, Grace Archer, died while trying to save her horse.

This led to one of the most astonishing events in the long history of radio. There was a national uproar; the BBC switchboard was jammed by callers; every major newspaper in Britain the next morning ran banner headlines: 'Grace Archer Dies in Stable Fire', or words to that effect; letters arrived in huge quantities at the BBC; there was a running public debate that went on for over a month about 'turning entertainment into tragedy', and hundreds of suggestions for ways of reviving Grace were received. Not by coincidence – in fact with Machiavellian calculation – Grace's death was on the same night that independent television began broadcasting in Britain, the first time in history that any mass medium other than the BBC had operated in the UK. This news was pushed into the middle pages by Grace Archer's death.

The event of Grace's death is recounted here to indicate the degree of following and involvement the series commanded, but it was not always necessary to be so dramatic to pass on valuable information to farmers. One technique that was commonly used was to have Dan Archer suffer some technical problem on the farm, but one that was serious enough to have financial repercussions – for example, the loss of 20 per cent of the potato crop through blight – and Dan having to talk to his bank manager about the season's gloomy financial outlook. Of course, the event was the channel for a lot of dialogue about control of potato blight, which, set in the context of Dan's losses and the sympathy they aroused, was much more effective than a normal radio talk on the subject.

The examples of the use of *The Archers* as a medium for passing on useful information are legion, and there is little point in providing others. It is enough to know that the series was an important influence in a critical period of agricultural and rural history in

Britain. The advent of TV was bound to reduce its audience and usefulness, and today's mainly large-scale, highly mechanized, and well-trained British farmers hardly need such a series. In effect, the series can be said to have worked itself out of a job as far as farmers are concerned, because it played a role in the rural trans-formation that has taken place in Britain and which has turned the relatively inefficient agricultural economy of the post-war years into one of the most advanced in the world today. But it has not worked itself out of a job as far as urban audiences are concerned, and almost half a century after it began, it continues to provide that information bridge by which town-dwellers can follow events in the countryside. *The Archers* was conceived and produced with a precise objective in mind, and with the utmost in professionalism and loving care. It was, of course, uniquely English in content, and had it not been so carefully crafted to reflect the reality of English farm life, it would not have succeeded as it did.

At one time or another over the years, many English-speaking countries tried to buy the series, but they were turned down by the BBC. The radio services in one country even wanted to translate the series and broadcast it. It is curious that no country ever tried to copy the idea and tailor it to its own audiences, with the exception of the United States and Italy. Both attempts failed: in the US it failed for lack of resources in a small private radio station, while in Italy, the programme was so badly produced, with farmers portrayed as being so backward and stupid, that their associations complained.

One is forced to the conclusion that few broadcasting authorities in other countries fully realized what the series was all about: they saw it as a first-rate piece of story-telling that was attracting enorm-ous audiences, but one must wonder whether they also perceived that, in its founder's thinking and practice, it was a subtle vehicle for promoting behavioural change in rural areas.

Today, countries might prefer to invest in rural television drama, as a number have done, but they have usually run into difficulties and failed after a relatively short period. There are certainly practical problems in television production that do not exist in radio. For example, as long as you are leaving your audience to imagine a crop hit by a hailstorm, as it is being described by the characters in a radio serial, there are no logistical problems to complicate programme production. However, when you need a crop that has really been hit by a hailstorm to satisfy the television camera and the needs of your story, all manner of problems beyond the control of man and television producers emerge. And just imagine the difficulties and expense of creating the scene for television of Dan and Doris Archer's Shorthorns being led away, slaughtered, burned and buried after the foot-and-mouth disease outbreak.

There are lessons in the experience of *The Archers* that could be applied to making radio drama a vehicle for information and learning in many parts of the world, especially as so many people still listen to radio while engaged in other things. Furthermore, it does not need to be confined to rural development: there are numerous themes of change and development that would lend themselves to the strategy. The fact that there are some 2 billion radio receivers in the world today, about one for every three people, shows that the potential for education by this medium is still phenomenal.

The One that Died – Radio Sutatenza and ACPO

In those same years after the Second World War, when Baseley was wrestling with rural broadcasting in the United Kingdom, and before he came up with his idea for *The Archers*, important events were beginning to take place high in the Andes of Colombia, more than 5,000 miles away. They ultimately led to Radio Sutatenza and Acción Cultural Popular (ACPO), the most widespread and important use of radio and other communication media for educating rural people ever seen. It became the subject of numerous studies and evaluations involving a variety of prestigious international development agencies and universities, and it created a model that was copied in 20 other countries. Despite its enormous size, its success in improving peasant life, and its international prestige, the operation collapsed after 40 years. The story of that operation, and the reasons for its collapse, are fascinating.

As in the case of *The Archers*, there was a gifted and committed person behind Radio Sutatenza. He was a village priest called José Joaquín Salcedo, a visionary of tremendous energy and organizing ability. He founded and then ran Radio Sutatenza for 40 years. He hardly fitted the usual image of a Catholic priest; in fact his religious calling often appeared faint. Rather, what inspired and drove Salcedo for the whole of his life was a single idea: for development to take place, one must first help people to develop their knowledge and intelligence, for they must be capable of knowing and discerning to be able to improve their lives.

To appreciate fully the story of the rise and fall of Radio Sutatenza, one needs to know something about Salcedo. Fortunately, before he died in 1994, an excellent biography called *Un Quijote Visionario* – 'A Quixotic Visionary' – was written by Luis Zalamea. We have culled much information from that work, as well as from other documentation and from people who worked with Salcedo and knew him well.

Salcedo was born in 1921 in a village called Corrales, 140 miles north of Bogotá, in the Department of Boyaca. Salcedo's grandmother on his mother's side was English. As a girl, towards the end of the nineteenth century, she had come to Colombia with her family. Her father was a steel production specialist, and he had been invited to help develop that industry shortly after the discovery of iron ore deposits near Bogotá.

Salcedo's parents were relatively well off. They lived in a large house in the centre of the village, but it was a peasant community, and Salcedo grew up knowing at first hand the abject conditions in which subsistence farmers lived. For his secondary education, Salcedo had to go to a school in Tunja, the capital of the Department of Boyaca. There, he became friendly with a priest who taught in the local seminary, and he later transferred from his school to the seminary to finish his secondary education. From that, it was a natural progression for him to continue in the seminary towards the priesthood. However, it took the intervention of his priest friend to persuade Monseñor Crisanto Luque, the Bishop of Tunja who later became Colombia's first cardinal, to let him study for holy orders, for he seemed to lack the necessary vocation and piety.

Bishop Luque, who was to play a central role in most of Salcedo's career and work, was of peasant stock, imbued with common sense, and with the conviction that the Church should play a role in the social and economic progress of the poor and oppressed. This was precisely the way Salcedo was beginning to think, and he and Bishop Luque soon became friends. Unusually for those years in Colombia, both were keen on sport, and they became tennis partners. This early friendship with the bishop served Salcedo in good stead because he was twice expelled from the seminary, the first time when he was caught reading Karl Marx, and the second time for teaching young army recruits in the local barracks to read and write. In his appeal, he told the bishop that, if he was going to devote his life to social work and human development, he must read Marx's doctrine in order to be able to know and fight the enemy. And as for teaching people to read and write, how could he prepare for his life's work if he were not allowed to meet the sort of people he was to help? On both occasions the bishop had him reinstated in the seminary.

Salcedo was so intensely concerned by social problems, so quick to rush to the defence of the defenceless, and to adopt impossible causes, that he earned the nickname of 'Quixote' in the seminary. Furthermore, his interest in cinema, and his holiday occupation of taking a 16-millimetre projector and films to rural communities in the region, at his own expense, were hardly thought fitting for an aspiring priest. Indeed, cinema was sinful to the traditional Church in those days. However, despite his free-thinking and rebellious attitudes, he endured the seminary, was ordained, and was sent out to be a village priest in the mountain village of Sutatenza.

The massive range of the Andes runs north from southern Argentina and Chile for more than 6,000 kilometres (4,000 miles) as a single chain of mountains, but when it reaches the southern border of Colombia, it splits into three separate ranges with deep valleys between them. The Department of Boyaca lies in the easternmost of these three ranges; some of its rivers flow westwards towards the central valley of the Magdalena, while others, on the eastern side of the mountain range, flow down towards the Amazon Basin. One of these watersheds leading towards the Amazon is the Tenza Valley, a fertile, sub-tropical area. In fact 'valley' is not really the right name, for that word conjures up the picture of a single, orderly vale lying between two ranges of hills, whereas the Tenza Valley is topographical chaos. It is a tortured jumble of hills and ridges, serpentine valleys and side valleys, only unified by being a single watershed that flows eastwards. High on the slope above one of the valleys of that watershed perches the white chip of village called Sutatenza.

From the square of Sutatenza you look out over an immense landscape of green slopes, broken here and there by other white villages, each with its church steeple. The landscape rolls on and on over ridge after ridge, each higher than the last, until the skyline is blocked by a towering mountain range, majestic and brooding. The skies of the Andes are seldom without some cloud, and this, and the strong rays of the high-altitude sun, create vivid patches of dappled light and shade over the rich green countryside.

Even today, the road to Sutatenza is unpaved and full of potholes, so in August 1947 it must have been horrendous, as a rattling, gaily painted bus ground upwards towards the village. Salcedo was among its passengers. Seated with the peasants dressed in their ponchos, and with their baskets of farm produce, chickens and the like, he seemed to come from another world. He was very tall, with a pale complexion inherited from his Anglo-Saxon ancestors. In fact, his gangling and awkward frame, his long face and large nose, and his thin lips, made him look more like an English aristocrat than a Colombian. He could hardly be described as handsome, but his appearance was certainly arresting. Penetrating dark eyes were set among his bony features, and he always wore the intense expression of a man with a mission, which he was going to fulfil at all costs. This is not to say that he was humourless; he had an ironic and subtle sense of humour that was often self-deprecatory.

Salcedo arrived in Sutatenza with his 16-millimetre film projector; and about a month later, a primitive amateur radio transmitter built by his brother also arrived. Sutatenza was a community of about 8,000 people, many of whom lived on isolated farms scattered up and down the slopes of the valley, often a long and arduous walk from the village. Salcedo had been sent to Sutatenza as assistant to the village priest, who was a very traditional cleric. His prime activities were to make sure his church's coffers were kept replenished and to scold his congregation during interminable Sunday sermons, which he sprinkled with Latin and Greek phrases to show his erudition before his ignorant flock.

Salcedo soon fell out with his superior. One Sunday not long after his arrival, the senior priest invited Salcedo to preach a sermon. Salcedo accepted, but once in the pulpit, he told the congregation that he did not intend to give them a sermon; instead he wanted to open a dialogue with them about improving life in the community. He told them that he could not do it alone, that they would have to work for themselves and with him, as a team, so that together they could lift themselves out of their backward state.

For the congregation to speak in church was totally forbidden by Salcedo's superior, and he was apoplectic at the unexpected turn of events provoked by his subordinate. But the more daring among the congregation began to speak up about the problems. They identified consumption of *chicha* – maize beer – on Sundays and the consequent drunkenness, violence, and quite frequent deaths caused by knifings, as a major problem. In their discussion, they came to realize that the cause of so much Sunday alcoholism was boredom, for after mass, there was nothing to do except drink. Salcedo proposed that they all get together and build a theatre; he would provide a film projector and the films. At the time, about 80 per cent of the peasants in Sutatenza were illiterate, so he also talked to them about literacy classes and other educational activities.

In the weeks while plans for the theatre and cultural centre were being drawn up and discussed, Salcedo began to project films in the square in front of the priest's house to tackle the problem of boredom. Then, once the plans were ready, he asked that each person contribute one chicken to raise money to buy tools and materials. The response was literally overwhelming. On market day, and starting at two o'clock in the morning, the peasants began to arrive at the priest's house with their offerings, until the place was overflowing with more than 1,400 live chickens. Ultimately, they were loaded into baskets and trucked to Bogotá where they were sold from hotel to hotel. When the construction began, so many volunteers turned up to help that there were not enough tools and tasks to go around.

Salcedo's superior tried to have him removed from Sutatenza, but the decision in such matters lay with Bishop Luque of Tunja, Salcedo's friend, who supported the social work he was beginning. And so did the community, who were enthusiastic about Salcedo's proposals. He was trying to help them to help themselves, to improve their lives here and now, while the traditional priest was only offering them recompense in paradise.

Salcedo went around from house to house in the community, which covered an up-hill-and-down-dale area of more than 100 square kilometres. He explained his ideas, telling people that they could improve their living conditions, that the old life of boredom and fatalism need not be, and that everyone could participate in his crusade for progress. He also inveighed constantly against the excessive consumption of *chicha* but at the same time he worked with the community to improve its recreational possibilities. He promoted a chess club, the community built basketball and football pitches, and once the theatre was built, skits, plays, and musical events were organized. Slowly the mentality and the basic values of the community began to change. The consumption of *chicha* dropped, and so did the violence and deaths by stabbing.

Pioneering education by radio

Salcedo's amateur radio transmitter, which arrived in September 1947, had an output of only 90 watts. After a few days of trial and error, he managed to transmit a signal two kilometres to one of Sutatenza's outlying houses, where he had placed a receiver with a peasant family. They could hardly believe it when they heard his voice coming out of the speaker. They were also somewhat alarmed, because anything they did not understand had to be supernatural, and probably the work of the devil.

Salcedo followed that first test transmission with others, experimenting until he was able to reach most of the community. In November 1947, he broadcast his first programme, which was music played by local people. Initially, to make sure that his transmissions were being received, he had an arrangement with a peasant family whose house, four kilometres away, was visible from the square in front of the priest's house, where the transmitter was installed. Before beginning his programme, Salcedo would wave a white flag to signal that he was starting to transmit; the peasant would turn on his receiver, and if the signal was coming through, would wave his own white flag to indicate that the programme could go ahead.

Initially, Salcedo provided four radio receivers for his programmes in the community. In the main, the programme content in those first weeks and months was aimed at motivating and preparing people to participate in the true educational broadcasts he was planning. Within only a few months, the number of battery-operated radio receivers in the community had grown to more than twenty. Large numbers of people gathered around them at five o'clock each evening to listen to the programmes. They were summoned by the keeper of the radio who would strike a piece of steel rail, donated by the Colombian railways and hanging from the branch of a tree outside his house, so that it rang like a bell.

Word of this totally novel approach to education spread fast and aroused much interest. After all, education by radio in a country with hordes of illiterates, who were often isolated by the tortured topography, was an appealing idea. And so, in early 1948, the country's president formally inaugurated the Radio Schools of Sutatenza, with much national and international press coverage. In the same year, UNESCO sent two specialists to help a local teacher draw up the content and design the educational programmes for the Radio Schools. These were in no way formal schools; each was simply a small group of people, normally numbering from three to ten, who committed themselves to come together regularly to listen to the educational programmes. They might all be members of one family, or they might be from different families in the neighbourhood.

Momentum began to build rapidly in the second half of 1948.

General Electric Corporation of the US donated Radio Sutatenza's first proper transmitter, a 250-watt professional unit, and 100 radio receivers. They evidently saw a huge potential market for radio receivers, and so they also invited Salcedo to New York, all expenses paid. Bishop Luque cannily refused permission for Salcedo to accept the offer; he said he should certainly go to the US, but he should not tie himself to General Electric when other companies, such as Westinghouse and RCA, could also be interested and might offer better terms for equipment. The bishop lent Salcedo the money for the trip.

In the event, General Electric continued to be the most generous supporter. They donated a 1,000-watt transmitter, 150 more radios, and antennae and other accessories to a value of US$60,000, a large sum of money in those days. Salcedo had been very astute in his contacts with US manufacturers, pointing out that the more powerful the transmitter of Radio Sutatenza, the more people it would cover, and by inference, the bigger potential market for radio receivers.

Thus Radio Sutatenza began its 40-year career. Within weeks of arriving in Sutatenza, Salcedo had challenged the peasantry from the pulpit to take up arms against the poverty and backwardness that afflicted them, and had offered his hand and vision in a partnership. They responded, and so a pact was formed. This later took on the form of a foundation with the name Acción Cultural Popular (ACPO). Although it was launched in 1947, its juridical status was not officially recognized until 1949.

In the following years, and from its tiny beginnings in Sutatenza, ACPO ultimately expanded to cover the whole of Colombia, becoming the most powerful radio network in the country. Its strategically placed transmitters also reached into all five neighbouring countries. This mighty network always remained faithful to its origins and kept the name of 'Radio Sutatenza'.

The philosophy and work of Acción Cultural Popular

Salcedo pioneered a concept known as integral fundamental education. This was similar to what today is often called 'life education'. The core of the concept is that the educational process must be the development of the individual as a whole person and as a part of society. It is founded on the belief that school education establishes only the basic knowledge on which the individual must continue to build throughout life, incorporating all those elements that are necessary for his or her life and development. The concept also emphasizes the need to help people to understand their own responsibility for improvement, to recognize their own potential for progress, and to know the value of their own resources.

A Bolivian colleague once said to us, in exasperation after some people in his country had not fulfilled their obligations and thereby wrecked our work programme, 'Under-development is a state of mind!' Salcedo believed exactly the same, but he put it the other way around, and it became an ACPO slogan: 'Development is in the mind of mankind'. Salcedo and ACPO were also bound to the notion that providing people with education in the broadest sense would enable them to make informed decisions, and become proactive in taking control of their lives.

Over a period of years, ACPO established fourteen objectives or areas of work to achieve its overall aims:

- development of the basic skills of literacy – reading, writing, and numeracy;
- improvement of individual and family health through better hygiene, nutrition, and utilization of available health services;
- increase in farm production through knowledge and practice of modern techniques of agriculture, animal husbandry, and soil conservation;
- acquisition of economic knowledge and skills and their application to the management of family, agricultural and other enterprises;
- improvements to dwellings, or construction of new ones, that would meet minimum standards of health, hygiene, and comfort and contribute to better family relationships;
- utilization of free time to participate in sport and other recreational activities;
- development of a critical and analytical capacity for confronting personal and social problems and needs, and for reaching decisions related to them;
- living according to ethical and religious principles and serving as a model to others;
- involvement in activities aimed at continuing education and self-improvement;
- development of stability, understanding, and improved human relationships within the family;
- recognition of the responsibilities of parenthood and the practice of responsible procreation;

- participation in community activities, association with others in organized groups, and cooperation for the improvement of the community;
- acquisition of knowledge about, and using the services of, other organizations within the community concerned with improving individual and community life; and
- development of political consciousness focused on the protection of human rights and the assumption by all individuals of their responsibilities in society.

Educational radio programmes alone could not achieve such far-reaching changes in the peasant communities of Colombia, so ACPO developed a highly organized and integrated multi-media approach that covered the whole country. This took some years to achieve, but by its peak, it had a wide range of publications and records, supported by a pervasive network of interpersonal communication channels.

Among its publications, ACPO produced six textbooks for use with the educational radio programmes. They covered literacy, numeracy, correct speech, health, agriculture, and community life. It also produced a Peasant Library, which was made up of a hundred books on a wide range of topics that could be useful in rural communities. Most of them were on technical subjects, but there were others on learning to play the guitar, on sex and marriage, children's stories, and civic rights. Initially these books were sold to peasants for one egg, but then the number of eggs that ACPO had to sell became a problem, because for long periods, the books were 'selling' at a rate of over 7,000 copies a day, and half a million eggs piled up.

In 1958 ACPO launched a weekly newspaper called *El Campesino*, and it soon reached a circulation of 120,000 copies, with an estimated five readers per copy. It was attractively designed and it covered news and items of interest for improving peasant life.

Correspondence between peasants and ACPO was another communication channel. Peasants who had completed the basic literacy course were encouraged to write their first letter to ACPO. Responding fully and properly to each and every one of the peasants' letters was a stringent ACPO principle, no mean task considering that 45,000 to 50,000 letters a year were being received by the 1970s.

Finally, an interpersonal communication network was created by training peasants, both men and women, for specific roles linked to ACPO's work. In each community, there was a leader who was responsible for promoting ACPO's services, for adapting those services to the local needs, for coordinating the activities, and for training the Radio School Monitors. These monitors were people with more experience and knowledge than the members of a Radio School – perhaps because they had already completed a course – and they sat in to help the school members. In addition, there were Community Workers who had been trained in four-month courses to be agents of change when they returned home. In a sense, they were also teachers in that their task was to promote the actual practice of what was being learned through the radio programmes and the publications.

ACPO also organized numerous short training courses in the communities. They were dedicated to some topic of local interest or concern, such as community organization, proper use of credit, or some agricultural technique.

Many of ACPO's field staff were volunteers, while others were paid. At its peak, ACPO had a total of more than a thousand paid staff.

Support for Salcedo's 'grandiose and divine obsession'

ACPO progressed mightily in its first two decades. It had started out well with its support from General Electric Corporation, but Salcedo's ambition – described by some as his 'grandiose and divine obsession' – to expand ACPO's activities to cover the whole of Colombia called for considerable resources. Since Salcedo was always wary of any arrangements that might politicize ACPO within Colombia, his first priority was to obtain financing from overseas institutions.

Salcedo first succeeded in enlisting overseas donors through Bishop Luque of Tunja, who in 1950 was named Archbishop in Bogotá, the head of the Catholic Church in Colombia. Through Luque and Cardinal Frinze in Cologne, Salcedo made his first trip to Germany in 1950. Frinze even took him to see Chancellor Adenauer, which provided him with a seal of top-level approval in his contacts with potential donors. During that trip, Salcedo opened the door for what turned out to be many years of financial support from German Catholic charities, particularly Misereor. This was supplemented by regular support from other Catholic groups in Europe. Moreover, international funding agencies such as the Inter-American Development Bank and the World Bank, and development agencies such as USAID, also became involved in supporting it. UNESCO, following its first assistance in 1947, continued to provide technical advice on such aspects as the content and presentation of texts and books.

Financial support from the Colombian government was more complex. Salcedo's concerns about a possible politicization of ACPO were confirmed as early as 1950, when the government offered ACPO all the resources it wanted, on the condition that its constitutional statutes were changed and that the president of the country named its board of directors. This was clearly an attempt to nationalize ACPO, and Salcedo, who tended to be plain-speaking at the best of times, was not over-courteous in his rejection of the offer, 'speaking in the name of the peasants of Sutatenza'.

However, with the next president, Salcedo struck lucky. He was Gustavo Rojas Pinilla, a general who took power by a coup in 1953. Rojas Pinilla had been the commanding officer of the barracks in Tunja when Salcedo was a seminarist there and had taught his young soldiers to read and write. They had been friends ever since, and ACPO received solid support, both moral and financial, from the Rojas Pinilla government. It was awarded contracts for specific educational projects; it was able to extend its radio transmission networks in the country; and tens of thousands of radio receivers were bought for the ever-expanding number of Radio Schools.

Relations were not as good between ACPO and Rojas Pinilla's daughter, who ran a non-governmental organization. She made a strong attempt to take over ACPO and incorporate it into her NGO. To prevent this happening, and also to protect ACPO from future political influences, Salcedo and Archbishop Luque changed ACPO's constitution to give it the juridical status of an 'ecclesiastical body'. This fought off the take-over bid by Rojas Pinilla's daughter, and her father later declared that his government respected ACPO's rights and would support it in every way. It would never permit a lack of material resources to hinder its literacy and educational work. Successive presidents of Colombia, some of them also friends of Salcedo, may not have been as generous as Rojas Pinilla, but most of them supported ACPO well. However, changing ACPO's status to that of an ecclesiastical body exposed it to Church pressure, and this was to have far-reaching consequences, as we shall see.

Salcedo also had important contacts in the Vatican, which he visited quite regularly in connection with international funding from Catholic groups. He became friendly with Cardinal Montini, who was later to become Pope Paul VI, and on one occasion he met privately with Pope John XXIII, who was enthused by ACPO's work.

Finally, Salcedo made friends with wealthy Colombian industrial-
ists, and they were also a source of funding. It should be remembered
that all this was happening when Salcedo was still in his mid-thirties;
little wonder his critics considered him a jumped-up village priest.

With all of this support, and with Salcedo's vision and immense
drive, ACPO became a large and complex institution. At any one
time there were some 20,000 Radio Schools in existence, with enrolment that normally ranged from 160,000 to 220,000 people. In its
first 20 years, more than 2.25 million peasants participated in the
Radio Schools.

In addition, ACPO had built or acquired important infrastructure
and assets. It had the most powerful broadcasting network in
Colombia, with its related studios and buildings scattered over different sites. This network was putting out almost a hundred hours a
week of educational programmes, and more than a hundred hours
of general programmes, including news, music and sport. Its audience
in the early 1970s was calculated at 10 million people, almost half
of the nation's population. This was a staggering achievement, when
one remembers the 90-watt home-built transmitter in Sutatenza of
only two decades earlier, and the signalling system with white flags
to confirm that it was working.

Among its other assets, ACPO had a publishing and printing
house that was the second largest in the country; it had a plant for
making records; it had a 14-storey modern office building in Bogotá,
which also housed its main radio studios; it had residential training
centres for men and women in Sutatenza and in other places, with
a capacity of 1,200 people a year, and it had the Villa de la Esperanza
– 'Villa of Hope' – in Sutatenza, a simple but attractive residential
meeting centre with capacity for 70 people. Over the years, numerous
heads of state, heads of major international development agencies,
high-level functionaries, and prestigious journalists came to see Radio
Sutatenza's operations and stayed there.

The usefulness of ACPO to peasants

There were regular internal evaluations by ACPO itself. In addition,
however, USAID financed a two-and-a-half-year evaluation by Florida
State University, which began its work in Colombia in 1976. With
ACPO colleagues, the team identified a series of indicators that
could provide a measure of behavioural change and human resource
development in rural communities. Some of the indicators were:

avoidance of the practice of burning to prepare land for cultivation; construction or improvement of animal shelters; planting of family vegetable gardens; practice of personal hygiene; ability to read and write; and participation in study groups.

More than six hundred randomly selected rural families, in randomly selected communities, were interviewed and studied. The conclusion was that ACPO's programmes had brought substantial benefits. When peasants were asked an overall question about ACPO's usefulness, 59 per cent said that ACPO had been of much help, 34 per cent that it had been of help, and only 7 per cent said it had been of no help. When asked the specific question of how ACPO's programmes had helped them in agriculture and health, 93 per cent of interviewees identified precise ways in which they had benefited from ACPO's work.

The why and how of the collapse

It is hard to imagine why something as large and successful as ACPO should collapse. True, there were changing circumstances in the country that called for modified strategies and methods. For example, the large-scale rural migration to the cities during the 1970s brought changing needs as poverty accompanied people from farms to the urban slums. The burgeoning of commercial media introduced serious competition for audience, for it would call for self-discipline from peasants to persevere with education by Radio Sutatenza, when there was music and entertainment available at the same time from other stations. Television was also expanding rapidly from its introduction in the mid-1950s. And finally, Radio Sutatenza's national coverage made it difficult to provide advice and information that was tailored to specific regional or local conditions. This was not serious in Radio Sutatenza's first decade or more, because peasants' levels of knowledge were so low that generalized information was valuable to them. But as their technology improved, especially in agriculture, they began to need information that was more locally specific and tailored to their production systems.

ACPO analysed all these problems and had proposals for overcoming them, so it was certainly not its strategy and methods that became outdated and caused the collapse. The real problem, in fact, was caused by ACPO's basic philosophy of motivating individuals and giving them the capacity to take responsibility for their own lives and destinies. This was a very serious threat to the conservative establishment in a country like Colombia, with its extremes of wealth and poverty, and of privilege and dispossession. And the more ACPO succeeded, the more the establishment perceived that its interests were being successfully undermined.

The Church oligarchy was an important part of the establishment. Salcedo always had its full support while Crisanto Luque was alive, but he died in 1959, by then a cardinal. After that, the Church was constantly sniping at ACPO. Salcedo was seen as an unguided missile who refused to conform to the Church's orthodox positions, and he was openly critical of them too. He once wrote: 'We consider that our [ACPO's] work is a sort of reparation for centuries of failings by the Church towards Colombia's rural population. The educational work of the Church concentrated on eternal life, and it completely ignored earthly realities. We think that a change of emphasis is necessary.'

Thus, Salcedo was in open conflict with the traditional Church and ACPO was an ecclesiastical body. This set the scene for trouble, which duly came in the late 1950s when ACPO precipitated it by doing the unforgivable: it introduced its chapter on 'Responsible Procreation' in its health education programmes. This effectively gave the Church real ammunition to use against ACPO.

Salcedo was later asked by an interviewer from the German Institute of Development in Berlin what ACPO's position was on birth control, and Salcedo replied:

We want women to open their eyes and learn to use natural methods to control their fertility. The main problem is to convince the masses that it is not a sin to discuss these matters. It is very difficult to educate people for human dignity and for responsible maternity in a country dominated by religious rules. ACPO does not enter into discussions about, or repudiate, chemical and physical methods of birth control. That is not our task. We want to create the basis on which every individual can take his or her own decision, with full responsibility.

Another of Salcedo's conflicts with the Church authorities concerned the visit of Pope Paul VI to Colombia in August 1968. The basis for that visit was laid in 1965 when the Pope went to make a speech at the UN General Assembly in New York. He invited Salcedo, as a friend and a communication specialist, to accompany him and report on how things went. One of Salcedo's comments to the Pope was that, thanks to the worldwide media coverage of his speech, an estimated 60–70 million people had followed it, and that it would take 30–40,000 priests 20 years to reach so many people with the same message.

Before they parted in New York, Salcedo told the Pope that he had now been to the rich America in the north and that he should think about coming to see the poor America in the south. Sure enough, the Pope later informed Salcedo that he was planning a trip to Colombia. It would be the first by any Pope to Latin America. Salcedo immediately began to plan for a grand open-air papal encounter with peasants, but the Church oligarchy in Colombia wanted to confine the Pope's activities to functions related to the sacraments and were against any rally with peasants. However, the Pope himself insisted on meeting with peasants, and on a fine August morning, he arrived by helicopter in a field in the high altitude plain that surrounds Bogotá. More than half a million peasants were waiting for him.

The Pope, who sat between peasants on a simple wooden platform, did not say mass. Instead he delivered a speech that stressed the need to improve the condition of the poor in developing countries. Then, he climbed into a jeep and drove slowly through the multitudes, the first time any Pope had done so. The people were respectful and orderly as they reached out to receive his blessings and greetings, and to touch his vestments. It was a dignified and moving occasion. The significance of this event must surely have shaken the Colombian establishment; ACPO, and its insubordinate village priest, had mobilized half a million peasants through its radio networks. This had been an occasion of peace and love, but what might happen in the future? ACPO and Salcedo were a potential menace to established order. Both the Church and high-level politicians took note.

In the late 1960s and early 1970s, the Catholic Church in Colombia was led by a cardinal who proclaimed that the only purpose of sexual intercourse between humans was to procreate the species. This placed ACPO's position in even greater discord with the Church power structure. It was hardly surprising, therefore, that the Catholic charity groups in Europe, which had staunchly supported ACPO for years, began to pull out.

On the other hand, international support from such organizations as the Inter-American Development Bank and the World Bank, channelled through the government of Colombia, continued, and up to 1975, ACPO was able to operate at full capacity. But the axe was not long in falling there as well. The minister of education under President López Michelsen, a man called Durán Dussán, cut all his ministry's contractual and financial arrangements with ACPO, and no amount of intervention by ACPO's friends was able to restore any of them.

In his biography of Salcedo, Luis Zalamea recounts that he tried to discover why this decision was taken and found indications that President López Michelsen was one of the politicians who had carefully noted ACPO's power in mobilizing so many peasants for the Pope's visit. He was the only president of that period who never visited Sutatenza or made positive public statements about ACPO. He also found that Durán Dussán had been receiving constant goading from the Church to do something about ACPO, and also from staff in his own Ministry of Education who were jealous of ACPO because it was doing work and using funds that they thought should be theirs. Durán Dussán had presidential ambitions and thought he could gain powerful friends by killing ACPO.

The personality of Salcedo did not help in conflictual situations. Like many truly great leaders who are fired by a sense of mission, he could be autocratic and demanding. Anything, within the bounds of honesty, that furthered the cause was justifiable, and he could be distinctly Machiavellian. Furthermore, he often appeared aloof and uncompromising, thereby adding to the tensions. As those who knew him say, he was a complex person who combined cool logic with impetuosity, and diplomacy with the itch to create crises. 'His friends venerated him and his enemies feared him, but everybody respected him.'

With a man like Salcedo, it was easy for his enemies to criticize him and start rumours about him. He was accused of using ACPO money for his life in high circles, though in fact that life was his tactic for obtaining moral and material support for ACPO. And no accusation of misuse of funds was ever proved; on the contrary, exhaustive audits by outsiders, invited in by ACPO, always found total transparency and rectitude in the way the resources were administered.

ACPO and Radio Sutatenza struggled on for several years after the loss of support from the Church and from international agencies. It used its own rather meagre income and borrowed funds, but in 1982 it had to start cutting staff. In 1983, negotiations were in course for the sale of its very valuable radio network to various government agencies. These fell through, but in 1985, Radio Sutatenza was sold to Radio Caracol, today one of the two most powerful commercial networks in the country. Finally, in 1987, ACPO folded, and most of its remaining assets were sold to pay off its debts.

By the end of its life, ACPO had broadcast more than 1.5 million hours of radio programmes from its various stations; it had printed 76 million copies of its newspaper; it had distributed about 6.5 million text books and 4.5 million copies of other books; and it had trained almost 25,000 peasant leaders and community development workers.

A peasant woman who had been trained as a leader in ACPO's field network, and who is still in Sutatenza engaged in what little remains of ACPO, wept openly as she recalled for us, a decade or so later, the sale of Radio Sutatenza and the demise of the institution that had lifted her out of her peasant poverty, given her dignity, and a life's mission.

One can only marvel at the advanced thinking of Salcedo. He was decades ahead of others in his educational philosophy, in his understanding of the potential of the media, and of the need to use multiple channels to achieve best results. To a great extent he realized his dream, even if small and mean-minded people finally destroyed it. In his last years, he lived in Miami and promoted the ACPO model in many other countries, but he realized that it needed modification, so it used mainly existing media channels to broadcast the educational materials it produced.

In effect, ACPO was an idea that had come before its time. The ideological tensions created between Marxist and capitalist models produced a climate that was unfavourable for something as essentially democratic and liberating as the ACPO philosophy. As Hernando Bernal, a sociologist who was for many years ACPO's director of planning and programming, and very close to Salcedo, said to us:

> That ACPO slogan 'Development is in the mind of mankind' was danger-ous. Some people on the left took it as being ingenuous and lacking revolutionary fervour. In fact, there was a leftist guerrilla movement called M-19 that accused Salcedo of betraying the peasantry by not fomenting revolution. They assassinated a labour-union leader for the same 'betrayal' and warned Salcedo that he was next on the hit-list. He didn't take it too seriously, but after somebody opened fire on his Volkswagen Beetle one day, and after there had been an armed raid on his house in Bogotá while he was not there, he moved to Miami.
>
> For other people, the ACPO slogan had the flavour of an obvious and irrefutable truth, but one that made them uncomfortable, because it was threatening to the status quo. None of these people could ever find any just cause for making an open and frontal attack on ACPO's philo-sophy. So instead, they used guerrilla tactics and ideological skirmishes,

and even theological ones, to bring down the institution, because it was too successfully putting its philosophy into practice. On the other hand, none of the people who were interested in seeing ACPO disappear have been able to defeat the ideas on which ACPO was based.

Hernando Bernal also told us that, in 1986, he was in a tiny village called Santa Inés, some 50 kilometres from Bogotá, and he went into the main shop, a small supermarket that was also the local distributor for ACPO's newspaper, *El Campesino*. The owner recognized Bernal from a recent photograph in the newspaper, and they started talking about ACPO. With obvious pride, the shop owner told Bernal that he had been among the first peasants who had attended ACPO's training institute when it was opened in Sutatenza in 1956. 'You know,' he said, 'I owe most of my human progress and my solid family life to ACPO.' He looked around his neat little supermarket, smiled, and added, 'And my economic and social progress too.' He continued:

What I learned in ACPO's training centres and from the Radio Schools over the years changed my life and helped me to change the life in this village. Today we have our schools, our own small church, electricity, telephone, a health post, a social centre and many other things we didn't have 30 years ago. ACPO taught me the importance of these things, and how to mobilize our community to create them. It also gave me the confidence to deal with the authorities to get things done that we could not do for ourselves.

Perhaps, with today's spread of democracy, multi-media and mass programmes of education for life and for the betterment of society could be tried again. They would have to use local media, and of course television, and they would do well to draw on a mixture of entertainment and education – as we saw Baseley did so successfully for *The Archers* – to compete for attention with the pure commercial media. They would also have to concentrate on the urban as well as the rural poor. But would such activities again be sabotaged by the privileged and the conservative? Are these people still too small-minded to realize that their real interests, and those of their children in the next century, would be best served by a more just and stable society around them?

CHAPTER 6

Of 'Condoms and Cabbages': Communication for Population and Family Planning

A Saturday morning in mid-1996, and we are driving along a valley high in the Colombian Andes. The road follows a small river, which tumbles over rocks in its headlong rush towards the distant Amazon Basin. It is a fine day, and the first white cumulus clouds are beginning to stud the blue vault of the sky. Here below, the white water of the river courses between emerald-green trees and fields. The scene, dominated by distant mountain crests, is one of stunning natural beauty.

We pass a peasant ploughing the black earth with a pair of oxen and a wooden plough, and then we reach a cluster of poor houses along the roadside. Close to one we see a crudely lettered sign: it announces *arepas con queso*. These are pouches of white maize meal filled with cheese and toasted over an open fire, a delicious hot breakfast or snack. We pull off the road and stop next to a ramshackle shelter with a tin roof. Smoke is wafting out from under the roof, for there is an open fire covered with an iron grill for toasting the *arepas*.

A peasant woman, aged about 30, is tending the *arepas* on her improvised grill. Her features and slightly slanted eyes show that she has mixed Indian and European heritage, as do many people in Colombia. Her dark hair is pulled back and tied behind her neck. Below the short sleeves of her blouse, her arms are brown and strong; she is no stranger to work in the fields. A small girl is standing at a nearby table passing cooked maize through a hand-grinder for the *arepas*.

The woman greets us with the particular courtesy common to Andean peasants, and we order our *arepas*. As she moves from foot to foot, tending them on the grill, we notice that her shoes are scuffed and broken. There can be no surplus of cash in her family. While we wait, a child comes toddling out of the hut behind the woman's *arepa* stall and approaches us. The small boy stops a few feet away, and gazes up at us, his hand to his mouth in an expression of wonder and curiosity. We greet him and ask him his name, but he is too shy to respond, and the mother provides the answer: he is called Juan. We ask him how old he is, and again his mother provides the answer: he is 3 years old. We comment that he is a fine, healthy-looking child. Our *arepa*-maker is evidently pleased by the comment, and a conversation is soon under way.

The girl grinding maize is her 8-year-old daughter, Maria Rosa, and she calls her over to say hello to us. She is an alert, bright child. She tells us that she attends a school that is a 30-minute walk up the road. Her mother breaks in: 'Maria Rosa likes school very much and she is one of the best pupils in her year. I want her to go on to secondary school, not like me. My father took me out of school after only three years.'

She reflects for a moment, and then goes on, 'But then, I was one of nine children, and my parents had to struggle to bring us all up. Our piece of land was small, and we were very poor – as I still am today.' She smiles cheerfully.

'So you only have two children,' we ask. 'Don't you want to have more?'

The women straightens from her *arepas* and looks straight into our faces, frankly and openly. She is easy in her response.

'No, two children are enough for us. We don't want any more.'

One of us (S.R.-E.) has considerable experience in communication for safe motherhood and reproductive health, and we are therefore curious.

'That's good, but what are you doing not to have more?' S.R.-E. asks.

'We've always planned,' the woman replies, and she pulls up the short sleeve of her blouse. 'Look,' she says, and there on her upper arm is a little patch of ribbing in the skin. 'That's a Norplant. I had it put in after Juan was born.' She says this with a tone of pride.

'How did you first hear about family planning?' we ask.

'I heard about it on the radio, not long before I got married. After Maria Rosa was born, I went to the health centre near here. I talked to the nurse, and then I told my husband what she'd said. We discussed it and I started with the pill, but now I prefer the Norplant.'

'And what does your husband say about family planning?' we ask.

'At the beginning, it took me time to convince him, but now he's pleased we only have two children. How could we manage with more?'

As we drive away, we reflect on this peasant woman in her roadside stall. In just one generation, in a simple rural family, the number of children has dropped from nine to only two. One might think that hers was an isolated case, but in fact, in a number of countries, especially in Latin America, Asia, and North Africa, the drop in the fertility rate – the average number of children women give birth to – has been dramatic in the last 25 years. Today, according to figures from the UN Population Fund, the fertility rate is 2.8 in Mexico, 2.75 in Tunisia, 2.65 in Brazil, 2.63 in Indonesia, 2.49 in Colombia, and 2.29 in Sri Lanka. A fertility rate of 2.1 is usually considered the population replacement rate, so these countries are well on their way to achieving it. Thailand and Jamaica already have. Yet, and this is the astonishing part, in the early 1970s, the fertility rates in those same countries ranged from 5.5 to 7 children per woman. Communication played a central role in achieving this rapid change in reproductive behaviour.

Unfortunately, not all countries have been so successful in bringing about these remarkable fertility rate reductions. Africa as a whole has an average fertility rate of 5.35 – compared to 2.89 in Asia and 2.83 in Latin America – but it peaks at over 7 in Niger with numerous other African countries in the 5.5 to 6.5 range. Many of these countries have population growth rates around 3 per cent per year, and at that rate, the population of a country normally doubles in under 25 years. And despite the successes in family planning that have taken place in some parts of the world, they have come too late to prevent today's situation in which 40–50 per cent of the population in many developing countries is under 16 years of age. They will soon enter the reproductive phase of their lives, creating the projected population growth mentioned in the first chapter.

Population growth depends on numerous factors linked to development in general, such as reducing infant mortality, levels of education (particularly of women), the availability of health services, and general economic progress. The poorer the country, the further behind it is in these aspects, and in general, the greater its population growth rate. And this is happening precisely in the countries least able to sustain larger populations.

At the other end of the scale, the countries that have achieved outstanding success in family planning are those where there have also been significant advances in these other aspects of development. In addition, however, they have all used communication intensely and systematically to promote family planning. Indeed, among all sectors of development, population is probably the one that has made the most use of communication, usually termed Information, Education, and Communication (IEC) in that sector. For example, the UN Population Fund (UNFPA),[1] which has provided assistance worth more than US$2.5 billion to developing countries since its founding in 1969, has allocated about 14 per cent of this amount – some US$340 million – to IEC. And other development agencies, in particular USAID, have also been highly active in supporting IEC for population. They promoted a series of communication activities in a variety of countries under a population communication umbrella project known as 'Popcom'.

IEC for population usually has three broad audiences: the political leadership, the service providers, and the general population, with special emphasis on couples of reproductive age and on youth. In addition there may be intermediate, or relay, audiences that can be induced to help spread the word, such as the religious authorities, teachers, agricultural extension workers, trade unions, and so on. Some of these audiences may be resistant, and that resistance will need to be overcome.

Gaining the Political Will

Gaining political will at the highest policy levels has always been a first step in population matters. In the 1960s and 1970s – and even later in some cases – governments were often unaware of the true implications of rapid population growth on their economies and societies. In fact, many governments were in favour of increasing their populations. This was because larger populations were often thought to be necessary for economic growth and power.

In Brazil for example, it was held that more people would help the country to exploit its enormous natural resources, while in Indonesia, President Sukarno was strongly opposed to family planning because the country had so many uninhabited islands that could be populated. In Thailand too, policy also favoured a larger population because the

---

1. It is still known as UNFPA because when it was founded in 1969 it was called the UN Fund for Population Activities.

government believed that the country should become another Japan, with some 80 million people. More people also meant that more taxes could be collected. And another element in official resistance to family planning was the perception at government level that easy availability of contraception would lower standards of public morality.

Thailand's policy in favour of a larger population stayed in place despite a census in 1960 which revealed a phenomenal population growth rate of 3.3 per cent a year, and despite a growing debate among economists, technocrats and politicians about the need for a population policy. In the end, the key element that changed the policy was a study among Thai women in 1964, which showed that vast numbers of them were eager to use modern methods of birth control. In the main, they were having their 6–7 children only because they knew little about modern family planning methods and had no access to services. It is highly significant that 80 per cent of the women at the time, even in rural areas, were literate, one of the most important of all the factors that determine women's interest in adopting family planning. As a result of that study, and a national population seminar that followed it, the government began setting up family planning services in 1965.

In Mexico, policies to increase the population had been in place since the Spanish conquest. They had gathered momentum since independence, because it was generally thought that a large population would provide cheap labour for industrial and economic development.

Military minds were often behind policies in favour of larger populations, for more people also meant more potential soldiers and more occupying presence in the national territory. For example, Brazil, while itself under a military regime in the 1960s, believed that the generals in charge in Argentina might be plotting to expand northwards. This feeling of insecurity even led the Brazilian government to pass a law giving a cash incentive to the parents of every child born.

The notion of a population time-bomb that must be deactivated, an invention of Western demographers, was generally dismissed by governments of developing countries with large land areas and low population density. The term 'birth control' assumed a negative connotation when used by people from rich countries with reference to the poorer. The term invoked the image of an elitist position, and in many developing countries, there was little understanding of what rapid population growth really implied.

Heads of state and other policy-makers needed to be made aware of the real issues of population growth through information, discussion, and debate. Thus a main influence in changing government perceptions in many countries was the first World Population Conference organized by the UN and held in Bucharest in 1974. This conference highlighted the significance of population issues in overall development, and many delegates went home with completely different perspectives. Policies began to change in a number of countries after that first UN conference on population, reinforced by many subsequent conferences on various development issues that have also dealt with population matters. However, it has not been enough for a head of state and his cabinet to issue a policy directive. The government administration at all levels has had to be motivated and mobilized, and opposition to family planning that has been present in certain sectors of society has had to be overcome.

Indonesia provides an interesting example of how this process can be achieved through well-thought-out communication. President Suharto himself attended the 1974 Population Conference in Bucharest, and this alone was evidence of the importance he gave to the issue. But building consensus and cooperation among decision-makers and government administrators had to follow. Every person who could contribute to a family planning programme, every institution, had to be convinced of its importance and of the need for their active involvement. The person who took the lead in this task of persuasion and conviction was Dr Haryono Suyono, a born communicator but also the holder of a Ph.D. in communication from the University of Chicago. He is now the state minister for population, and also the chairman of the National Family Planning Board, which is known under its Indonesian abbreviation of BKKBN.

As a result of Indonesia's remarkable reduction in fertility rate, BKKBN has gained wide international fame and prestige for its achievements, as well as for the training programmes in population and family planning issues which it provides for people from other countries. Dr Haryono is equally famous and respected, and perhaps, after the president, the best known national figure in Indonesia.

We went to interview Dr Haryono in Jakarta. The building where he has his office is modern but in traditional style, white with red-tile roofs and surrounded by immaculate gardens. The total informality of the place astonishes us. After all, we are going to see a minister, but we are not asked to produce personal identification papers for passes to be issued. We are simply told by a smiling receptionist to go to the third floor. On that floor we are sent in the right direction by someone we meet by chance as we get out of the lift, and we arrive at the end of the building where Dr Haryono has his office. There is nobody in sight, so we poke our heads around an open office door to enquire for Dr Haryono. A friendly man shows us to a sofa in the corridor and asks us to wait a moment.

After less than five minutes, a door at the end of the corridor opens and a man in a dark suit, with black hair, just greying at the temples, horn-rimmed glasses, and a moustache comes out briskly. 'Come in, come in,' he says jovially, with a broad smile. The first thought is that he must be an assistant to the minister, for such people usually surround themselves with pomp and protocol. But no, it is Haryono himself, totally informal apart from his dark suit, and totally unassuming.

We go into a light and spacious office, but it is not particularly luxurious. When Haryono hears during the introductions that one of us is from Colombia, he immediately says, 'Como está Usted?' He tells us that he wanted to learn Spanish while at the University of Chicago, but that phrase is the only one he knows, and he laughs heartily at his own Spanish limitations.

During our interview, scheduled to last for half an hour but which runs double that, Haryono laughs easily and frequently. He is an extrovert, who obviously enjoys people, and he is highly articulate and funny at the same time. He pokes frequent fun at himself while talking about his experience and work, and about the grey hair at his temples. He exudes charisma. 'The foundation stone for building family planning programmes in Indonesia was creating political will, institutional linkages, and operational networks, and this required intensive communication,' he tells us.

He explains that during his first ten years with BKKBN, he dedicated most of his time to this task; he needed to persuade everyone and every institution that could play a role in family planning of its importance and obtain their commitment and involvement. As a professional communicator, he knew he must keep a low profile in those early years, for otherwise, the people he was trying to convince could easily have thought that his main aim was self-aggrandizement, and this would have defeated his purpose. His highly developed sense of self-deprecatory humour must also have been a major weapon. It disarmed potential resistance to his pleadings and proposals as he buttonholed people to appeal for their support and involvement. He exploited all possible occasions, whether they were formal meetings, informal work gatherings, or even chance encounters and parties. The framework for his basic message was: 'Population is vitally important! Too many children weaken people and their position. What they must have for development is education. Education, especially for girls, is a prerequisite for human development.' Haryono's communication skills were fundamental to Indonesia's family planning success, and we shall come back to them later.

Also in the domain of creating political will, there was an interesting initiative by the World Bank in Mali. Mali's population and development situation is critical. Its population in 1996 was 11.1 million, which might not appear much for such a vast country, but the fertility rate was 6.6, the population growth rate was 3 per cent per annum, and the projected population by the year 2025 is 24.6 million, an increase of more than 120 per cent. The country may be huge, but much of it is desert, and it is among the poorest countries in the world.

Katherine Marshall, an American and the director of the World Bank's Sahelian Department, told us how, in 1993, she had arranged for the cabinet ministers of Mali to spend three days together in a retreat, which she named 'Days of Reflection'. The purpose was that, during those days, they would discuss the situation in their country and consider development options and plans in an integrated and coordinated way. She said that few of the ministers had thought seriously about the population issue: they had assumed that, since the country was enormous, population growth was mainly irrelevant.

However, during the 'Days of Reflection', the ministers began to consider it more carefully, taking into account the many related aspects. Mali's situation gave plenty of scope for serious reflection: just providing education for a burgeoning population was an enormous task; already, only about 75 per cent of Malian children were completing primary school, and only about one boy in ten, and one girl in twenty, were completing secondary school. And what about providing employment in the future – even in the quite near future, because more than 45 per cent of Mali's people were under 16 years old? Unemployment was already a problem, and creating work for *today's* children would be difficult enough in Mali's circumstances. Thinking 25 or 30 years into future, when the offspring of today's adolescents were entering the job market, the problem would be magnified beyond imagination.

Population growth would also put added strain on food production capacity. Desertification was already a problem and to push crop production further into marginal areas could have serious environmental effects. Sand from the Sahara was already invading historic places like Timbuktu and the arable land around them. Even today, the daily calorie intake of the people was 4–5 per cent below the minimum established for full health, so how would so many more people be fed? And talking about health, what about providing health services for all those people in future, when even today only about a third of Malians had access to health services? Faced with such realities during their 'Days of Reflection', government ministers had the opportunity of becoming acutely aware of the population issue, even in a 'vast country with plenty of space'.

Another interesting example of winning commitment among policy-makers and government officials for population activities involved communicating about the links between population and natural resources. A USAID-supported project in Guatemala, Costa Rica, and Ecuador used sophisticated communication technology, based primarily on computer graphics and modelling. Satellite imagery of the earth's surface from Landsat, showing the status of the natural resources in the countries, was combined with data from population surveys. This was processed into computer-generated graphics, videos, interactive computer presentations, mathematical models simulating the relationship between population and environment, and informational brochures. These materials were used in seminars involving policy-makers and other influential sectors. They were presented to high-profile audiences by carefully chosen people who had strong communication skills and status equal to that of the audience – for example, ex-ambassadors, university deans, and other people of similar calibre.

The seminars and the materials had a strong impact. In Guatemala not long afterwards, a newly elected government issued a policy statement, part of which analysed the relationship between population growth, economic development, and the environment. It drew heavily on the points made by the communication materials.

In Ecuador, the materials concentrated on the environmental consequences of rapid population growth in urban areas. The mayor of Quito became so concerned after the presentation that he declared an emergency plan to decrease levels of garbage production, improve sanitation and waste treatment services, and undertake better city planning to reduce the impact of population density on the local environment.

These are just some examples of the way communication efforts, using interpersonal and group channels and often supported by communication materials, have helped to bring about the policy changes and created the institutional linkages that have led to good family planning programmes.

Overcoming or Circumventing Resistance

In some countries, specific sectors of society were against family planning using modern contraception methods, and these resistance points had to be overcome or circumvented. The Roman Catholic Church was, of course, such a sector in most Latin American countries, but in Muslim countries too, the religious authorities were often initially hostile. What happened in Indonesia provides an example of how the religious authorities were won over.

In Indonesia, President Suharto in person began the process with the Islamic authorities. He realized that family planning was a cultural and social issue as much as a medical one, and when he returned from the Bucharest Population Conference, he immediately met with one of the country's top religious leaders to explain the population problem and ask for his help.

This started the ball rolling, but as Haryono told the Indian journalist Rajul Singh, when he was researching his book *Family Planning Success Stories*, BKKBN made some mistakes when first trying to overcome possible religious objections from people. On the basis of outsiders' advice, BKKBN staff were told to memorize certain passages from the Koran for use when talking about family planning. In practice, this was ill-conceived because their superficial religious knowledge was unconvincing, and it put them in competition with the *ulemas*, the local religious leaders. Haryono realized that BKKBN was beginning to make enemies; he could see it in the eyes he faced during his meetings in the communities, and with the religious authorities, and it was confirmed by the qualitative research his staff were doing.

BKKBN has always used an admirable degree of flexibility in its work, and when something is going wrong, they quickly change tack. In this case, the new tack was to involve the *ulemas* by asking the leaders for advice on how best to promote family planning and how to get people involved. Any *ulemas* who were still hostile to family planning were told that the people's representatives, the parliament, and the highest Islamic leaders had already approved it as an essential part of national development.

The *ulemas* responded by providing their advice on how best to proceed, and BKKBN supported them in organizing seminars or whatever else they needed to prepare the religious sector for promoting family planning. In addition, Haryono deliberately gave the religious leaders prominence and importance by inviting them to appear on television and radio so that their participation in the programme became known nationwide. They were made to feel that they were working for the country and for its people, rather than for BKKBN.

In this way, BKKBN was able to win the Islamic authorities over completely, but there remained a few stumbling blocks regarding the methods of contraception. From the beginning, the religious leaders had made known their opposition to abortion, sterilization, and the intra-uterine device (IUD). This opposition was recognized and accepted by the BKKBN, but Haryono also began a tactful and patient dialogue about the IUD. It turned out that the religious authorities objected to it because they thought that it functioned by provoking an abortion, and because they did not approve of male doctors inserting it. BKKBN was able to convince them that IUDs do not provoke abortions, and agreed that only women doctors or paramedics would insert them. If, in an emergency, a male had to insert one, a woman would always be present. The religious authorities, pleased that their concerns had been taken into account, and by the way that the negotiations had been handled, actually became promoters of the IUD by issuing a *fatwa*, or religious edict, approving its use. Insertions of IUDs soared as a result.

Haryono's strategy of not confronting the religious leaders, but rather of entering into a give-and-take dialogue, was masterly. And once consensus had been reached, the religious authorities set family planning in the context of Islamic teaching and of the Koran to justify and explain its benefits, especially in terms of the health and well-being of mother and child and of the family in general. They thus became preachers of family planning, its allies and supporters.

People sometimes express surprise that Roman Catholic countries such as Mexico and Colombia have achieved such enormous reductions in fertility rate in the last 25 years. In truth, the position of the Catholic Church in Mexico was never strong enough to have much influence in family planning matters. Mexico had introduced reforms towards the end of the last century to curb the then enormous power of the Church and to separate it from the state, and during the Mexican revolution, the Church's influence was further reduced.

In Colombia, the Church has considerable power, at least in theory, and initially it did all it could to stop family planning programmes. It mounted its last attack in 1984, when a young woman, who was mentally retarded and already had two children, was sterilized when she attended a mobile family planning unit that was visiting the poor rural area where she lived. Her parents claimed that she had been forcibly sterilized.

The Church leapt on this opportunity to allege that Profamilia, the outstanding NGO that was leading family planning in the country, was receiving secret funding from other countries to carry out forced sterilization programmes on Colombian women. These accusations by the Church provoked a national uproar, whereas until then, and despite Church opposition, family planning had been expanding steadily and quietly. The government immediately withdrew its support from a joint programme it had with Profamilia, and amid recriminations from all sides, the outlook for family planning looked bleak for several months. Finally, support from the press, the mass media, and the medical profession won the day, and eventually the Church gave up.

Today, it seems that at the community level, few priests take the Vatican's position against family planning very seriously. This is probably because they are in daily contact with their community and see at first hand the health problems and hardships that result among the poor when families are not planned. As a highly placed Jesuit said to us:

> The Church establishes its positions based on an ideal, a Utopian vision of how the world should be, and propounds that moral position. In the case of family planning, one of its concerns is doubtless that it can open the door to libertinism. But at the pastoral level, a priest faced by the social and economic problems of a family in his congregation will go along with, or even recommend, what he considers is best for the happiness and well-being of that family.

Even among practising and fervent Catholics, it seems that the awareness of the problems generally caused by large and unplanned families far outweighs any moral scruples they might have about disobeying a religious edict. As a woman in Ecuador said to us, 'I am only going to have two children, because that is all I can support properly, and I will do whatever is necessary to see that happens. The saying that you can feed three as easily as two may have some truth, but you can't dress or educate three as easily as two.'

The Indian journalist Rahul Singh asked a practising Catholic woman in Colombia for her religious views on using modern family planning methods, and she replied: 'It is more of a sin to have a baby you cannot look after.'

It appears that the influence of the Roman Catholic Church worldwide on modern contraception is less than might be expected, if one takes into account its strong position against it at central level and in world conferences. For example, it is fascinating to see that, in UNFPA's publication *The State of World Population* for 1996, the lowest fertility rates in the world, with the exception of Hong Kong, are in those cradles of Catholicism, Spain and Italy – 1.23 and 1.27 respectively – while Portugal is not far behind at 1.55.

In retrospect, it is clear that resistance to population programmes from religious and other groups was overcome once stress was placed on the benefits of family planning in terms of the *health* of mothers and children, and on family well-being in general. In effect, and in the terms that would be used by social marketing specialists, contraception was 'repositioned', just as is done for marketing commercial products. That is to say, its advantages were presented differently, to appeal better to its potential 'buyers' and supporters, but there was no change in the 'product' of contraception itself.

A Focus on Information, Education, and Communication

Communication programmes for family planning were begun in the late 1960s to help people change their often strongly held traditional beliefs and practices about birth and contraception. Initially, most of these communication activities were targeted towards married women and couples of child-bearing age, but it was soon realized that the audiences had to expand to cover men, adolescents, medical and paramedical staff, as well of course as policy-makers, religious and other leaders, as we have just seen. Specific messages and media strategies had to be developed for each specific audience. This led to increasing emphasis on research with the different audiences, and to careful pre-testing of messages and materials before widespread distribution.

Research in many countries showed that men were often a barrier to family planning. A first reason for this was that they believed that if their wives were protected from pregnancy, they would be more likely to have extramarital relationships. A study in Zimbabwe showed that men's suspicions in this respect were increased by the fact that their wives had to continue taking the pill, even when they were separated from their husbands for some time. Many men also believed that if their wives took the pill they would be made permanently infertile, or that they would have deformed babies after they stopped taking it. Yet another factor in creating men's resistance in some countries was the traditional image of virility and manhood attached to fathering many children.

Both in Bolivia and in Ecuador, we have been told by women that they adopted family planning without telling their husbands. There, and in many other countries too, women wanted men to be reached with more information and motivation about family planning. This resulted in campaigns specifically to reach men. For example, in Zimbabwe, which is by far the brightest star in the gloomy firmament of family planning in black Africa – if one excludes South Africa – special efforts have been made to influence men, beginning with a 'Male Motivation Campaign' in 1987. This reached into men's places of work, beer halls, and sports grounds.

Similar IEC activities to involve men have been conducted in numerous countries in recent years. For example, in the Minya governorate of Egypt, a conservative rural area with low contraception prevalence, a mobilization campaign was organized in 1992–93, with men as its prime audience. There were hundreds of public meetings that attracted mainly men. Religious leaders, teachers, and workers were brought together for discussions, and for traditional media presentations of poetry and skits, and several thousand men attended a play on the benefits of family planning presented by an all-male troupe. As a result, four out of five men who attended a meeting reported later that they had discussed family planning with their spouses, and 16 per cent of women arriving at family planning clinics said that their husband's encouragement was the prime reason for their visit.

Social marketing of contraceptives was a strategy used in many countries, often with support from USAID. One such project began in Pakistan in 1985 with the specific aim of promoting condoms and the pill among married couples. The target audiences totalled about 11 million people in the middle to low socio-economic sector of the population, mostly poorly educated and rural. A survey before the project began had shown that only 60 per cent of urban men and 26 per cent of rural men knew about condoms. Research also showed that messages should stress male responsibility.

The project introduced a brand of condoms called Sathi, an Urdu word for companion, and priced them above the government-subsidized brands but below other commercial brands. The Sathi packaging was attractive in order to avoid perceptions that the product's low price might be linked to inferior quality. A marketing organization was set up to distribute through commercial outlets.

Initially, the government was against the advertising of condoms in the mass media, but when it finally gave its approval, full-scale, multi-media promotional campaigns were launched. One objective was to make the name Sathi the generic name for condom, since the word 'condom' was relatively unknown. About 300 cinema halls screened a Sathi advertisement; radio and TV spots were broadcast nationwide; metal signs were posted outside about 20,000 shops, and there were displays in about 35,000 sales outlets. As a result, the sale of Sathi condoms rose from 30 million in 1987 to almost 74 million in 1990, and by the end of 1994, a total of more than 350 million condoms had been sold.

Social marketing of contraceptives has continued in many countries, and the spread of AIDS has given added importance to promoting the use of condoms, often with notable success. One USAID-supported programme in Peru, starting from zero in June 1994, sold 3 million condoms in the following 18 months. In Bangladesh too, where the fertility rate has dropped from 7 to 3.9 in about 25 years, social marketing of contraceptives has played a major part.[2] In general, however, the communication strategies for population have been gradually shifting, with the emphasis increasingly being focused on the benefits that child spacing and limiting their number can bring in terms of mother and child health, and of family well-being. This leads to awareness that stimulates people to adopt family planning, as opposed to placing the stress on selling contraceptives. And more recently still, other approaches have been introduced, especially in rural areas, which relate population to the environment

2. Bangladesh appears to be something of an exception to the rule that fertility rates begin to drop when a country achieves a certain level of socio-economic development. For example, the country has not made very significant advances in literacy levels in the last 25 years, and only 45 per cent of the population is estimated as having access to health services. Similar processes may now be starting in Africa. According to Professor Bill Gould of Liverpool University in a BBC interview in January 1997, fertility rates there are beginning to drop, despite little advance in socio-economic development.

and to the availability of natural resources at the community and family level.

Mixing entertainment with education about population has been extensively used in many countries. This technique is sometimes called 'enter-educate'. The experience with *The Archers*, described in the previous chapter, was the first major application of this technique via mass media, in that case radio, but TV dramas have also proved enormously valuable. Mexico was the forerunner in the use of TV dramas for social aims. A gifted television producer there, Miguel Sabido, had the idea in the mid-1970s. One of Sabido's most successful early series included well-embedded messages about adult literacy, with the result that enrolment in literacy courses soared.

In 1977–78, he turned his attention to population with a series called *Accompañame* (Accompany Me). The series was broadcast over a year, and during that time, there were half a million new adopters of family planning. Sabido later produced series on other themes related to population, such as responsible parenthood, teenage sex education, and gender equity.

The educational strategy in Sabido's series was based on the social learning theory that positive role models should be rewarded in a story, while negative role models should be punished. A third type of character should change from a negative to positive role model as he or she is influenced by others, or learns through personal experience, as the story unfolds. This process of conflict and change of heart naturally allows for good human drama, and individuals in the audience who identify with the characters in the series will be motivated to change their own behaviour.

Sabido added an element to this general strategy: at the end of each instalment, there was a 30-second epilogue, delivered by a highly credible authority, to sum up the main educational message and interpret its meaning in the everyday life of the audience. This epilogue frequently included factual information – for example, the addresses of family planning clinics.

Sabido's experience was picked up by several North American groups working in population communication, particularly by the Population Communication Services of Johns Hopkins University. They have since helped spread the TV drama strategy to more than 40 different family planning communication projects in some 30 countries. When the technique has worked well, the family planning motivation has been inserted in a subtle and natural way into the programmes, at the same time as unobtrusively showing the leading

characters, and therefore role models, as having small families. However, some countries that have tried to promote family planning
through TV drama series did not take the necessary subtle and soft-
sell approach. For example, *Hum Log* (We People) in India began
with 13 episodes that were a hard-sell for family planning. They
produced a generally negative reaction because they came over as
exhortative; later episodes were made more subtle, but their content
was still too high in preaching and teaching, and the overall conclusion was that *Hum Log* did not achieve as much as hoped.

Sometimes too, excellent creative talent went partly to waste
because it was used without sufficient understanding of communication processes than can bring attitudinal and behavioural change.
For example, in Algeria, one of the most talented film directors
made a one-hour television programme about two friends working
in the same factory; one was the father of only two children while
the other had a very large and still growing family. Everything that
could possibly go wrong in a family teeming with children happened
in the TV drama. The poor mother even got into rows with her
neighbours in the apartment below because water from the vast
quantities of children's clothes she had to wash dripped on their
balcony. The film swung from being hysterically funny to being
deeply moving in its portrayal of the problems of the large family.
Our criticism was that the entertaining and thought-provoking
material was so concentrated in a short programme that many of its
important points could be lost. And as a film transmitted once, or
maybe twice, by TV its impact would certainly be limited. It could
easily have been extended into a series, which would have spaced
out the events that had significance for population issues so that
people had more time to absorb and reflect on them. In addition,
each episode would have probably attracted increasing numbers of
viewers as word got around about the series.

Mixing education with entertainment has also been used successfully for young people, who have become a priority audience for
population issues in recent years. Steeply rising rates of teenage
pregnancies were one reason for this, but another is the new attention
being given to reproductive health and sexually transmitted diseases
– particularly AIDS – as part of the overall family planning and
reproductive health spectrum. Given the wide following of pop music
among adolescents, several countries have managed to involve pop
stars in family planning communication, providing an excellent and
attractive mixture of entertainment with education.

For example, in the Philippines it was thought that publicity about the pregnancies of well-known entertainment personalities was influencing the behaviour of young Filipinos. So it was decided to mount a campaign using teenage celebrities as role models and aimed at almost 1.5 million adolescents in the middle to lower social sectors in Metro Manila. The main objective was to increase their awareness about problems related to teenage pregnancy and the benefits of responsible parenthood. In addition to mass media exposure with teenage celebrities, a telephone and face-to-face counselling service was set up.

Two songs were the core of the campaign. One was a solo telling young people that they should approach relationships seriously and that their future was in their own hands; the other was a duet between a boy and a girl who are attracted to each other, but they are still very young, and they should be cautious because 'love must stand the test of time ... I don't think it's right to need me just for a lonely night.' Video and audio recordings of these two songs were used by television and radio stations. They were supported by TV and radio spots that explicitly stated the risks and consequences of teenage pregnancy and gave the telephone numbers and contact address where adolescents could obtain counselling.

An evaluation of the campaign showed that 70 per cent of the listeners interpreted the messages correctly, and 25 per cent of the target population said they sought information about contraceptives as a result. About 147,000 adolescents tried to telephone the counselling services, but the four lines available were insufficient for the demand. Even so, more than 8,000 calls were logged in the first five and half months, and 60 per cent of youths said they would use the service in future if the need arose.

A significant secondary achievement of the project was that it managed to trigger sponsorship from corporations in the Philippines. Ultimately, this brought in revenue worth four times the cost of the project. The importance of this corporate sponsorship will be referred to later in this book, for it seems that this source of funding for communication to achieve social aims has remained largely untapped.

A more ambitious 'enter-educate' project was launched in Mexico and ten other countries of Latin America in the second half of the 1980s. Again it was aimed at adolescents, but this time in the 12- to 18-year-old range, and again it used songs as its centrepiece. The problem that the project addressed was that young men in Latin

America often feel that it is socially and culturally acceptable for them to experiment freely with their sexuality, while leaving the responsibility of pregnancy to women. Thus, the aim was to generate discussion about sexual responsibility and promote attitudes favourable to responsible sexual behaviour.

The campaign used Tatiana and Johnny, young and popular singers, who performed two original songs. The first was called *Cuando estemos juntos* – 'When we shall be together'[3] and the second was called *Detente* – 'Wait', or 'Hold back'. The social messages in the songs were clear and direct, and an evaluation showed that they were well understood by adolescents. They concerned the need to reflect before engaging in sexual activities, and postponing sex until teenagers were more mature.

Music videos were the centrepiece for presenting the two songs, but they were supported by four TV spots, four radio spots, 11,000 45-rpm records and the same number of posters/record jackets. A press kit including colour slides, black-and-white photographs, and seven press releases was also produced. The record album was sent to 3,000 radio stations in the 11 countries; the music videos were sent to 250 TV stations, and the press kits were sent to 350 publications. Following the mass media exposure, contacts were made with youth organizations in all 11 countries asking them to provide information on teenagers' perceptions of their needs and problems in the area of sexuality. Later, all the materials were supplied to youth centres, which provided further information and services.

The 'Tatiana and Johnny' project attracted a great deal of attention as being particularly imaginative. The first song quickly rose to the top of the charts and remained there for several months in most of the countries, and the second song rose to the top ten in several countries. Both songs reached the top twenty in all 11 countries involved. About a million hours of free air time was devoted to playing the materials and discussing them. Media executives found it relatively easy to support a social campaign which had commercially viable materials that could be incorporated into regular programming.

Unfortunately, as is so often the case, there was no systematic evaluation of the project, but a survey among 2,000 Mexican teenagers showed that they were aware of the key points made within the songs and that they felt the advice to be helpful. It is also known that teenagers discussed the issues raised by the songs among

---

3. This phrase in Spanish also has a connotation of being together sexually.

themselves and with their mothers, and thousands of letters poured in to the youth counselling centres in the participating countries.

The whole 'Tatiana and Johnny' project cost about US$300,000, confirming that 'enter-educating' via the mass media is generally able to reach people at very low cost per person. For example, a radio drama series in Zimbabwe cost US$0.16 per person reached, which worked out at US$2.42 for every new family planning user, whereas by comparison, pamphlets given out by clinic workers reached less than 7 per cent of the number of people reached by the radio dramas and cost US$28 per new user.

Linking interpersonal and media communication

It is usually a mixture of interpersonal channels and media that has brought the most success, and Indonesia deserves special attention for the way it manages integrated IEC for population. According to a USAID report, BKKBN excels in its IEC, and even the commercial marketing and advertising agencies in the country envy its achievements in arousing broad public attention and interest, as well as recognition for its slogans, logos, and messages. Doubtless Dr Haryono's communication expertise has been one of the reasons for the success, but he is also supported by skilled staff in BKKBN's Information and Motivation Bureau. Its head, Masri Muadz, explained to us that the communication strategy is divided into two elements: what he termed 'basic', which is to build and maintain overall support for population programmes, and 'operational', which is to build support and motivation for actual family planning activities. The communication work also aims to be top-down, bottom-up, and horizontal; in other words, information flows in all directions.

Qualitative research, using individual interviews and Focus Group Discussions in selected areas, provides the basis for the specific strategies for each audience. Key criteria for communicating with any audience are to produce transparent messages, work through multi-media channels – including interpersonal communication – and use credible sources for the information.

The strategy also includes reaching intermediate audiences that can, in turn, reach couples eligible for family planning. These intermediate, or relay, audiences include government institutions, NGOs, professional organizations, community institutions, and formal and non-formal leaders.

There is a Media Production Centre in the capital, but each of the 27 provinces in the country has a similar production unit. The central production unit usually confines itself to developing the main communication strategy and materials, while the provincial units either modify those materials to meet their specific needs or produce their own, but within the overall strategy set by the central unit.

For many years, BKKBN used the mass media mainly for slogans and direct messages. Thus its slogan of the 'small, happy, and prosperous family' reached the whole country. In the last five years, BKKBN has adopted 'enter-education' and has turned to TV drama series as a main communication tactic. These series are produced by private companies. Haryono briefs the producers and script-writers, who submit a draft for discussion before shooting begins.

Finally, another plank in the communication strategy is to use public events, which themselves gain wide mass media coverage, for example occasions on which people are given awards and medals for family planning achievement. The most important of these takes place every two years, when there is an enormous ceremony to which each of the country's 300 districts sends its champion family planning couple to meet the president in his palace, have lunch, and receive a gold medal and certificate. They also receive rewards, including a free trip to Mecca for couples who have two children and ten years of family planning.

Haryono, with his ebullient personality, shines on these occasions, but later, as he says, people from the Ministry of Health tease him that all he does is talk, preach and preside over ceremonies, and that he is always on television and in the newspapers getting the credit for everything. Haryono's response is that doctors and health personnel like to do things quietly because their interest is in curing disease, but that he, as a social scientist, cures the mentality and changes attitudes and behaviour. To do that, he creates demand among people by provoking them and giving them information.

Professor Santoso Hamijoyo, who is the head of BKKBN's International Training Programme and a highly respected academic, summed up the Indonesian use of IEC when he told us:

> Entrenched and traditional culture can be the stumbling block in development. Perceptions and feelings are very complex, and IEC is crucial to understanding them and changing them. You mustn't use only media or communication packages. In the early days, we relied too much on the media and didn't pay enough attention to social networking. But because the issues are cultural, IEC must use all possible channels and permeate

the social fabric. The channels here in Indonesia are the bureaucracy, the religious network, the political network, and the military network. It is particularly important to get the bureaucracy involved in IEC because it has all-pervasive lines of communication to people. We try to flood the country with information all the time, keeping the networks alive. And we also flood the country with contraceptives.

We have been able to create a social support system for family planning and that has been possible because we are lucky in having a structured society. In Pakistan and Bangladesh, for example, the structure stops at the sub-district level, whereas here, our villages are real villages, in the economic, social, and cultural sense, with elected village leaders. There are even sub-villages with their elected chief, and neighbourhood associations. You can't get things done without a structure. In Pakistan, the local authority is the landlord, not an elected chief. [Santoso makes a gesture of hopelessness with his hands.] Here, we have many, many meetings, down to the grassroots level, and people often ask us why we have so many. But meetings down to that level are central to managing a programme like ours, for reaching collective decisions.

Certainly, the cohesive social structures and long traditions of community volunteer work and mutual self-help in many parts of Indonesia were an enormous advantage. BKKBN, faced with the logistical and economic problems of providing the necessary density of family planning services in thousands of islands scattered over an arc of more than 3,000 miles, decided to mobilize volunteers in the communities. As a result of this strategy and of the social traditions in the country, there are today more than one million volunteers complementing BKKBN's 35,000 family planning workers. And they are truly volunteers, for they receive no pay. They have all been trained in interpersonal communication and in family planning counselling, and they have IEC materials to help them as they go from door to door in their communities. They are also supplied with contraceptive pills and condoms to distribute, but they refer more complex methods of family planning, such as the IUD, to medical or paramedical staff. Most of these volunteers are women aged about 30–40 and already have two children. With the formal BKKBN staff and the private medical sector, they have created a vast communication and service delivery network for family planning throughout the islands.

Given BKKBN's perceptions about participatory management and social mobilization, and the way it has to put them systematically into practice, it is not surprising that it won the very prestigious

Asian Institute of Management's award for excellence in development management in 1992. Nor is it surprising that BKKBN's strategies and excellent use of communication have been able to reduce the fertility rate from 5.6 in 1970 to 2.63 today.

Breaking taboos

In all countries that have achieved major advances in family planning, an important aspect of communication has been to break down the social taboos of talking about it, and at the same time to draw widespread attention to it. Thailand made a great breakthrough in this area, largely because of one person, Mechai Viravaidya, who possesses communication skills similar to those of Haryono.

In 1974, he launched a project called the Community-based Family Planning Services to complement the family planning efforts of the government. A main thrust of the project was to set up unconventional campaigns to spread the family planning message nationwide. One of Mechai's dictums is: 'If you can make people laugh about family planning, half of the battle is won.' Since the Thais generally have an excellent sense of humour and fun, Mechai's strategy was to use it as a way of making people familiar with family planning and to remove the sensitivity that surrounded it. So he and his family planning volunteers managed to attract huge publicity by a variety of stunts: they regularly handed out condom keyrings at formal functions; they organized condom-blowing contests, family planning carnivals, and vasectomy festivals on the king's birthday; they armed policemen with condoms to hand out as part of a 'cops and rubbers' project, and so on. They also produced T-shirts, sheets, and pillowcases with humorous family planning slogans. Mechai himself was always in the public eye through his media appearances, larger than life, joking and laughing, but at the same time preaching his family planning doctrine.

People at the formal functions who received condom keyrings were initially somewhat shocked, but Mechai's humour and jokes, and those of his volunteers, about family planning gradually had the desired effect. His Community-based Family Planning Services grew into the Population and Community Development Association, which today has about 12,000 volunteers working with about a third of the country's people, and it is involved in a range of community development initiatives. To help finance its activities, it has an excellent restaurant in Bangkok called 'Condoms and Cabbages'. As you leave, there is an elegant lady standing by the door with a bowl in her hands. As you approach, you assume it contains mints or some other sweets, but no, it contains condoms, and she graciously invites you to help yourself.

Promoting debate in the community

In recent years, and especially in rural areas, IEC has tried to promote social dialogue within communities about the link between population, the environment, and natural resources. This approach is part of the more subtle type of IEC for population that has been emerging, and it has been generally successful in arousing awareness of the local effects of population growth as a first step in creating interest in family planning.

Whenever we have done participatory rural appraisal work with peasant farmers, they have almost invariably raised points about declining crop yields and loss of soil fertility. They have also commented on the decreasing size of land holding. In Bolivia, for example, several groups of peasants in the Altiplano made comments to the effect that their *minifundios* (mini-holdings) of the past had today become *minisurcos* (mini-furrows). In such circumstances, it is relatively easy to bring the relationship between population growth and natural resources to people's attention, for it is there for them to see, in their own community, in their own fields, right before their eyes.

FAO and UNFPA have had a number of joint projects in a variety of countries in recent years that have used this communication strategy. One was among the upland forestry communities in the Philippines, where a dialogue about family resources, population and the environment was successfully established using communication materials produced in the locality to show the immediate reality of the situation.

For such work at the community level, folk and other group media are naturally more appropriate than mass media. FAO and UNFPA have made folk media a feature of much of their joint activities, especially in Africa. These media, using local culture and art forms, have inherent advantages for stimulating debate and awareness. Properly used, they can also entertain, inform, educate, persuade, and influence values and behaviour.

When use of folk media for population communication began in the 1970s, it was a rather hit-and-miss affair, but since the mid-1980s, it has become more scientific. As applied by FAO and UNFPA, the process begins with qualitative research among the local population as the basis for developing a communication strategy and plan. Once the main themes, say population, environment, and natural resources, have been identified, a one-week workshop is organized. This brings together a wide variety of artists such as rural story-tellers, poets, dancers, singers, bands, comedians, and drummers.

As a first step, the artists are informed about the basic population situation and the results of the qualitative research. They are invariably quick to master these issues, after which they are left to make the links between them and their particular art form – stories, songs, theatrical skits, poems, and so on. They then begin to write and compose their productions, which are frankly discussed between the artists as they go along. At the end of the workshop, there is a public performance to test the songs, dances, stories, and skits. After further refinement and testing, they are finalized and used in various community situations. When properly integrated into a carefully designed communication strategy, which spells out the media mixes, the messages, the audiences, and the specific communication objectives, folk media have proven invaluable, especially for dealing with sensitive issues, as well as for reaching men who had often been neglected in family planning and health issues.

The Importance of Other Factors

Although it is of vital importance, it would be incorrect to create the impression that family planning hinges entirely on IEC, for experience in the countries where it has taken off on a massive scale generally shows that a certain level of social and economic development had already been reached. Health and family planning services, whether provided by government or NGOs, were available and expanding, and other conditions had also been created, such as a reduction in infant mortality to the point where parents no longer felt compelled to have numerous children to ensure that enough would survive.

Improved roads and transportation also played a role. In many countries, as rural isolation was broken, people were exposed to external ideas and made aware of consumer goods available in urban markets. Consumption patterns changed as people entered more fully into the cash economy, and as they became more conscious of the cost of rearing children, their values changed too.

However, perhaps most important of all the complementary conditions in the countries with successful family planning has been education, particularly of women. One UN study showed that women who have seven years or more of education tend to marry four years or more later than do women with little or no education. Other studies in several countries have shown that one extra year of schooling for girls reduces fertility rates by 5–10 per cent.

A more specific proof of the influence of education can be seen in Mexico. There, between 1984 and 1986, women with no education at all had an average of 6.11 children, while those with secondary and higher education had only 2.51. Even among women who had only completed primary school, there was a drop in fertility rate to 3.66. Fortunately, ever since the Mexican revolution, education had been a high priority, with the result that literacy rose from only 28 per cent of the population in 1930 to 80 per cent by 1980. Similar improvement in literacy levels among women has been the foundation for successful family planning almost wherever it has happened. In Indonesia, the literacy rate rose from only 12 per cent in 1949, when it won its independence from Holland, to almost 80 per cent today.

On the contrary, in many other developing countries where the fertility rate is still in the 5–7 range, literacy levels have remained disappointingly low, especially for women. Men may have progressed to some extent but women have lagged behind. To take just one example from many: in Sierra Leone between 1970 and 1990, men's literacy rose from 18 to 40 per cent, while women's rose from 5 to 14 per cent, and in 1996, the fertility rate was still more than 6. In sum, when women are empowered through education, they gain the confidence, status, and authority to stand up for their reproductive rights and take decisions about the size of their families.

In some countries, a series of factors favourable to the adoption of family planning all came together, creating a popular demand for it, even when there was no government population policy or programme. This was the case of Brazil, where the fertility rate was 5.7 in 1970, but dropped to 3.3 by 1985, and to 2.65 by 1996. How and why this happened in the absence of any real government involvement, and without any major NGO taking a leading role, is curious.

It seems that general economic progress, including several aspects of communication, were the foundation for the behavioural change in Brazil. Physical communication certainly played a part. As in

Thailand, which launched a mammoth road-building programme in the 1960s, rural isolation in Brazil was greatly reduced through road and air connections. This opened the possibility for people to reach medical services more easily, and also increased the numbers of women who had their babies delivered in hospitals and clinics. This introduced people to the medical culture, and also reduced infant and maternal mortality. Furthermore, since most medical people are professionally in favour of family planning, women who went to medical facilities found themselves exposed to information and motivation about it. And the key factor of women's education was also favourable, with literacy among adult women approaching 80 per cent.

Communication via the mass media was another, though unintentional, cause of the behavioural change. Radio and television coverage expanded widely in the 1970s, and television now reaches more than 75 per cent of the urban and 30 per cent of rural households in Brazil. But almost 80 per cent of the total population is now urban, so in effect, access to television is widespread indeed. The significance of television in fertility rate reduction was mainly through its drama series, which have always been enormously popular in Brazil; it is estimated that about half of the population watches them regularly.

From their beginning, these series have invariably shown all their protagonists, the beautiful people, as having small families. Unlike in Mexico and in many other countries in more recent times, there was no deliberate attempt whatsoever to build this message into the dramas; it just happened that way as the writers and producers showed the typical situation among the educated and the privileged ranks of society. But of course, the circumstances of the popular screen characters implied that success and prosperity were linked to small families, and people naturally wanted to emulate them.

Mass media advertisements for consumer items, rising prosperity, and easier access to urban markets also played a role in Brazil, as elsewhere, in changing people's priorities and consumption patterns, especially as they took into account the expense of rearing and maintaining children. So, even if not deliberately planned, communication also played an important role in Brazil. In most other countries with successful family planning programmes IEC has been an integral part of the activities and has been strategically planned and implemented. This is especially true for Asia and Latin America.

Although in many countries of sub-Saharan Africa the general level of development is certainly not yet conducive to success in family planning, it is also true that IEC for population did not get off to a good start. Even if it has certainly improved in recent years, one study completed in 1990 by UNFPA's regional IEC adviser for Eastern and Southern Africa was depressing. It showed that of 248 population communication and education projects in his region, most had failed to follow basic communication principles and practices. The majority of the projects did no proper audience research; only half pre-tested their materials; and most projects used a top-down and exhortative approach. Among the projects that had the objective of behavioural change, nearly half did not investigate obstacles to such change, and more than 70 per cent did not attempt to measure whether behaviours actually did change.

Fortunately, in the last few years, a fully professional approach has emerged. The folk media experiences described earlier, and which have taken place in the Comoros, Malawi, Burundi, and Uganda, are one example of a professional use of basic communication principles and practices. But there are others under way in numerous African countries, including Nigeria, Ghana, Kenya, and Zimbabwe. Many of these IEC activities are now using 'enter-educate' strategies.

Nevertheless, one must wonder whether poorly planned and conducted IEC in the past is one of the reasons for the continuing high fertility rates still evident in many African countries, and for the continuing attitude in favour of large numbers of children. Even in a relatively prosperous country like Zimbabwe, as a recent survey showed, the average couple still sees four children, preferably two boys and two girls, as the ideal family.

The role of communication for population has been so important that the Cairo Conference on Population and Development in 1994 fully recognized it and expanded its role well beyond IEC for family planning only. As the Action Plan states:

Information, education and communication efforts should raise awareness through public education campaigns on priority issues such as safe motherhood, reproductive health and rights, maternal and child health, family planning, discrimination against and valorization of the girl child ... More education is needed in all societies on the implications of population–environment relationships, in order to influence behavioural change and consumer lifestyles and to promote sustainable management of natural resources. The media should be a major instrument for expanding knowledge and motivation.

CHAPTER 7

Tambuli: the Electronic
Carabao Horn

Gambling is a passionate pastime for many men in the Philippines, especially in the poor rural areas where cockfighting is one of the commonest diversions. On this, and on other gaming activities, even poor men wager relatively large sums of money, often disregarding the impact on their families' well-being when they lose.

Attempts to outlaw gambling have not succeeded and one might think that the gambling lust was so entrenched by tradition that it would be impossible to bring it under control. Yet, in a poor rural area of the Province of Camarines Sur in the Central Philippines, the men voluntarily gave it up. The key to this change of heart was the work of a community radio station that had been set up in March 1995. It repeatedly broadcast programmes and discussions about gambling, its economic effect on the community, and its negative impact on families. It also became clear too that gamblers were generally wasting their money for the benefit of the gambling lords. Over a period of time, increasing awareness about the true nature of gambling and its effects took hold, and the people began to see it as socially unacceptable in their circumstances. The gamblers also discussed it among themselves, and the final result was a group decision to give it up.

This occurred in one of several localities in the Philippines where the innovative Tambuli Community Radio Project has created pressure and triggered community action. Some of the results of such action may, in themselves, appear trivial to an outsider, but in the context of the prevailing rural poverty in the Philippines and seen against the people's traditional fatalism and inertia, they are indications that the radio is inspiring new vibrancy and the will to bring about change in the communities. Some of the early community achievements, after debates and appeals over the radio, have been: a prohibition on butchers bringing live animals to the local market and slaughtering them there; cleaning up of a large poultry farm to reduce its smell and pollution; dredging of creeks; putting up a footbridge and extra lighting, and the creation of a day-care centre for children by the local authorities.

This interesting community radio project was several years in gestation before it became operational in the second half of 1991. Initially, it was to be called Radyo Pintig ('Radio Heartbeat') with the radio in close contact with the villagers, listening to their 'heartbeat' and re-transmitting it. But during the research and planning stages, it changed its name and became the Tambuli Community Radio Project. The *tambuli* is the traditional carabao horn or sea conch used by the *baranggay* (village) chief to call the people for an assembly. It is used only for serious matters, particularly for gathering villagers to make important decisions. For this reason, the *tambuli* invariably commands respect and authority. The name Tambuli has also been turned into an acronym in Filipino, which in English means 'Voice of the Small Community for the Development of the Underprivileged'.

In recognition of its successes, in 1996 the Tambuli Community Radio Project won the UNESCO Rural Communication Prize, worth US$20,000, from among 22 other international contenders. It won because of the advances it had made in empowering people through their direct involvement in decision-making. This is noteworthy in a country where the social structures often stand in the way of democratic process and where there are numerous development problems.

The Philippines Scene

The Philippines has characteristics that create particular development constraints. For a start, the country is made up of some 7,000 islands spread over an archipelago that measures about 800 kilometres (500 miles) from north to south. Not all of the islands are inhabited, but even so, the population of almost 70 million people is widely scattered over many of them. Over 60 per cent of the people live in rural areas, and mainly gain their livelihood from farming, fishing, and other traditional activities.

In addition to the dispersed population, a further complication is that 93 different languages are spoken, and even if Filipino is the national language, it is spoken as their mother tongue by less than a third of the population. For example, in the Sulu archipelago in the south of the country, the Muslim population of about 5 million speak 15 different languages, while in the remote mountain and river communities all over the country, dozens of local languages are spoken.

The image of the Philippines as a bustling economy, another 'Asian tiger' in the making, is based on the affluent cities and growth centres, but there are larger and impoverished areas where growth, opportunities, and incomes are severely constrained. The distortion in the balance between these two Philippines has been growing, with ever-increasing marginalization for the rural millions who have been left out of the mainstream of development.

The Marcos regime, which lasted from 1965 to 1986, was marked by his autocratic and elitist style, a crony system, and dubious ways of operating. Today's political system still takes the form of a centralized presidency, and the power structure, whether national or local, is often based on a condescending system of patronage and *clientelismo*. This usually leaves the poorer sectors of society with no real voice in community matters or in how to improve their situation.

The mass media have hitherto done little or nothing to propel national development or to promote democratic processes. There is a plethora of media, especially in the urban centres such as Manila and Cebu, while remote areas often remain uncovered. The majority of the media outlets are commercial, and show little interest in anything but increasing their audiences to be able to command higher advertising revenue. The competition for listenership in the urban areas has left the rural people as a peripheral and marginal audience, and the programming has little relevance to their needs.

There are 17 radio stations owned by religious organizations, and some of these do some development broadcasting, but their main thrust is evangelical. The government-owned media channels are widely seen as being part of the patronage system, for they pander to the establishment and reinforce the interests of certain families, political parties, or businesses.

It is hardly surprising that with this lack of appropriate media coverage in many rural areas, the people are deprived of the information that could help them to improve their lot, defend their rights, and maintain their cultural values. For example, the following actual situations are typical: the Ilongot tribe in the Cordillera mountains are losing their ancestral lands to unscrupulous land-grabbers because they are ignorant of the existing laws that could protect them; farmers have no access to price information so middlemen can pay what they like for their produce; a farmer travelled by sea and land for seven hours to buy seeds, not knowing that a fellow farmer, only three kilometres away, had the same seeds for sale; people in remote villages discuss some national or international event they have heard about over government or commercial media channels, but they have not heard why the construction of the bridge connecting them to the nearest town has been suddenly stopped; young village people have mastered the latest Western dance craze, but they can hardly identify, much less show, the steps of any local folk dance; and one survey revealed that children would rather have an American or Japanese child next to him or her on the school bench than a fellow Filipino.

These are just some of the sorts of problems that could be alleviated by an appropriate communication system in the rural areas. However, against this rather negative situation, it is curious that the Philippines is one of the most advanced countries anywhere in some aspects of communication for development, especially in its availability of competent development communicators. The University of the Philippines, in its Faculty of Agriculture at Los Baños, has been running courses in communication for development for years, one of the few universities in the world to be doing so. This so-called Institute of Development Communication at Los Baños is a well recognized centre of excellence in this discipline and attracts students from many other countries to its fine campus, set in lush tropical countryside next to the International Rice Research Centre. There is also a prestigious College of Mass Communication, again part of the University of the Philippines system, in Manila, and this college has shown much interest and activity in communication for development over the last two decades or so.

Planting a Seed

It almost always seems to be the case that individuals rather than institutions catalyse important development initiatives. There is a highly experienced rural broadcaster in the Philippines called Louie Tabing. He is an amiable, round-faced man in his forties who speaks calmly and softly, but in a measured and convincing fashion. For several years he ran a public service programme for a Church-owned station called Radio Veritas. This station played a central role in supporting the popular revolution that ousted President Marcos in 1986. For many years, Louie Tabing was also the executive director of the Rural Broadcasters' Foundation of the Philippines.

Shortly after the election of Corazon Aquino, and when the demand for change was fresh and strong, Tabing wanted to do something about the media situation in his country. In part, he was motivated in this by a critical situation that was developing with Radio Veritas. The station had served as a credible, non-commercial media outlet for more than a decade, but its management had begun to discuss turning it into a profit-making organization. Tabing was deeply disappointed that the 50-kilowatt station would become yet another commercial operation, convinced as he was that commercialism in the media had done nothing whatsoever to advance the socioeconomic state of the country.

In that same year of 1986, an informal lunch meeting took place that was to have significant later importance. Louie Tabing recalls that it was a casual foursome that got together to talk about the media situation in the country. In addition to Tabing, there were two other prominent Filipino communication specialists present. One was Felix – known as Lex – Librero, at the time the director of the Institute of Development Communication in Los Baños. The second was Carlos – known as Choy – Arnaldo, who had been a radio and TV journalist in the Philippines before joining UNESCO's Communication Division in Paris in 1973. Arnaldo is a humorous and relaxed individual, in many ways atypical of an international bureaucrat. And the last person in the foursome was Martin Allard, an Englishman who designed and built small and economical FM radio transmitters and was a regular consultant to UNESCO.

'If I had my way, I'd bulldoze the whole of our media system,' Tabing said over that lunch. 'It is run as PPPP: Profit, Propaganda, Power, and Privilege. Communication is an important resource and basis for power, and here it is in the hands of an elite who are already powerful and overloaded with resources. What we need are new public media structures that are owned and controlled by the people.'

Tabing told his companions how he had been involved in promoting Integrated Pest Management (IPM) as part of a crop protection project supported by Germany. IPM uses traditional and biological methods of pest control and farmers are taught to spray chemicals only when the level of pest infestation makes them truly necessary and when their use is economically viable. This significantly reduces farmers' costs, chemical pollution, and damage to useful insect life. But when Tabing sent materials promoting IPM to numerous radio stations, many of them refused it, saying they could not broadcast it because it would 'turn the chemical companies away from advertising on the station'.

Choy Arnaldo was not optimistic about Tabing's proposals. 'You won't get far by simply going to our politicians and demanding that they change the system,' he said. 'Don Quixote died a long time ago. You want to fight the whole system, Louie, and that won't work. We should try an experiment on a small scale to show that there are ways in which media can really provide a public service and help development.'

The discussion continued and Lex Librero suggested that, if they were ever able to start community radio in the Philippines, the first place to begin would be in the island Province of Batanes, in the extreme and very remote north of the country. Librero was a native of that area, so he knew it well.

Martin Allard, who had begun building small and cheap FM transmitters in his garage in the small fishing town of Brixham, in south-west England, remarked that he had just completed upgrading his basic transmitter to 20 watts stereo, and that this would be perfect for a start in the Philippines.

Thus the seeds of an idea were sown during that lunch, but they took several years to grow. In fact, the Tambuli notion was certainly not new; it drew on UNESCO's serious interest in community radio as a means of propelling local development that went back to the late 1970s. The Allard transmitter had sparked much of that interest, for it seemed to offer enormous possibilities for developing countries. In flat terrain the earliest versions could cover a radius of about 25 kilometres. The device was so robust and light that it could be put into a car and taken to the countryside for instant mobile broadcasting.

UNESCO and Allard worked closely together and UNESCO began providing a few of these transmitters to developing countries. They were accompanied by some training in how to use them and make simple radio programmes. The results were mixed, especially because the media were state controlled in many countries, and governments were highly allergic to decentralizing their media to places where they could not censor what they were doing. For this reason, one Allard transmitter installed in 1982 at Homa Bay, on the Kenyan shores of Lake Victoria, was closed down by the national authorities after only a few months. The pretext was that the tiny transmitter with its local coverage was increasing tensions between the various tribes.

Other community radio transmitters provided by UNESCO to Burkina Faso were more successful, but the real breakthrough came in Sri Lanka when DANIDA (the Danish International Development Agency) the government and UNESCO got together to establish a community radio service for people being resettled on newly irrigated areas created by the construction of the Mahaweli Ganga dam.

The Mahaweli Development Programme brought almost a million people from different parts of the country and settled them on the newly irrigated land. Although media support was not originally foreseen among the various rural development inputs, it was later realized that a community radio service could help the settlers to integrate and to motivate them to take initiatives to improve their living conditions. As a Danish specialist, Ole Aabenhus, wrote in a 1985 essay about the Mahaweli Community Radio:

> The radio cannot possibly make every listener rich, but it might improve knowledge, help its listeners to think in a long-term perspective, take more factors into consideration, give or point out channels of access to authorities, inform them of their legitimate rights, and maybe even give them a pride in their own history and culture, which is not family-related, but community-related, and thus could generate a feeling of 'we-ness' which could contribute towards future cooperation.

A 1988 evaluation of the Mahaweli Community Radio concluded that it had made a significant impact, creating awareness and understanding of the development programmes. The report stated:

> It has animated settlers into participation in activities that not only encouraged self-actualization but community identity and development. In tandem with Mahaweli development workers, it has motivated the settlers to try innovative practices in agriculture and health. It has likewise motivated local development workers to take the settlers and their problems more seriously, ensuring a more palpable degree of service to the people.

Thus it was that UNESCO, which was successfully breaking new ground in Sri Lanka, was ready to use that experience in the Philippines. The seed that had been planted in that 1986 lunch meeting began to germinate. To help it grow, UNESCO provided US$25,000 to cover the cost of a first 10-watt Allard transmitter, basic studio equipment, and accessories for a community radio station in Batanes. This area was so cut off from everyday life in the Philippines that it received no radio or TV services. People could only tune to radio programmes from China and Taiwan. The College of Mass Communication of the University of the Philippines assumed responsibility for setting up the station. So, in 1990 Radio Itavan in Basco, on the Island of Batan, went on the air as a precursor of what was to become the Tambuli Community Media Project a year or so later.

The Context and Concept for Tambuli

The proposal for the Tambuli Project was based on a situation analysis that established its potential contribution to rural development. This analysis pinpointed the fact that, even when development requirements such as credit, machinery, fertilizers and other farm inputs are available, villagers in the poorest sectors are not always prepared to take advantage of them. They are often apathetic towards opportunities, sceptical towards banks and other lenders because they have incurred critical debts in the past, and even more sceptical of political leaders whose promises too seldom materialize. So they easily find it safer to take refuge in fatalism and inertia.

This situation is made worse by the city-based commercial media, which often entice poor listeners and readers into buying consumer goods they cannot truly afford and often do not really need. Thus these media create demands but do little or nothing to help rural people satisfy those demands through inspiring or motivating them to improve their production or engage in profitable enterprises.

The analysis emphasized that a cause of rural inertia could well be lack of information about opportunities and the lack of communication with leaders, in the sense of dialogue, rather than the usual top-down imposition of demands and admonitions. The local information systems that could fill these gaps did not exist in most municipalities and their sub-regions.

The proposal, therefore, was to create just the sort of localized information network that would link villagers to development resources and knowledge, and also establish two-way communication with leaders. The primary target was *not* to set up radio stations or newspapers: they would only be a *means* towards reinforcing communities and motivating them to organize socially. This would require setting up a community organization to control and run the local media, and the body foreseen for this would be a Community Media Council (CMC). This in turn, it was hoped, would lead to the creation of a local development foundation – if one did not already exist –

and this foundation would be the community's main interface with development bodies and authorities.

The local radio stations and newspapers would be non-commercial and non-profit-making in character, and all those working with them would be unpaid volunteers, at least in the early years. And the communication expertise available within the Philippines would be used, rather than so-called international 'experts'.

Finally, in 1991 and after several years of looking for funding, DANIDA agreed to finance a first phase of Tambuli through UNESCO's International Programme for the Development of Communication. The cost was US$900,000 for an initial period of four years, with a probable follow-up. There was to be a pilot stage in two communities that would last for two years. Following that, the experience would be expanded to other communities, to reach a total of twelve over the project's two phases. Each community would be expected to make a significant contribution through providing land or buildings, labour and other inputs to create what would become a physical Community Media and Training Centre (CMTC). Arrangements were made with several Filipino institutions working in communication to guide and help the implementation of the project, and Louie Tabing was named as project manager.

In the event, the work programme was changed. The so-called pilot period ran from September 1991 to December 1994, and there was more support from communities and local government than had been expected, resulting in savings in the international project funds. This, and the project team's belief that having only two pilot operations would not provide the necessary experience in varied settings, led them to set up more community media systems than originally foreseen, so that by the end of 1994, there were six of them in operation, including the one in Batanes which had been integrated into the project.

The second phase of the project, again with finance from DANIDA, was scheduled to begin in early 1996, but there were bureaucratic delays until mid-1996 in getting it started. Its planned duration is three and a half years, with international funding of US$575,000.

The selection of sites for Tambuli operations would be of great importance. A series of criteria were drawn up to determine what would make suitable locations. These included that the geographic area should be approximately 10 to 30 square kilometres, with a population of between 10,000 and 100,000, and preferably isolated

by mountains, sea or difficult terrain. It should be poor in communication media services but, nevertheless, show a potential for building
and managing a radio station and community newspaper. It should
show a potential for social organization, community consciousness
and cooperative work. The community should be willing to pool
resources and offer land and buildings for a community centre to
house the radio station and the newspaper office. The potential for
interaction between communities, groups of towns or islands should
be taken into account. And finally, Tambuli should only agree to
step in once the people had expressed their enthusiasm and support
for having a local communication system.

Louie Tabing and his small team of three people have been
extremely cautious and methodical in selecting sites. Suggestions have
poured in and the project staff visit each site for several days for an
initial assessment. The local priest is normally an important inter-
viewee in this early assessment and in several cases has turned out
to be a key figure in helping to get the radio station established and
operating. But during one reconnaissance mission, the local priest
said that he could not see how such a community radio would help
him in his evangelical efforts and said bluntly that he would not
cooperate with it, even if it were set up. By mid-1996, more than
twenty reconnaissance missions had been carried out.

Since FM radio waves travel along the line of sight, some areas
have been rejected for reasons of terrain. Hills present problems
unless the antenna can be placed high enough for the line of sight
from it to reach into the valleys, or unless relay transmitters can be
installed on ridges.

Once a site has been selected, a full research programme with the
people is conducted. This uses mainly Focus Group Discussions
and key informant interviews to determine how people would like
the radio station and the community newspaper to operate, and
what their main communication thrust should be. But the times and
duration of broadcasts, their content and form, are just part of the
research. Just as important is determining how the social and economic relationships in the community function, and identifying the
people who should run the media operation, based on their abilities
and their acceptability to the community.

The guiding principle is that the Tambuli Community Radio must
meet the interests and the expectations of all of the various sectors
in the community. Therefore, the Community Media Council which
will run the media system must be made up of representatives of

as many of these sectors as is practicable. In effect, the objective of Tambuli is to help establish an interactive communication system that is owned and controlled by a broad base of the citizenry and not dominated by any vested interests.

First Line Management by the Community

Today, the Tambuli Project has three levels of organization and management. The first and by far the most important is the local one made up of the CMC and the Local Development Foundation. Typically, the CMC consists of 12–15 people and includes representatives of farmers, fishermen, women, youth, tricycle drivers, market vendors, the Church, and a balance of local political leaders. The CMC promotes the free flow of information, especially to the grassroots level in the community and, just as important, enhances the feedback of information to the leaders and policy-makers. It also promotes wide participation of ordinary members of the community in the media activities. The longer-term intention is that the CMC should gradually evolve into the basis for cooperative ownership of the community centre, the radio station, and the newspaper.

The proper establishment of the CMC is so critical that the project has established guidelines, based on experience, for making the selection of people to form it. The guidelines are very perceptive about what may go on in a community. For example, they state that care is needed to avoid 'token representations that have been conveniently set up by dominant groups or individuals who have vested interests and might have the intention, or temptation, to try to rig decisions'. In addition, project staff must use care, tact and diplomacy when dealing with an 'assertive, glib-tongued minority of individuals capable of imposing on the timid or reserved majority'.

Some comments about the Church in the guidelines are also worth quoting:

> The Church, which normally carries a certain level of integrity and clout in the community, is a veritable ally in setting up an independent and credible media system. Aside from the solid, stable, and neutral image that it relatively projects, the Church can harness the services of individuals on a volunteer basis, which the Project [needs because of] the non-commercial, non-profit character of the media operation.
>
> The Christian Church is also laden with the unlimited task of communicating not only with respect to religion but [also] to social and

development activities. Still we must be on guard against Church officials and leaders who forge 'unholy' alliances with some vested groups of politicians, businessmen, lobbyists, and propagandists. It also happens that different Church leaders have varying interests, understanding and attitude with respect to the media centre.

Despite these calls to be on the alert, the project expressly tries to maintain a high level of Church involvement.

Working in tandem with the CMC for local management is the Local Development Foundation, which is usually made up of community leaders. Its role is to help plan and implement development actions, in many cases after they have originally been identified, discussed and decided upon through the work of the radio. The foundation also forms the body with which outside institutions can have a formal working relationship for funding, technical assistance, and the like.

The second level of organization is a management team selected by UNESCO and its Philippine National Commission to provide support, technical advice, training, and research. It draws on expertise from professional and academic institutions in the country and also from several radio stations and newspapers.

Finally, a high-level Advisory Panel provides overall policy and directional advice. This small panel is made up of the president of the University of the Philippines, the chairman of the UNESCO Education Committee and a few other notables, but it also includes a prominent broadcast practitioner.

Tambuli at Work

The first step taken by the Tambuli Project was to improve the operation of Radio Ivatan in the Batanes Islands, which had been set up before Tambuli itself became operational. It needed to be adapted fully to the Tambuli model of community decision-making in its operations, and its broadcast power increased to cover a wider area. The original 10-watt transmitter was therefore replaced with one of 20 watts coupled to a 100-watt booster. Training in radio and print production was conducted by the project and extra equipment was provided for the preparation and publication of a bi-monthly newspaper.

Curiously, not long after Radio Ivatan went on the air, the governmental Philippines Broadcasting Service decided to install a medium-wave station in the same area. Fortunately, once the station had been installed, Radio Ivatan was able to start a dialogue with it, for the benefit of both. The government station was serving mainly as a relay for centrally produced and broadcast programmes, with little capacity for local programming, mainly because it was having trouble finding staff willing to be assigned to those remote northern islands.

Radio Ivatan, despite several periods of being off air because of breakdowns, had built a faithful audience for its entirely local programmes, and so the two stations were able to agree to cooperate, with the result that the better of Radio Ivatan's programmes were regularly broadcast by the government's AM station to the whole province. And staff from the Tambuli radio help out in the government station. By the end of 1993, the cost of running the radio station and of producing the local newspaper had been taken over by the community and the Batanes Development Foundation.

The second Tambuli station established was in a place called Laurel, in the province of Batangas. It is only about 85 kilometres south of Manila, but over a bad road, and the journey takes about two hours. The road skirts the shores of Lake Taal, with a regular view of the cone of Taal Volcano, one of the most active in the world.

Despite its proximity to the capital, Laurel is a depressed area, mainly because it lies at the dead end of the road. Construction of an extension could connect Laurel to the farmlands of the neighbouring province, as well as to the lower valleys of Batangas province itself, turning Laurel into a transit and trading centre, with significant impact on its economy. This is one of the goals of the community, which had already created its own Development Foundation before the Tambuli Project made contact. The foundation was quick to realize the potential of a community radio station, and once the decision to go ahead had been taken, it immediately formed its CMC. The research phase to determine people's priorities and expectations soon followed, and the station went on air in March 1993. It was located in a classroom of a secondary school. Experienced professionals were brought in to provide training in radio production. In addition to the basic grounding, the training put special emphasis on the dramatization of messages, the production of short materials, and participatory-type programming in the neighbourhood. Training was also provided in newspaper production.

A local newspaper, called *Abot-Tanaw* (Within View), was launched. It had a print run of a thousand copies, produced at a cost of US$200 in a local offset printshop. Most copies were sold at cost, but the production team also had the ingenious idea of marketing it to people originally from the community who had emigrated overseas and would be willing to pay about US$20 per annum to have news from their old home town.

The third Tambuli initiative provides an interesting example of building community radio into an existing institution that is already doing important development work. This happened on the island of Panay, in the central Philippines, where there is a State College of Agriculture in the town of Banga, province of Aklan. The president of this college, a dynamic and progressive man, took the initiative of asking for Tambuli involvement to help the college's outreach programme to farmers in the area.

The town of Banga is relatively prosperous, and it is quite close to the provincial capital of Kalibo. Radio stations from there, and from other larger towns even further away but using powerful AM transmitters, were reaching Banga. For these reasons, Banga did not meet the Tambuli site selection criteria properly, and in discussions with local leaders during a reconnaissance, it was suggested that a town called Ibajay, with about 35,000 people, lying some 33 kilometres west of Kalibo, might be more appropriate.

When the project team went to Ibajay, they found a large economic gap between those living in the comfortable and well-built houses of the town itself and those living in the tattered palm huts in the depressed villages, or *baranggays*, in the surrounding countryside. In addition, insurgency problems were beginning to manifest themselves in some of the remoter *baranggays*. It was obvious that a Tambuli action in Ibajay could be more important and useful than in Banga.

The president of the College of Agriculture, who had been hoping that the project would help him with his outreach programme to the farmers close to Banga, not only accepted that Ibajay was a better site but also offered the help of his college for training of rural people as a follow-up to the communication actions of Tambuli. Furthermore, he offered to make Ibajay the central point for the college's island-wide extension thrust. In Ibajay, the project helped to organize a multisectoral core of leaders who quite quickly became a Development Foundation, which in turn created a Community Media Council.

The simple production studio was installed on the second floor of the rectory. This was a provisional measure while the community was left to solve the problem of raising funds to build the permanent station on a nearby lot. The new station's antenna was hoisted on to the church belfry to give it the height it needed for line-of-sight broadcasting. A UHF base station was set up in the studio, and two handsets were provided so that the broadcasters would be able to cover live events in the communities and make their programmes more dynamic.

The project organized a three-week crash course in radio production for trainees, who included a farmer, a fisherman, two municipal workers, a schoolteacher, a church worker, a bank employee, and several recent school-leavers. Immediately after the training, the station went on the air on a test-broadcast basis from 05.00 to 08.00 hours each day.

The response from the town and the 38 villages surrounding it was overwhelming. Literally bags and bags of letters began to arrive. When a mailbox was placed at the door of the rectory, it would overflow each day with requests for songs, dedications, public service announcements, suggestions, comments, and news items. Sometimes the envelopes also included banknotes to support the broadcasting operation.

The broadcast hours were soon extended to midday and, touched and propelled by the public response, the foundation and the CMC worked hard to find ways to finance the operation, provide some incentives for its volunteer staff, and build the permanent station. The wealthier sections of the community pledged financial support, and a campaign was launched to persuade people in full employment to contribute to the operation. The College of Agriculture was true to its word and offered all its competence and experience for the content of radio programmes dealing with farming and rural technology. This led to the idea of setting up a small production studio in the college itself, and from there it was a small step for the project to offer a transmitter to the college.

In this way, the College of Agriculture, or Banga where it is located, became the fourth Tambuli station. The transmitter and antenna are perched at the base of a cross on a mountain top from where the signal reaches Banga and most of the ten other municipalities in the area. The Tambuli team took the decision to install this station because they wanted to experiment with community radio as part of a well-established institution that was doing outreach work in the surrounding communities. They also saw possibilities for linking the programming of the Banga and Ibajay stations, another area in which they wished to experiment. From its side, the college took the matter very seriously: the Tambuli studio was installed in a new development communication centre built by the college, which also offered to finance some of the expenses and manpower costs of the operation.

A three-week intensive radio production course, similar to the one conducted in Ibajay, was held. The trainees included a beautician, a farmer, a policeman, a handicapped person, a market vendor, a government retiree, the municipal secretary, a midwife, a student, and two of the extension staff from the college.

Banga and Ibajay were also keen to get their community newspapers started as soon as possible. A training course for those who would produce it was held and it was one of the very few occasions in which an international specialist was involved. A graphic artist recruited by UNESCO gave guidance on newspaper layout and graphic design. The first publications for the two towns were produced immediately after the course. They were mimeographed, but plans were soon made to upgrade the quality through more sophisticated printing techniques.

After Banga, which was relatively central and accessible, Tambuli turned its attention to the island of Olutanga in Zamboanga del Sur, a location in the south that is about as remote as Batanes in the north. Reaching it involves an arduous eight-hour road trip from Zamboanga City to the town of Alicia, and a boat trip across the strait to the island, which takes another one and a half hours.

This geographical isolation has been a principal factor in Olutanga's social and economic stagnation. It was also the scene of severe unrest about 15 years ago when the Muslim separatist movement in the south was in conflict with other armed groups. As one result, the then flourishing town of Mabuhay, one of only three communities on the island, was razed to the ground. Mabuhay today has a population of about 13,000 people; the other two municipalities of Suba Nipa and Talusan have populations of 16,000 and 8,000 respectively.

The Tambuli staff held initial meetings with the local leaders on Olutanga, and they immediately showed enormous interest in the project and enthusiasm for getting it under way. They quickly organized a CMC and an Olutanga Islanders Development Foundation. The latter was headed by a very dynamic and efficient woman, who was a town councillor in Mabuhay.

The three-week intensive training course in radio production organized in Olutanga included 15 people who, as usual, came from a wide variety of sectors in the local society. Two of the participants had to walk 11 kilometres each way to get to the training site. Two others walked 5 kilometres morning and evening along dark and muddy paths. Since test broadcasts were beginning at 05.00 hours, this meant that some had to leave their homes anything up to three or more hours earlier for their long walk in the dead of night. They later recalled fondly that they got used to having breakfast not long after midnight.

As a provisional measure, the station was installed in a Catholic convent in Mabuhay. The local government then donated a nearby building plot of 400 square metres, and the community set about raising the money to build the station on it. A raffle was organized to raise some of the funds. As in other sites, some listeners also included banknotes with their letters and requests for programme items. Ultimately, with some limited help from Tambuli, and from the provincial government for materials, and with all the labour provided by the community, the building was constructed. It is a small but sturdily built studio and next to it stands its red-and-white steel antenna, towering over the palms and other lush tropical vegetation of the island.

However, even if that antenna looks impressive, it was not high enough to cover more than the northern part of the island. So, with the station in Mabuhay progressing well, a 20-watt relay transmitter was set up in the southern town of Suba Nipa, 18 kilometres away. This provides coverage of the whole island, and the facility in Suba Nipa can also produce programmes for its own people that are separate from the island-wide programmes. A novelty in Olutanga is that the broadcasters have managed to harness local two-way VHF radio communication systems belonging to amateurs, businesses, and even the police, to feed information and news into their programmes.

By mid-1996, Tambuli had established media operations in three more sites, bringing the total to eight. An early lesson learned in setting up these community media services was the importance of using a participatory approach in all the planning, including the research in the community. This helped to give the people a sense of ownership and commitment. In addition, the research findings were more authentic when people from the community, fully familiar with its linguistic and cultural peculiarities, were the ones gathering the information. Involving the community during the research phase also gave more opportunities to explain the Tambuli Project through key people.

The Tambuli radio style

The basic purpose of the Tambuli Project, as we have seen, is the empowerment of people through information so that they will be motivated to take better advantage of existing development opportunities, as well as identifying and pursuing their own development opportunities through media-supported discussion and debate.

For Tambuli to achieve such a process obviously requires a high level of community participation in the communication system. One of Tambuli's programming precepts, therefore, is that ordinary people should be encouraged to speak out and to develop their capacity for self-expression. This is done during normal interviews and discussions, but in addition Tambuli has developed a special programme format, known as *Baranggayan sa himpapawid*, which translates as 'Village on the Air'. This programme format was originally developed by the station in Banga, but it was then copied by all of the others.

'Village on the Air' programmes are actually produced in the village or neighbourhood, using a karaoke music player/recorder. Karaoke machines are very common in the Philippines because many overseas contract workers and professional people buy them to indulge their typical Filipino love of music. As a result, there are karaoke machines in many homes, and they are well-known even in remote villages. The use of such familiar equipment by Tambuli for radio production in the communities relaxes people and demystifies the electronic medium of radio.

'Village on the Air' is normally a lively one-hour programme. Much of it is made up of local songs sung by villagers, debate in verse form, poetry and declamations. The villagers are encouraged to address social and development issues in their artistic presentations, but certainly not to the exclusion of entertainment.

The programme also has an important discussion portion during which the members of the village raise their concerns and talk about important issues. Local leaders and authorities join in, providing their points of view. Alternatively, the discussion section may begin with an interview with a local personality followed by questions and comments from the community and general discussion. Regular 'vox pops', or interviews with the ordinary members of the village, are solicited. These quite often put the local leadership under pressure to explain and justify its priorities and actions.

The 'Village on Air' programme is recorded live in the village and broadcast from the station studio the next day. Thus the whole area is entertained, and at the same time made aware about social and development issues of concern in the village where the programme was made. They also learn about the local leadership's views and actions. The issues discussed in any one 'Village on the Air' programme may be specific to that village or they may be similar to those in most of the other villages that are listening. When they are similar, which is usually the case, the foundation stone for inter-village cooperation may be laid. It may also happen that a listening village has already met and resolved a particular problem and can therefore provide information to others on how they did so.

Generally, 'Village on the Air' is broadcast once a week, but in some Tambuli stations, the programme is aired two or three times a week. Initially, trained people from the radio station give villagers guidelines and assistance in producing their programme, but the aim is that the villagers should learn to plan and conduct the whole process themselves. They normally acquire that capacity rapidly.

In their other programmes, Tambuli stations try to provide messages that are useful to their community. Some examples have been: information on local legislative measures; information on agricultural products and services; death announcements; warnings about an escaped convict; returning a lost child to its parents; returning a carabao to its owners after it had strayed into another village; improving employment through announcements about labour availability and requirements, and so on.

Educational and religious programmes, and others to promote cultural values, have been introduced in some stations. In Banga, the station airs daily educational programmes for out-of-school children on various topics such as history, natural science, and language. Also in Banga, a midwife hosts a weekly health programme, and the beautician-turned-broadcaster, who loves reading fairytales to her children, introduced this programme format to the radio. She mastered the art of varying her voice to capture the characters in her stories. In Laurel, the local police sergeant hosts a weekly hour on law and order. Also in Laurel, teenagers used the radio to help them raise funds for a basketball court.

The radio in most sites also functions in the place of a telephone system; for example, messages can be broadcast to advise someone that a relative in another village is ill, or to call someone to a meeting or celebration.

A livelihood component

Tambuli's interactive communication system has shown that it can introduce information about new technology, provide a forum for discussions about possible income-generating ideas, identify sources of inputs, help build economic units such as cooperatives, inspire communities, and spread and exchange beneficial concepts and experiences. However, the best information and motivation are not always enough to trigger action and income-generating activities, for they may need initial investment and other inputs.

This was one of the reasons for the importance Tambuli gives to having a local development foundation, which can be a channel for funds and other inputs from outside. It is also the reason for Tambuli complementing its communication functions through a component known as Livelihood Assistance. Under this, Tambuli can provide several types of support, such as initial capitalization through an interest-free loan, training, and bringing technical information to the community.

Under the interest-free loan arrangements, a Tambuli community radio station can lend a maximum of Pesos 120,000 (about US$4,600), with up to Pesos 60,000 for any single project. The maximum loan to an individual person is Pesos 5,000 (about $190), so larger amounts must be to a group. The period for repayment is up to 30 months.

Tambuli requires detailed proposals for loans and has drawn up guidelines for the type of requests it prefers. The general objective is to foster endogenous and self-reliant development, so the use of locally available materials and the harnessing of untapped local resources are preferred to acquiring inputs from outside the community. Similarly, there is preference for products and services for which there is a local demand, as opposed to reliance on markets and patrons outside of the area. The most acceptable activities spread their benefits over the greatest number of people and have a relatively small initial capitalization. They should also be innovative and have a potential for replicability. The risks – natural, political, economic, and managerial – should be assessed in the proposal and mechanisms foreseen for coping with them.

The initial loan can also be converted into a grant to the community after two years, but only if certain conditions are met. These are that repayments must be 95 per cent up to date but taking into account any natural and unforeseen calamities; that the original loan has been used only for the purposes agreed when it was made; and that there is a sound proposal to use the grant money to expand the programme to a greater number of people, or to improve the original livelihood project. This possibility of turning the loan into a grant is obviously a considerable incentive for the borrowers to have their projects perform and to repay the loan on schedule.

Livelihood projects can also be started by people working in the radio stations. Since they are all volunteers, and many are either unemployed or underemployed, this gives them a chance to earn a living while continuing to work in the stations. As could be expected, there has been quite high turnover among the volunteer broadcasters, and livelihood projects aim to reduce this.

The Tambuli broadcasters and their families on the island of Olutanga have made particular progress with livelihood projects that can serve as models for the community while, at the same time, generating income for themselves. Their projects include fishing, pisciculture, duck raising, an upholstery shop, a mechanical workshop, a piggery, and other small industries. In Ibajay, the broadcasters created an informal cooperative to mill and trade rice. Tambuli provided Pesos 60,000 as seed money, which was supplemented by the CMC and the foundation. The activity has gone very well and provided substantial material rewards to the staff. And equally important, the staff acquired interesting insights into livelihood activities and organizational skills, which they then talked about in their radio programmes for the benefit of listeners.

However, in general terms, the livelihood aspects of Tambuli were rather slow to take off, which is understandable because the processes triggered by the community media take time before they can lead to good proposals for livelihood projects.

Tambuli's Impact

This chapter began with some examples of the sort of changes that were beginning to happen in communities as a result of the community radio. So far, not very much has been done to evaluate Tambuli's impact systematically, although the project did commission an assessment of five of its community radio stations in the early part of 1994. This was conducted by Delia Barcelona of the College of Mass Communication.

She visited the project sites and communities in Batanes, Laurel, Banga, Ibajay, and Olutanga. She found the volunteer broadcasters enthusiastic and dedicated. They were motivated to provide so much of their time without material benefit generally because they found that doing service for the community was rewarding, but so also was being known and hearing one's own voice on the radio. Many of them said that they were often approached by local people who praised their programmes and congratulated them for their efforts, and that they enjoyed this recognition. Nevertheless many broadcasters hoped that, one day, it would be possible for them to receive some monetary compensation for their work.

The resourcefulness of the station staff was often noteworthy. In Banga at one Christmas, they went carol singing from door to door to raise the funds to buy a karaoke machine for their 'Village on the Air' programmes.

An indication of the broadcasters' prominence in the community is that a number of them stood as candidates in local council elections and won seats, but they all voluntarily stopped working in the radio station during the electioneering period, or were temporarily suspended by their CMC. In this way, no accusations of bias or conflict of interests could be levelled at Tambuli or at them.

In quantitative terms, the success of the radio stations so far can really be measured only by the number of listeners who send in all kinds of requests for announcements, greetings, public service plugs, and notes of appreciation. These letters and notes still regularly overflow the boxes provided for them. Furthermore, all the Tambuli stations have achieved very large and regular audiences, far in excess of competing stations, where they exist.

Qualitative information about the impact of Tambuli is more plentiful. In many areas, the 'Village on the Air' programme is so popular that the radio station cannot cope with the number of invitations it receives from villages to visit them and record programmes. The priest who is chairman of the CMC in Laurel said: 'The medium has been instrumental in raising the consciousness of the people. They are now aware, informed, and concerned.' In a similar vein, the station manager in Banga declared: 'Were it not for Tambuli, the people of Banga would still be lying back passively.'

Perhaps one of the most interesting aspects of Tambuli's operations has been the way they have helped to promote moral rectitude. The project has drawn up a code of conduct for its staff. It covers all aspects of the ethics and professionalism of broadcasting, such as fairness, truthfulness, objectivity, verification of information sources, respect for the rights of all, innocence of the accused, and the like; but in addition, it also covers conduct both in the studio premises and in the community. If the behaviour of a broadcaster is in any way considered to be tainting the integrity of the radio station, his or her services can be suspended or terminated by the CMC or Development Foundation. Thus Tambuli has succeeded in creating a sound reputation for morality and principle.

At the same time, a public medium of communication has provided ordinary members of the community with access to a wide-reaching forum where they can express their grievances. This has a community watchdog effect that has made officials more conscious of their public responsibilities. For instance, in the town of Laurel, the public market was dirty and unsanitary until an item in the newspaper called the market administrator to task. There was an immediate and sustained improvement.

Most Tambuli stations have a programme such as 'Report it to Rusty' (or the appropriate broadcaster's name), and this is the normal recourse for people who sense misdoing or irregularities among public officials. Tambuli stations have also helped to stop illegal activities, particularly logging, and fishing in prohibited areas. People who had seen what was going on reported it to the broadcasters, who immediately raised the issue to a level of public concern and protest, so also goading officials into action to stop it. Behaviour patterns in communities have also improved. In Batanes, the incidence of drinking in the streets dropped after the topic was the subject of a radio programme. A resident in Batanes said, 'Beware, we could be the subject on the air!'

The instances and examples of impact cited here are qualitative and anecdotal. However, they do seem to show that Tambuli is playing a very important role in the communities where it works. But unfortunately, a proper methodology for the evaluation of the impact is still missing as we write. There will be more about evaluation of communication impact in Chapter 8, but the fact is that it is difficult to measure social and human change; it calls for special methods to identify what role was played by communication – in relation to other factors – in bringing it about. Perhaps some advances in this complex area will be achieved by Tambuli, for in late 1996, it commissioned a highly experienced university academic in the Philippines to try to develop a series of social indicators that could be used to measure change.

Whatever the outcome of more formal evaluations, there are already signs of official recognition of the value of Tambuli's work. In 1996, the provincial government of Aklan awarded plaques of citation to the Banga and Ibajay stations for their outstanding contribution in the field of public service. The Banga station also received the Binhi Award, a trophy and a cash prize worth the equivalent of about US$600, from the association of Philippine agricultural journalists.

What Prospects for the Sustainability of Tambuli?

One might easily think that setting up community radio stations in remote rural areas of the Philippines was doomed to create yet another graveyard of sophisticated and expensive equipment, lying around useless because no replacement parts are available, or because there is no one who knows how to repair it. In fact, this scenario does not apply to Tambuli. The equipment is simple and also cheap. The Allard 20-watt transmitter now costs about US$2,000 and the amplifier to boost its output to 100 watts costs the same. An antenna can be built from local materials by any competent metalworker. Indeed, as a provisional measure in Laurel, one was even built out of copper brake-pipe and PVC water-pipe, both bought in a local hardware shop.

And there are even cheaper transmitters than the Allard on the market today. Some, which Tambuli is now trying, are built by Free Radio Berkeley in California. They make one model of 250-watt output that costs less than US$3,000. At the other end of their range, there is a 6- to 8-watt transmitter that costs about US$325 and would be ideal as a small relay station to pass a signal from the main station into a village hidden behind a ridge.

The Philippines has a surprising level of self-sufficiency in electronics. Even in remote villages, there is usually some technical expertise available. Martin Allard, after a visit to the project, made the point that it was refreshing to find technicians who were so willing to try working on any type of electronics. They often needed, he said, to be restrained from taking on jobs that were beyond them, whereas in some countries they had to be encouraged to work at all. He added that operating simple Tambuli stations did not call for sophisticated engineers. Rather, commitment and creativity were the main requirements, and these were abundantly available in the Philippines.

Although Filipino technicians are often very competent, they have benefited from the technical assistance they have been receiving from Tambuli. For example, during a visit that Martin Allard paid to Radio

Ivatan in Batanes, he found that the broadcast signal from the 10-watt transmitter barely reached the outside of the town, a distance of about 1 kilometre. The Batanes technicians, thinking that the problem was one of low transmission power, had added a locally built power amplifier. Allard suspected that the problem was related to the antenna, a commercially available unit called the 'Penetrator' – falsely named, as he found out. He connected the new 20-watt transmitter he had brought with him to the Penetrator, and he found that the signal began to fade within walking distance from the station. He then installed a provisional antenna, and even though it was only about 20 feet up the 60-foot mast, there was a twenty-fold gain in signal strength; it could even be heard faintly in the next island, 37 kilometres away.

Thus an antenna made from locally available materials had solved the signal problem, but it had certainly not resolved all of the problems of FM broadcasting in Batan Island. It is so rugged, and there are so many inhabited inlets around the jagged coastline, that even an antenna on the highest mountain could not gain line-of-sight to the many clusters of houses nestling at the foot of the cliffs.

Allard and the Filipino technicians were doing a reconnaissance along these clifftops one day when one of the Filipinos jokingly said, 'What we really need is a station out at sea!' They all laughed, and then someone said, 'What about on Sabtang?' nodding towards the neighbouring island to the south, which was in full view from most of the coastline on which they were standing. From that exchange, the idea rapidly developed of setting up a relay on Sabtang, but with a simple facility for some production of its own programmes. This could begin the process of linking the islands of Batanes, which traditionally have had very little communication between them. In late 1996, proposals for setting up relays in Batanes still exist, but there are problems of transporting the equipment there and ensuring maintenance on a regular basis.

With regard to costs, UNESCO estimates that it requires about US$90,000 in total to establish and support a Tambuli operation until it is fully up and running. About US$55,000 of this covers transmission equipment (two transmitters on average), studio equipment, two-way radio links, the antenna and mast, studio construction or renovation, and installation of the equipment. The remainder is spent on training, management support, operational assistance, securing the broadcasting licence, livelihood assistance and contingencies.

The point must be made, however, that Tambuli is a pilot operation with attention being paid to every detail, and with relatively high investment and operational costs as a result. A bare-bones station for a small community could be set up for less than US$5,000, and this figure is within the reach of many local organizations or governments, schools, and cooperatives.

The early years of Tambuli's operations have shown that the communities and local authorities have already been willing to make important contributions in cash and kind. Provided the Tambuli strategy and operations can continue to meet a felt need, and provided they can stimulate local development, it should become increasingly easy for the community, local government and other interests to assume the cost of running the media system. It is interesting, too, that other organizations have been inspired by the Tambuli experience and are planning to copy it. One of these is the Philippines Peasant Institute, an NGO identified with progressive farmers, which has been in close consultation with Tambuli staff and intends to set up three 20-watt stations in three different locations.

Sustainability in human terms is also an important factor. Certainly, in terms of commitment and resourcefulness, the project team is outstanding. This was shown by what happened when the second phase of the project was due to begin in very early 1996 but was delayed several months because the government had not signed the Project Document. The Tambuli team kept things running for almost four months by borrowing funds from the Philippine Foundation of Rural Broadcasters, and also by financing many operations from their own pockets.

However, Tambuli is not without its uncertainties on the human side, beginning with its volunteer broadcasters, normally numbering about 10–15 in each station. There are advantages in having volunteers for this type of work, mainly because people usually only volunteer for something to which they feel committed. Certainly, in the case of Tambuli, this has led to highly motivated and active teams of broadcasters. Most people admire and appreciate good voluntary work, and this is certainly true also for volunteer broadcasters who gain in prestige and credibility among their listeners as a result. In many cases too, listeners and the local authorities have shown their appreciation by donating small gifts at Christmas or by turning up at the station with refreshments for the staff.

However, the question must be asked whether it is in the best interests of community radio to have volunteers with no regular compensation except the prestige of working for their community. It would seem that in an ideal situation, the broadcasters should receive some financial recompense for their work, but not enough to make it so attractive that it loses the advantages of its essentially volunteer character. Some recompense might also reduce the relatively high staff turnover, which has been a feature of Tambuli in the past.

Training can also be a good incentive, for it enhances people's job satisfaction when they can take pride in their professional skills. Furthermore, although it may not be in Tambuli's immediate interests, good technical skills open up job opportunities. For example, two Tambuli-trained broadcasters were recruited by the new government AM station when it opened in Batanes. In the past, there has been a greater demand for training than the project has been able to meet. It is to be hoped that training can be expanded, both to create more skilful and satisfied broadcasters, and also to have more of them.

Despite all the positive aspects of the Project, it is not immune to conflicts in the community. Fortunately, only one Tambuli site, Laurel, has been seriously affected in this way. The problem occurred mainly because there were changes among the local leaders who had originally worked to set up the community media system. One of these was the mayor, but he was later accused of murder and gaoled to await trial. Meanwhile, a new priest was assigned to the community. He at once became very active in promoting development activities, working very closely with the radio team. Unfortunately, he trod on a few toes in the process, particularly those of the acting mayor, with the result that there was a breakdown in working relationships between key people in the community. In effect, the mayor's removal to gaol took away the energizing spirit of the community media experience, and it slowly declined until, after about two years on the air, the transmitter broke down in 1994. Despite the supply of a new transmitter about three months later, the station remained silent because the local leadership never managed to reach agreement on the necessary mechanisms for managing the media operation.

In 1995, a group of communication students from the Ateneo de Manila University completed a case study, submitted as their thesis, called 'Has Laurel Lost its Voice?' Their research showed that the people in Laurel had much appreciated the community radio station's work and wanted it to go back on the air. They preferred its programming to that of the commercial stations in Manila that were also reaching Laurel. But the management problems have persisted, and by late 1996, the Tambuli team were considering relocating the transmitter and other equipment to another site.

Endogenous conflicts in a community are always a possible obstacle to community radio, but in addition, the Tambuli staff have identified a number of possible conflictual situations which could be triggered by the media operation itself, and which could affect its continued success. For example: a more aware citizenry in a locality might threaten to destabilize the traditional leadership, which might have been accustomed to wielding power through patronage; as productive and commercial enterprises increase, the know-how and capacity generated among ordinary people could upset monopolistic business and trading arrangements and at the same time expose some of the abuses of the existing systems; the open forum for ideas, and also for criticism, offered by community media might disgruntle local officials and the establishment; people beyond the law, such as those responsible for gambling and illegal logging, might find that their interests were being damaged by the media system. Any, or all, of these sectors in a community, feeling themselves threatened or criticized, could be stirred to take hostile measures against the initiators and operators of Tambuli.

However, these are the risks that any innovative and truly democratic initiatives, leading to the empowerment of the underprivileged, must face. Louie Tabing has the following dictum: 'Community radio is more than radio situated in the community – it is radio about the community, for the community, and by the community.' Putting such a philosophy into practice will always have its built-in hazards.

On the positive side, it is possible that the success of Tambuli will lead to many other organizations copying and expanding the experience. This could snowball to the point where government policies and trends in media ownership could change radically. In fact, in addition to the possible involvement of other groups, Tambuli has formulated a well-planned proposal for an integrated campaign that would create more awareness of the development role of community media and lead to new legislation in its favour.

Tambuli's campaign partners are the College of Mass Communication and the Institute of Development Communication, both of which enjoy the prestige and influence of being part of the University of the Philippines. The campaign will include regional policy symposia, advocacy through a group of trained spokespersons, the production of TV and radio documentaries, posters, pamphlets and press kits. All this would be supported by congressional lobbying and it is hoped that the end result would be a Community Communication Reform Bill, for signature by President Fidel Ramos before the end of his mandate in May 1998.

It is too early to know the final outcomes of Tambuli and its related activities, but certainly the project is blazing an important trail in showing how to change the four Ps – Profit, Privilege, Power, Prestige – of the existing mass media into the modified four Ps of community media – Participation, People, Power, and Pluralism.

A Communication Agenda for the Next Century

Part Three will identify common elements in the case studies presented in Part Two and suggest some possible guidelines for applying communication to change and development in the future.

CHAPTER 8

Towards Successful Communication Strategies

The case studies in Part Two of this book have a number of common factors that can provide guidance for the future. However, the first of these factors may be the most difficult to replicate, for it concerns the people behind each of the experiences described. In every case, they were individuals with a deep understanding of the human dimension of development and of how communication can influence people and bring about behavioural change.

The executive director of UNICEF, the late James P. Grant, who was the mastermind behind social mobilization for child immunization (Chapter 3) understood how societal forces could be brought to bear to achieve an aim. He was also convinced of the power of communication and the media to help sensitize people and stimulate them to action. On a personal level, he was also an outstanding communicator, articulate, personable, and very persuasive, and this led to success during his interventions with heads of state and other decision-makers. His vision was made reality by dozens of highly competent people working in communication in the countries where UNICEF has offices. Of course, the theme of child survival was an attractive one, which made convincing people about it less difficult than is the case for many other of today's issues.

For PRODERITH in Mexico (Chapter 4) there was Santiago Funes, the FAO communication adviser, and truly a rural development intellectual. The conceptual aspects of PRODERITH's communication approach were all based on his understanding of how rural communities function and of how, through communication, they can be helped to reach decisions that reflect a collective will and ensure their participation in putting it into practice. He also realized the importance of helping rural people to acquire knowledge and skills that they could apply in their production processes and in their daily lives in order to improve their well-being. Finally, he developed excellent personal relations with Mexican policy-makers and was able to convince them to put resources into communication for rural development.

Godfrey Baseley and José Joaquin Salcedo (Chapter 5) used entirely different strategies but they were inspired by a similar view of the information and education needs of rural people and of how meeting them could bring about development. Baseley's natural gifts as a communicator led him to understand that imitation among farmers is a spur to innovation. This was the starting point for pioneering a new radio-drama formula based on creating role models, and which mixed education, in small but effective doses, with entertainment. Salcedo was an ardent advocate and practitioner of what we would now call human development and life education decades before anyone else. He fought the establishment and entrenched interests for years, and even if he was ultimately defeated by them, his ideas have been vindicated by today's concepts of human development.

For population communication (Chapter 6) people like Haryono Suyono in Indonesia, Mechai Viravaidya in Thailand, Miguel Sabado in Mexico, and similar people elsewhere, applied enormous creativity and imagination in their use of communication. They raised population issues to a high level of national concern and action, mobilized service providers, and helped couples towards the adoption of family planning.

In the Philippines, Louie Tabing (Chapter 7) fashioned a framework for community media and other inputs that successfully promotes local action towards self-sustaining development. The establishing of community media services could easily have become an aim in itself, but Tabing has never lost sight of the larger objective of empowering the poor to take their own initiatives and break out of their mould of apathy and inertia. (In this, the inspiration for his work is similar to Salcedo's.) Tabing has come up with the subtle formula of an open community media system, controlled by the community, with radio programming that opens the door to addressing the community's social and development problems. This is supported by the possibility of providing seed loans in a carefully controlled manner, and under conditions that are designed to promote responsibility in the way the funds are used and repaid.

All these people have had an inspired concept of how to use communication to help people to help themselves, and at the same time to help society. In addition, they have all been possessed of enormous energy and tenacity in pursuing their vision until it was realized. Indeed, as in many other areas of development, for example in the founding and running of development NGOs, success often depends to a large extent on the single person who is the driving force behind the operations, and once that person moves on, the initiative may well decline, and even disappear. This has often happened in communication work too, so the problem of institutionalizing communication for development, making it a routine part of development operations, remains generally unresolved. The PRODERITH experience, and what has been happening lately to Mexico's Rural Communication System, epitomize this situation.

Considerations for Future Communication Work

Even if the success of communication for development is often the result of the talent and drive of a few people, there are many other elements that lay the foundations for success. Certainly, all of the experiences described in this book, as well as examinations of failures – of which we have seen plenty and been involved in some – show that there are certain prerequisites and considerations for achieving good results.

Strategic planning

Communication succeeds when it is an integral part, from the very beginning, of a development programme, playing a full role during the identification of the problems and priorities, as well as during the detailed planning, implementation, and evaluation. When communication processes can be established from the beginning, they help to determine the areas of common need and interest among governments, people, development workers, and donor agencies. This leads to projects that are viable and sustainable because of the converging interests of all the parties involved. The communication inputs need to be continued throughout the life of the development initiative to enhance participation of all concerned, to help people to acquire new attitudes, knowledge and skills, and to ensure that the monitoring and evaluation activities reveal opinions from all levels of participants.

Communication needs clear objectives, identification of different audience groups, qualitative research with the audiences, careful message design and choice of channels, and monitoring and feedback, as detailed in Chapter 2. It needs to be based on an integrated approach, rather than a series of piecemeal or independent actions.

The addition of a 'communication component' to a development programme that has already been planned or is actually operating, is seldom cost-effective. Furthermore, communication inputs are often only thought of when the project is already suffering misunderstandings – and even hostility – from its so-called beneficiaries. It is usually too late to recover from this situation, and in any case, no amount of belated communication can 'sell' a project to people if it has been planned without them and does not meet their needs as they see them.

Multi-media approaches

Even if there are cases where really clever use of a single medium works well – for example, radio for the drama series *The Archers* – using different communication channels in a mutually reinforcing way usually gives better results. This calls for careful planning and coordination. For example, when dealing with a health issue, radio programmes about it will attract people's attention, but radio is not good for providing specific instructions about how to do something. So radio should be supported by wall-charts and other printed materials, and if possible by educational audio-visuals, to provide more explanations. Posters could be used to promote the recommended action and to serve as a reminder, over time, of the need for it. Health workers should also be briefed and trained to counsel people on the same topic. In this way, the same basic information will reach the audience from a variety of sources concurrently, and maximum effect will be achieved.

Communication media in orientation and training

The usefulness of communication materials, such as flip-charts, videos, slide sets, and pre-recorded cassettes, to improve the quality and impact of orientation and training of groups is well established. This applies at all levels of training, from illiterate peasants or urban poor, to field development workers, technicians, and government officials. However, the most difficult aspect of this use of communication is the design and the educational structure of the materials, especially when aiming to reach poorly educated groups. Research with the intended audiences, the incorporation of their concepts and language into a framework that fits their logic, and good pre-testing call for understanding, patience and flexibility from producers of materials.

There is no place for productions that try to be artistic and, in the end, satisfy the pride of their producers more than the needs of the intended audience. There was, in our opinion, an example of this problem a few years ago, in a pilot project in India to use television for agricultural information in selected villages. TV receivers were provided and placed in the school or other public place, and people would crowd in to watch TV in the early evening. However, an evaluation after some time showed that when the agricultural programme came on the air, a large number of people used to get up and leave.

We subsequently saw some of those programmes. They were very professional in terms of their shooting and editing, and any TV producer could have been proud of them. But perhaps the way they presented information and their content were the reason many small farmers did not care to watch them. For example, one programme showed how to plant sugar cane. It started well enough, but when it came to fertilizer treatments, it filled the screen with names and figures for several minutes. Another covered an agricultural fair and most of it was devoted to showing magnificent Sahiwal bulls, with their coloured rosettes attached to their heads, being led around the arena. Yet another showed a farmer building a mushroom production unit, an operation that obviously needed a considerable sum of start-up capital. These programmes seemed to have been produced without taking into account the capacities and needs of the small farmers they were intended to help.

When working with groups, those who are going to use communication materials need solid training in how to present them and lead a discussion. The presentation of communication materials is only part of a group communication process; the verbal introduction before an audio-visual presentation sets the context and should arouse the interest of the group, while the discussion that should follow is when the group interiorizes the information and decides whether to act on it.

Reaching a critical mass

A critical mass of communication activities is needed if they are to have an impact, and they must operate over an appropriate length of time. First, this implies having sufficient resources to employ qualified people and to have equipment and materials on hand, or to be able to contract competent private-sector organizations to conduct the work. And second, it implies having enough resources to be persistent. No one-off, single-shot effort will ever succeed in bringing about social change, for people need time for reflection and for the internalizing of information before they modify their perceptions and behaviour patterns. It may take repeated exposure to information to start the process.

Media hardware

Media hardware such as video-recording and playback equipment may be required, but those responsible for development programmes often believe that buying hardware is the main factor in solving their communication problems. For this reason, there are cameras, recorders, projectors, and video equipment gathering dust in cupboards all over the world. Equipment purchases should be made only after determining clear communication objectives, the needs, and the local conditions. Compatibility with existing equipment in the country, and the availability of repair and maintenance facilities, are important considerations.

When considering video equipment, the compatibility with nationally used television formats may become an issue. If the aim is to produce purely educational materials for peasants or urban poor, it may even be a disadvantage to go on major television channels. This is because the style of educational video is different from broadcast television, and if such programmes go on air, intellectual viewers will apply their urban and normal television criteria in judging them. As a result, they will probably complain that they are slow and boring, and ask why the producers are turning out such rubbish! If such a project needs a television programme or spot, it will probably be preferable to call in a commercial studio to produce it, with television-compatible equipment.

However, there are occasions when video equipment must be compatible with TV. In one African country where we worked, the Ministry of Agriculture's Communication Unit, which was being modernized and re-equipped by a development project, was supposed to produce a weekly farming programme for national television. An equipment consultant brought in by the project specified and supplied a video format that could not be used by the television station.

Careful thought must be given to this question of compatibility with television, taking into account the objectives of the project.

A particular problem is when a project budget contains a 'communication component' only to buy equipment. In the past, financing agencies, such as the World Bank, have often been major offenders in this regard. A particular example that continued for many years was the financing of very expensive mobile film or video units without considering whether there were existing and suitable films or videos to show, and if not, how they could be produced, and by whom. We have seen many of these vehicles in the hands of governments, with their audio-visual equipment stripped out, being used to transport people and goods. Fortunately, lending agencies are now becoming more aware that investment in communication equipment needs more thought.

Producers need training and time

People not conversant with the production of communication materials often imagine that it is a simple operation, quickly done, in the same way they operate their pocket camera for family snapshots. In fact, to produce really good informational or educational materials, which will convey their content effectively to the target audiences, is a skilled area of work. And it takes time. It is no accident that advertising agencies can spend weeks conceiving and producing a short spot for television. Yet development projects that buy equipment often indulge in the optimistic belief that someone in the project team, who has no specialized training, will produce informational and educational materials, often in addition to their normal duties. Of course, this seldom happens, and even if it does, the educational and communicational quality is usually poor. If equipment is to be bought, it should be clear beforehand who will be expected to use it, whether they have the professional competence, or whether they need training, and then they must be given the time necessary to produce quality materials.

The 'quality' question

Quality is strictly related to the function that a piece of communication material is expected to achieve. For example, a spot for a major national television channel to promote, say, breastfeeding, will need to be just as creative and well produced as the spot for the detergent or carbonated drink that appears in the same time slot. Otherwise, it may appear second-class and thereby lose impact. In addition to the general competition for attention from other television spots, there may also be occasions when there is a direct confrontation, as in the case of advertisements for infant formula and promoting breastfeeding, or advertisements for pesticides and promoting integrated pest management – which uses fewer chemical pesticides. The quality of the television materials in these circumstances will be crucial.

At the other extreme is what might be termed the 'quality of relevance'. A video which is technically bad, with poor shooting and editing, but which shows a situation that is highly relevant to the audience, and with which they identify, can have enormous impact.

We were once involved in a communication programme among milk producers in Argentina. The issue was whether or not the farmers should group together to add value to their product by making butter or cheese. The video produced to show both sides of the argument was technically very bad; there had been equipment compatibility problems and it was roughly edited. Nevertheless it sparked a very lively discussion when shown to groups of farmers. During the discussion in one group, we asked what they thought of the quality of the programme. The question was brushed aside with dismissive hand gestures, and one farmer said, 'The quality doesn't matter. It's what's in the video that's important.' And they resumed their animated discussion.

Thus, when communication materials are being used among a group of equals to spark off a discussion or analysis, formal quality is of little importance provided the content is relevant, but formal quality assumes increasing importance for materials that are trying to promote new ideas or actions, especially if they have to compete with commercial materials that are also appearing in the mass media.

Interpersonal and group communication

Good communication for development can not be done by media alone, and the quality and skills of technical staff making interpersonal contacts in the field and in the community play a central role. In Chapter 1, we looked at some of the problems that afflict the working relationship between farmers and agricultural extension staff. Those same problems apply to any technical staff trying to work with the poor, whether in rural areas or urban slums. Major improvements are needed in the way technical assistants work with their clients, whether they are dealing with agriculture, health, or any other development theme.

As a first step, it should be realized that providing technical advice calls for special personality traits and skills. At present, it is usually assumed that any person with specialized technical training can be a good agent of change at the community level. It is just not so, but there is seldom a screening process of potential technical assistance staff before they are despatched to work in the community. In addition, they seldom receive any special training, nor do they receive much guidance from more experienced people. A screening process should take into account a number of the important personality traits that are attributes of good development agents. Among them are humour, humility, patience, empathy, and a genuine interest in, and respect for, their client population.

Humour is important because a ready smile and a shared laugh are invaluable to bridging distances between people. It also helps to reduce the apprehensions the poorly educated may feel during their early contacts with technicians and other 'experts' from outside.

Without humility it is difficult for technicians to establish a good working relationship with people and to build a partnership for sharing knowledge and ideas, and for communicating as equals in trying to solve problems. Humility and respect for client populations go hand in hand, and unfortunately, it is difficult to develop either of these essential characteristics without a strong sense of self-assurance. For it is the confident people who do not fear loss of 'authority' by talking as equals with their 'inferiors' and listening carefully to what they have to say; it is the confident people who, when asked a question to which they do not know the answer, can say quite naturally that they do not know but that they will find out and return in a few days with the information. People who suffer from serious problems of insecurity will usually appear autocratic and dominating in their relationship with their clients.

Patience is essential, especially in rural areas, where people often live and work to a rhythm different from that of someone who was born in, or has spent much time in, a city. The pace of change is also much slower, and it may take considerable time before people agree to try something suggested by a technician. Of course, great patience is also required to make sure that people are really understanding the technician's point of view, and that he is understanding theirs.

Empathy is another requirement. A technician must be able to put himself in the shoes of the client, looking at the technical, social, and economic constraints in the same way as the client does. In the case of agriculture, farmers often make the point that technicians are not farmers themselves, and that when they recommend something, they are not taking the risk that the farmer must take if he accepts the recommendation. With very poor farmers, risk may be a major consideration, for a failure may tip the finely weighted balance of economic, or even physical, survival the wrong way. If the technician does not have the empathy to understand such a situation, he will never be successful.

Skilful listening is essential too. To listen carefully, with real interest, and to understand truly the thoughts being expressed by another person is an art that must be acquired. And leading group discussions also calls for special skills in which the leader stimulates and facilitates the process without ever dominating it.

Interpersonal and group communication skills, linked to certain personal characteristics, therefore lie at the heart of successful advisory work at the farm, community, or family level. Some people have a natural gift for relating to others and need a minimum of training, while others can have these skills considerably improved through training and experience. However, there will always be some people who are too insecure and introverted ever really to enjoy working with others. Even if they are technically well qualified, they need to be screened out early on. It is noteworthy that in Holland, the annual evaluation of agricultural advisers is now conducted with help from their client farmers. Salaries and career prospects depend on this performance evaluation. The result of this process has been that about a third of all the farm advisers have lost their jobs in recent years.

The question of organizational support and career development for technical staff working at the community or farm level is not truly part of the theme of this book. Nevertheless, it impinges so directly on communication for development that it cannot be ignored. For in effect, technical advisers working with their clients are at the cutting edge of development; they are the people who, in the final analysis, must help individuals and communities towards change and development. However, in many countries, work in the field is truly a hardship post. In much of Africa, for example, the facilities in rural areas and small towns are very poor, and the availability of educational facilities for children limited in quality. This naturally means that a government or NGO employee will want his or her children to be in a school in a main city while he or she is working in the countryside or in a small town. This often implies the extra expense of having two homes and paying for weekend travel.

These facts need to be recognized and compensated for accordingly, with prestige, career prospects, and conditions of employment. At present, a government development agent in the field, in addition to being low on the government pay scale, usually gets less total income than someone on the same scale living in a major city. This is because total salary packages usually include a cost of living element, which is lower for people in the countryside or small town. No account is taken of the extra costs of having the family divided. All in all, there is little incentive for good technicians to work in the countryside and communities, which is where they are needed.

Certainly, governments are under pressure from institutions like the World Bank and the International Monetary Fund to spend less on state services. In some cases we have seen, this has led to the ridiculous situation in which governments have fired large numbers of field extension staff without firing anyone working in the ministry headquarters, thereby leaving extension supervisors with hardly anyone to supervise. Of course, policy decisions are not always this ridiculous, but nevertheless, governments seldom seem to think of ways to make work in the field as attractive and rewarding as possible, but without having to pay out extra cash in salaries. For example, would it be so difficult to arrange for people doing good work in hardship areas to earn added seniority while they are there? This could take the form of faster promotions, or longer holidays, or even that each year spent in a difficult rural area could count for, say, 15 months of service.

Fundamentally, what is needed in most countries is to turn the hierarchical pyramid of technical ministries upside down and provide the maximum training and support for carefully selected people who are in contact with their clients in the communities and on the farms.

Communication for development is a specialized field

Communication for development has become a specialized field of work. It can be described as part science, part art, and part craft. It is part *science* because it draws heavily on the theory and methods of social and behavioural science, on individual and group psychology, and on principles of adult education; it is part *art* because it incorporates artistic talents and skills such as graphics, photography, radio and video production, instructional design and the like; and it is part *craft* because it involves manual skills with a variety of aids and equipment such as cameras, projectors, video recorders and editing suites, computers, and the paraphernalia of telecommunications and broadcasting. This mixture of knowledge and skills is not always readily available. Therefore, in many cases, a programme that is going to incorporate communication for development will need to call for technical assistance on other sectors in the country that have more experience, from neighbouring countries, or from international development agencies.

A holistic approach

Particularly among the extremely poor, a holistic approach is needed to help them change and develop. As we saw in Chapter 4, the case study of PRODERITH in Mexico, poor peasants do not see their problems in terms of separate components; rather, they see their reality as a single continuum in which the elements are interrelated.

Poor peasants, therefore, expect an integrated approach to helping them solve their problems. So in rural areas, it is not enough to deal only with agricultural production. Health, habitat, nutrition, and so on, will also need to be taken into account. As we have seen, this presents a major challenge to the compartmentalized government structures that are usually in place. Better communication between them is a first need, although some reorganization into cross-sectorial working groups would also be ideal.

Management, monitoring, and evaluation

The best communication programmes have always been extremely well managed, that is to say, proper coordination has been achieved with the various sectors and institutions involved, and the human and equipment resources have been well used. Without such rigorous management, it is easy to waste time and effort: equipment will become unserviceable; staff productivity will drop; and there may be institutional conflicts that damage the whole operation.

Monitoring is essential to ensure that the communication process is having the desired effect, and to identify any changes or adjustments that may be necessary, whereas final evaluation should provide information about the overall impact of the communication programme and its cost effectiveness. At the same time, evaluation should be the basis for future improvements in similar operations.

It is unfortunate that not enough has been done to evaluate the impact of communication programmes. In late 1994, we conducted a survey, sponsored by UNICEF and WHO, among high-level decision-makers in a large number of international development agencies to obtain their opinions about communication for development. All the interviewees stated that communication was of extreme importance in development, but they added that it had still not proven its economic effectiveness. The decision-makers wanted chapter and verse of the costs and benefits, with one respondent saying: 'You must demonstrate the power of communication if you are going to raise resources and support. You need proper evaluations, with an analysis of costs and benefits.'

Unfortunately, it is not easy to provide impact evaluations and the related economic costs/benefits of communication programmes, because human change is almost always also linked to other inputs as well, and it is difficult to separate out the effects of each. However, there are some types of social change and development that do lend themselves to impact evaluations, and it must be admitted that most communication specialists have been seriously negligent in even trying to develop evaluation instruments and methods. They sometimes blame lack of budgets, but where there is a will, there is a way, and only now are development communication specialists beginning to take evaluation as seriously as it deserves.

When evaluations have been done, especially of campaigns, they have often shown striking results. In 1983, there was a well-planned and well-executed campaign in Bangladesh, supported by FAO and the government of the Federal Republic of Germany, to reduce the damage done by rats in the wheat crop. It was planned and run along social marketing lines, and the objective was to convince producers of wheat on 1.5 million hectares to control rats in their fields with poison. Specifically, the aim was to raise the percentage of farmers applying rat control from the existing 10 per cent to 25 per cent in the first year.

About 4.6 million farming households were reached by the campaign. The cost for the production and distribution of communication materials was US$17,000, and poisoned rat-bait worth $23,000 was made available to farmers. In one year, the percentage of farmers who controlled rats in their fields rose from the existing 10 per cent to 40 per cent, well above the target. In that same year, the gain in wheat production from controlling rats was estimated at 5,045 tons, worth US$834,000 on the market. Thus an investment in communication and rat-bait worth about US$40,000 brought a benefit of US$834,000.

A similar rat campaign in Malaysia on 477 hectares of rice fields in Penang in the mid-1980s produced a return of US$2.6 for every dollar of campaign costs. Also in Malaysia, there was a campaign for integrated weed management in the Muda Irrigation Scheme. There were 30,000 farming families as the target audience, and the campaign was run between January and September 1989. It used radio and printed materials and, of course, interpersonal contacts. The evaluation conducted in 1990 showed that the total cost was US$46,400, and that rice production increased by 9,500 tons, equivalent to US$2.33 million, a return of 50:1.

Campaigns have also been applied to integrated pest management in rice, with major impact. In 1986, the government of Indonesia banned 57 of the 66 pesticides commonly used to protect the rice crop and adopted a policy of integrated pest management. The campaigns were used to motivate farmers and provide them with information about the techniques. The results were dramatic. The average number of pesticide applications on rice dropped from 4.5 to 0.5 per year, saving the country about US$35 million in pesticide costs. At the same time, average rice yields rose from 6.4 tons to the hectare in 1986 to 7.4 tons to the hectare in 1988.

These impact evaluations of campaigns are obviously important, but what are required in the future are cost–benefit analyses of other types of communication programme, for example for participatory planning and implementation of development projects, and for health. Communication for health has brought important social benefits. We only have to consider the children's lives saved by communication and social mobilization for UCI–1990, described in Chapter 3. An estimated 12 million lives were saved in the six years after the drive for Universal Child Immunization began in 1984, and after 1990, an estimated 3 million or more lives a year have been saved. How can this be translated into economic and cost–benefit terms? Surely, economists could establish some ways of reaching figures. The same should be true for breastfeeding campaigns, which in many countries have increased the number of mothers who breastfeed and expanded its average duration. It should not be impossible to calculate the positive benefits in terms of cash saved on infant formula, heating costs for the water, better health and fewer medical costs for the child. On the other side of the scale, there may be certain disadvantages, such as the loss of flexibility to undertake jobs outside the home in circumstances where employers still do not provide facilities and time for mothers to breastfeed their infants during the day. Such possible drawbacks should also be weighed in the balance.

The costs of communication

The cost of effective communication as part of development pro-grammes has normally been about 10 per cent of the total budget. For large programmes, especially those with a major investment in infrastructure such as PRODERITH (Chapter 4), it can be as low as 1 to 2 per cent of the budget. Communication for small projects working intensively with communities and people may require up to 15 per cent for communication.

For several years, there were attempts in the UN system to have 1 per cent of project budgets automatically assigned to communica-tion. When this actually happened without a proper analysis of the communication needs, and therefore without a communication strat-egy, the money was usually spent on equipment that was seldom put to good use. A fixed percentage is not, therefore, a solution. It is much better to examine the communication needs and possibilities from the very beginning, as an integral part of the whole of the project's life, and design and budget the communication component accordingly.

In conclusion, much has been learned about how to plan and imple-ment successful communication for development; what remains to be accomplished is that policy-makers recognize its importance and provide the relatively modest resources necessary for it to be the catalyst without which other development inputs are often wasted.

CHAPTER 9

Towards Communication Policies

Any successful attempt to make communication a part of national development and change will depend on a democratic spirit among decision-makers and on the political will to make it happen. Only then will all the other elements such as legislation, organizational structures, operational methods, training of staff, and financing be able to fall into place. Furthermore, a lack of political will, or a reluctance among government staff to engage in democratic processes with their so-called client populations, can nullify communication efforts and create frustration among those populations.

We had a personal experience of such government reluctance quite recently. We were working in Uganda on a Farming Systems Support Programme funded by the European Union. The programme was essentially involved in helping small-scale coffee-growers, but an evaluation of the project had found that the work was essentially top-down in nature, and it did not involve farmers sufficiently. The evaluators recommended that any follow-up project should be planned with farmers.

Our assignment was with the Agricultural Communication Unit in the Ministry of Agriculture, and one of our tasks had been to provide training in qualitative research and Participatory Rural Appraisal techniques. Thus the evaluation mission's recommendation about planning with farmers was the cue for us to go out and do qualitative research to find out how farmers saw their coffee production problems, what they could do to help themselves, and what help they needed from outside. We and our Ugandan colleagues spent several weeks in the field working with numerous groups of farmers.

Somewhat to our surprise, the farmers themselves identified a number of actions they could take, especially with regard to selling their crop. Their common experience was that the buyers cheated them. For example, buyers used a variety of different containers, ranging from buckets to sawn-off oil drums or baskets, and declared that their particular container held, say, 8 kilogrammes of coffee. But the farmers had no way of checking. During the discussions, many of the farmers' groups themselves came to the conclusion that they could improve their bargaining power with buyers if they brought their coffee to a central place and sold it together. On the other hand, they wanted the government to license the buyers and establish a standard measure for determining the weight of the coffee they were selling. In addition to this particular finding, the field research brought to light a wide range of other valuable information for future development actions.

The plan was to bring all this information to a seminar in the ministry that would be attended by senior policy-makers and planners. About ten days ahead of time, invitations were sent to 18 of these functionaries. Written reports of the field findings were prepared, and the flip-charts recording the conclusions of each farmers' group were hung on the walls of the seminar room, with a photograph of each group to add authenticity. Two farmers' representatives were invited to participate in the seminar, so that they could vouch for the research findings and add any other pertinent information.

However, of the 18 invitees, only 6 turned up on the day, and they were relatively junior. There was no meaningful discussion that could lead to decisions, and the lack of interest and commitment from the ministry side in the presence of representatives of the farmers, who had devoted so much of their time and goodwill to the operation, was deeply embarrassing. As long as governments continue to behave in this way, it will be extremely difficult to achieve sustainable development.

The situation was even worse with ACPO in Colombia (Chapter 5), when there was active hostility from the establishment. The collapse of ACPO shows clearly what can happen when grassroots-level democracy and empowerment are taking place in a national context that is fundamentally undemocratic, even if the country may officially call itself a 'democracy'.

Fortunately, however, genuine democracy has been spreading in recent years, and this, coupled with decentralization processes gathering speed in country after country, provides real opportunities for people to play a full part in their own development. And another positive element for the future is that, as democracy grows, many governments may well realize that the people and popular movements are better able to identify and propose solutions for social, environmental, and other problems than governments themselves. This could open the way further for the encouragement of social communication to tap the capacities and energies of society.

As mentioned in Chapter 1, all the recent summits or world conferences on development issues have called for governments to make use of their educational structures and mass media facilities to help promote change and development. However, they have been less than explicit as to how this might be achieved. Only Agenda 21 from the Earth Summit made a practical, if somewhat vague, suggestion when it called for a 'special cooperative relationship with the media, popular theatre groups, and the entertainment and advertising industries to mobilize their experience in shaping public behaviour and consumption patterns'.

In effect, all the summits implicitly echoed the opinion of Paul Kennedy, in *Preparing for the Twenty-First Century*, that 'nothing less than the re-education of humankind' is called for. The issue was put differently, but with a similar sense, by Dr Soedjatmoko of the UN University in Tokyo when he said: 'If development is not growth, not resources, not wealth alone – what is it? I think it is, above all, learning. The learning needed by individuals, communities, and nation states to prepare themselves to live in the future.'

But how? We are living in the midst of an information and communication revolution. Governments, national and international institutions, societies, and communities need to grasp the concept and opportunity of using that revolution to stimulate change, sustainable development – and perhaps, in the ultimate, survival.

Since the collapse of Marxist systems of government, the US models of market economies and commercial media, with their related cultural values, are being exported everywhere. So what is happening in the media scene in the USA will probably have repercussions on what happens in other countries too. But unfortunately, US media operations, with their usually unbridled commercial interests, are hardly a suitable model for all countries to follow.

An article in the *Washington Post* of 5 March 1996 by Edwin M. Yoder Jr described some of the programmes that were on air in the USA during the daytime when children are often at home without parental supervision. He singled out the *Sally Jessy Raphael Show*, which specialized in 'sexual voyeurism'. It included items such as 'Teen Sex – Better in the House', 'Mom, I'm a Teen Prostitute', and 'My Daughter is a Tramp'. On another programme, the *Montel Williams Show*, a recent item had shown 'a row of louts explaining, with a smirk, why they had a right to "rape" any woman who disappointed their expectations on a first or second date'. Yoder commented: 'Either they misconstrue the word rape (no wonder, given its continuing trivialization) or the Visigoths are indeed at the gates.'

But as we write this, a quiet revolution seems to have begun in the USA. Objections against the violence and sex on the screen have been mounting from all sides of the political spectrum, as well as from the general public. For decades, the mass media in the USA and in other Western countries vigorously denied any causal effect among young people of violence and sex in their programmes, and they were quite often supported by academic studies. But now, people seem to realize that excessive media presentation of acts of violence and sex *must* legitimize such acts as normal and acceptable behaviour; perhaps it even becomes *desirable* behaviour for young people wishing to emulate their heroes.

A new Tele-Communications Act, which became law in the USA in February 1996, gave power to the Federal Communications Commission to impose a rating system for television programmes – similar to those for cinema films to denote their suitability for child and adolescent audiences – if the media industry itself failed to introduce such a system. This, and the so-called V (for violence) chip, which is to be introduced into all new television sets to allow families to block out programmes they find objectionable, are the first legislative steps to attempt to limit harmful effects of mass media. However, the press has already pointed out that the rating system and the V chip will make no difference when children are watching television alone, as so many do.

Jim Hoagland, the well-known *Washington Post* commentator, wrote an article published on 4 March 1996 in the *International Herald Tribune* about the fundamental values in United States society, the choices facing it, and the mass media. He stressed the point that in the last 50 years, Americans of all political colours had made a series of choices that had culminated in a society in which the freedom to choose and to consume were the ultimate values, turning the country into the 'greatest national bazaar that history has ever known'.

He wrote that the Americans were now facing 'epochal economic and cultural choices' about which the politicians and the media had done little to enlighten the nation. The fundamental choices were between 'unfettered consumerism and the social discipline that a more regulated and structured society can achieve'. He went on to write:

Nor have we Americans been prepared to accept the trade-offs that would have been involved in serious regulation of the most powerful non-military technology ever invented, television and the cinema industry, so as to set a national cultural and political tone, and to encourage values guided by something other than the marketplace.

Hoagland thus identified the potential power of the mass media to sway, in a positive direction, the values of a society and the way it functions. However, it is not only in the USA that this perception has been missing.

The Dislocation Between National Media and National Development

It is indeed curious how governments almost never link the objectives of their communication sector with their social, human, and economic development objectives. In most countries, ministries of information and/or communications confine their concerns to the development and maintenance of telecommunication infrastructures, running of state-owned broadcasting systems, and granting licences and frequencies to commercial broadcasters. Their work seldom, if ever, takes into account the broader social issues that the communication sector could influence.

We came across a classic example in Bolivia in 1995 of this dichotomy between mass media policies and national development policies. To be more precise, they were actually in opposition to each other. The country, which is one of the poorest in Latin America, had recently launched its Popular Participation Law. In effect, this is an important decentralization programme that will, over time, delegate most decisions to the local level, and provide funds to implement them.

There are a total of 519 radio stations operating in Bolivia, and many of them are of an educational, peasant, or community nature. In fact, the country has one of the longest and broadest experiences of community radio anywhere, beginning with small stations in mining communities in the 1950s. Obviously, in the framework of the new decentralization programme, local radio could play a particularly important part in arousing community interest and participation in local policy and development decisions.

However, despite the potential importance of community radio in the country's new policy circumstances, the government passed a new Telecommunications Law in August 1995 under which, in future, licences will be granted only to radio and television stations of a commercial character. They will have to be 'enterprises organized in accordance with [the country's] Commercial Code', which in practice means public or private limited companies.

The licences of existing and well-established educational radio stations, most belonging to the Church or to NGOs, will be allowed to run for another 20 years before they fall under the new law. But the numerous community and peasant stations in existence, many of which in fact do not have licences, were debarred from operating after May 1996, at least legally, unless they had their papers in order. If they are closed down, their frequencies are to be awarded to the highest bidder, which of course favours the powerful commercial networks.

On the face of it, this new law seems to be contrary to all logic; a country that is committed to community participation at the same time makes it extremely difficult, if not impossible, for community radio to play its classic role of being a forum for discussion, consensus building, and democratic local decisions. The only glimmer of hope on the horizon is that those pressuring the government not to pass the law in its existing form managed to obtain a concession that any broadcasting law that might be passed in the future would override the 1995 one on telecommunications.

Colombia provides an interesting example of a similar dislocation between the media and national development. During the last two decades, successive governments have launched various national plans to eliminate absolute poverty, to improve health, to provide integrated development for peasants, to promote national reconciliation, to decentralize many government functions to the municipal level, and, most recently, to bring about a 'social leap'.

However, during most of those same two decades, the analysis of these social and development problems, and the plans to resolve them, contained no reflections whatsoever on how the national communication system might play a role. To be more specific, the National Planning Office – equivalent to a ministry – never ever referred to the potential of the communication media in areas such as generating or distorting consumption patterns, creating internal demand, enlisting citizens' participation in the decentralization process, or improving basic education and health. Nor was any mention ever made of the possible effect of the mass media in the home, the basic unit around which the various actions to eliminate absolute poverty were to be centred.

Another indication of this dichotomy between the communication sector and the social, cultural, and economic development goals set by the other parts of government is that the Communications Division of the National Planning Office was located in its Infrastructure Department, and this deals only with the technical aspects of telecommunications.

Finally, however, in the late 1980s, Colombia began to address the problems just described. The social mobilization efforts for child immunization and other children's interests had been particularly successful in Colombia, and the country was in many ways a model for others in this respect. Stimulated by these achievements, the government, with advice from UNICEF, began to reflect on its successful communication experience and how it might be furthered and expanded for broader areas of social development. The result was the setting up of a Division of Social Communication in the Ministry of Communications.

This fledgling operation has not had an easy time. Its relatively junior staff have not always been in a position to exert the necessary influence, either within their own ministry or in the many others that are involved in social development issues. However, by 1996, better progress was being made. The division had been entrusted with a number of national and international contracts. One was for communication about drug-crop substitution; another was for a water and sanitation programme in the very poor and isolated area of the Pacific Coast; and another was to provide policy advice regarding new legislation for local and community radio stations.

A major problem the division faces is that of trying to develop activities that cut across many different government sectors. It also has to be on its guard against possible attempts at political influence. So far, most of its work has been in support of individual programmes for a single sector. It will be interesting to see, over time, whether it will be able to influence national policies to merge the objectives and activities of the communication sector with those of human and social development.

A New Development Paradigm?

Proper attention to communication and the human dimensions of change and development would call for some radical rethinking of the way things are done and organized at present. Bernard Woods, who spent 15 years working in the field in rural development, followed by a further period of 15 years in the World Bank head-quarters, is the author of a book called *Communication, Technology and the Development of People.* He calls for nothing less than a new paradigm, based on changes in concepts and a new framework for thinking and acting about development.

Given that the pursuit of modernization and higher GNP does not necessarily lead to improvements in human and social development for all, Woods states that a more meaningful aim in present circumstances is the development of people, and of groups, communities, and institutions. However, even if a lot has been written about the need for human and social development, an adequate conceptual and practical basis for achieving it has not yet been established.

A principal obstacle in the path of human and social development, and the use of communication to help achieve it, is Western society's reductionist thinking and the structures it has created. As infants, we naturally learn holistically. That is to say, as we explore our environment and gain experiences, we quite naturally apply what we discover in one field to what we know in another. So we start life by building a multi-disciplinary thinking style, and many traditional societies maintain it through adulthood. For example, people living in difficult circumstances, such as in deserts or harsh mountains, survive because their holistic approach, based on ancestral and present experience, allows them to bring together numerous elements into knowledge and skills that perfectly meet the needs of life in their circumstances. Many of these elements come from what in Western society have become specialized and professional fields, such as botany, zoology, hydrology, meteorology, and so on.

When children go through formal education systems, they get forced away from holistic thinking. There is a vast body of knowledge to be taught in schools, so it is categorized and organized for convenience and to make things easier for the teachers. In this way, subjects and disciplines are created. This reductionist process is such that as education proceeds, more and more is learned about less and less. Knowledge and disciplines are put into separate compartments. As Woods says, 'Our education systems have created our conventional disciplines – and the barriers between them.'

Reductionist thinking and compartmentalized knowledge have led to structures, both in government and in international development organizations, that are similarly divided into compartments, and frequently there is little interaction between them. During an interview we had with a high-ranking official in a UN agency, he pointed out that development institutions are staffed by economists, engineers, and technicians, and added:

> Our training for development work is fractured. I am a development economist, and I can tell you that few of us are focused on the fact that economics cannot work if people don't know what it is all about. We have to train development technicians to realize that their work can only have relevance if people know what is required and to what ends. Yet our training does not include communication.

The result of the compartmentalization of disciplines, of development institutions and government structures, is that the multi-sectoral approach needed for human and social development is difficult to achieve. To quote Woods again:

> We all, naturally, seek solutions in our own field of specialization and through the organizations and institutions through which we work. Information is generated and received within each discipline and sector. Budgeting processes, existing mandates, and staff profiles perpetuate existing organizations. We all accept information that reinforces our current way of thinking and reject information that appears to undermine it. These and other forces tend to maintain the status quo. Few people are rewarded in governments, large bureaucracies, or academia for questioning traditional disciplines and existing organizational structures. To suggest that conventional disciplines and the organizations in place for development are part of the problem is heresy!

Among the various technical fields of development work, communication is in a particularly difficult situation. It is not yet recognized as a sector, and partly in consequence of this, there is no obvious place to locate the function in the existing organizational structures in such a way that it could help all the other sectors.

Technical ministries in many countries have established their own communication units, but seldom with much degree of success. There are, of course, exceptions, an outstanding one being the Indonesian population communication unit in BKKBN, described in Chapter 6. But for the most part, on government pay scales, and with the usual administrative constraints of most government services, few really creative people ever stay with government communication units for long. They can generally find much better pay and more dynamic conditions in the private sector. In addition, most of these units just produce materials of an informational nature about health, agriculture or whatever. They have rarely, if ever, become involved in the whole communication and human dimension of development, from analysing the attitudinal and behavioural situation to devising an appropriate communication strategy and putting it to work.

This ministry-by-ministry approach has also tended to fraction what ever communication activities for development were actually in process. This has reduced the impact of each, and in some cases it has led to conflicting, confusing, or at best incomplete information reaching the public. When, for example, have we ever seen a joint effort between a ministry of agriculture and a ministry of health to communicate together about irrigated agriculture and the waterborne diseases its expansion can cause?

It is true that social mobilization for child vaccination, as described in Chapter 3, brought together many different government and non-government sectors to work and communicate jointly, but that was a rare situation, and the success in reaching Universal Child Immunization by 1990 is a good demonstration of the impact that can be achieved when sectors can be brought together to focus on one specific social aim.

A new development paradigm, which integrates communication routinely, would have many of the features of what was done for child immunization. Some important organizational changes would perhaps be necessary to institutionalize such cross-sector cooperation and have it become the norm rather than the exception.

Mali Making History

Mali is establishing a national policy of communication for development. It is a pleasant surprise to find such an initiative in a country of the Sahel, one of the poorest areas in the world, and with enormous natural problems. The country is landlocked, and most of its vast area is desert and scrub. Of its estimated 10 million people, almost 80 per cent live in rural areas, most of them as little better than subsistence farmers. Livestock is a vital element in the national economy, but when drought hits, as it often does, the animals die like flies, and much of the human population needs food aid to escape death by famine. To add to all of its natural problems, the country has for several years been under a draconian structural readjustment programme, imposed by the international community, which has greatly diminished resources for government spending.

During the 1980s, the country lived through an economic,

financial, and political crisis that finally blew up in severe social disturbances in March 1991, leading to the overthrow of the government. A new transition government took over, pending democratic elections. It organized consultations with representatives from among the rural people, and learned some interesting things.

It became clear to the new government that after years of an authoritarian regime, during which the media had been used vertically to give instructions, and government agents in the field were equally despotic, the peasantry had become thoroughly disaffected. The lack of any form of dialogue with government staff had led the peasantry to hide their ideas and opinions behind what was termed a 'mirror of protocol' in all their contacts with officialdom. Rural people felt alienated by the government's imposed development programmes and preferred to have nothing to do with them. The agricultural extension staff had lost all acceptability and credibility because of their working methods.

From those consultations, a new principle for rural development was founded: in future, it would take into account the peasants' concerns and aspirations. With this focus, when the newly elected democratic government came to power in May 1992, it declared its interest in establishing a national policy of communication for development as part of its overall economic, social, political, and cultural plans for the country.

This new emphasis in national development policy hinged on the following points: to break with the earlier system of vertical communication and replace it with communication aimed at participation and feedback; to design information and communication strategies and plans that would help to achieve national development objectives; to establish a dialogue between decision-makers and the people about the objectives and scope of development; to disseminate and replicate successful village-level development experiences; and to associate people in the design, implementation, and monitoring of development projects.

A first practical step towards realizing its objectives in communication for development was a series of 'national days on information and communication' during which the issues were reflected on and discussed by representatives of all sectors concerned. The outcome was a decision to create a High Council for Communication, and legislation was passed for this at the end of 1992. However, it proved difficult to agree the composition of the High Council and some months passed before the problem was finally resolved.

FAO and UNDP had a long-standing interest in what was taking place, for they had been supporting a project for rural communication and training based on the same video methodology used in PRODERITH, Mexico (Chapter 4). This methodology, as noted, was begun in Chile in the early 1970s and then developed in Peru with FAO help spread over almost ten years. In fact it was two Peruvians, originally trained under that project, who went to Mali as international advisers to set up the project there. It is known as CESPA, initials in French for Centre for Audio-Visual Production Services. The successful experience of CESPA was certainly one of the elements that influenced the government towards its decision in favour of communication for development.

In October 1993, a national workshop was organized to discuss a policy for communication for development. FAO and UNDP provided technical and financial support for this workshop, which was the first of its kind ever held anywhere. The objectives were to hammer out details of the policy and to agree activities and a timetable to have the policy become operational. The workshop began by establishing certain principles, for example that one function of a national communication policy was to create a climate of trust between the country's internal and external partners in order to achieve concerted action for tackling Mali's problems. Another principle was that the communication system should provide a space in which all the actors in development could dialogue and work towards consensus, transparency and equity within the country's overall development policies. It was also recognized that, within the decentralization process that the government was launching, communication would be essential to help people towards participation in decision-making and the management of their own affairs.

The workshop identified main objectives for a national system of communication for development. These were: to help establish agreed guidelines for rural development policy; to feed the dialogue desired by the government, civil society, and development partners; and to assist the emergence of a legislative framework that would permit and promote dialogue between the public sector and rural people, and at the same time improve the quality and responsibility of that relationship.

Specific areas of development that were identified for action by the communication system were: the use and protection of natural resources, with special attention to fighting the desertification that afflicts much of the country; the promotion of girls and women in

Malian society; the evolution and adaptation of the school system to meet the real needs of the people; improvements in health; population programmes; and urban environment and sanitation.

Many practical problems were identified by the workshop. Among them were: to decentralize the Malian national radio and television services; to create appropriate juridical and institutional arrangements; to recognize the profession of 'communicators for development' and provide training in it at the University of Mali; to improve the communications skills of intermediate-level professionals working in development programmes; to create a communication unit within each ministry; and to define its strategies and implement communication programmes.

A major problem would be coordination across the different development sectors. The workshop decided that the best solution was to set up an Inter-Sectoral Coordinating Committee, under the aegis of the High Council for Communication, to deal with day-to-day planning and operational aspects of communication for development.

Other countries are following Mali's example in beginning to create national policies for communication for development. Guinea Bissau has gone through a process very similar to that in Mali. The main difference was that in Guinea Bissau, instead of creating a policy unit in the form of a High Council for Communication, as in Mali, a coordinating committee was set up in the office of the prime minister. In 1997, it is expected that the Central African Republic, the Congo, and Burkina Faso will also follow the earlier examples.

FAO has been instrumental in instigating these processes, and they appear to be on the right track. FAO has correctly identified some prerequisites for establishing national policies of communication for development. Among them are: a socio-political environment that is conducive to participatory development and democratic decision-making; political support at the highest level, as in Mali from the president; a focal point, with a secretariat, to initiate and conduct the process; a series of preliminary studies and surveys of communication needs, available resources, and existing legislation; and a national workshop, with the participation of all stakeholders, to define the policy and action plan. FAO also makes the important point that a national communication policy cannot, and should not, be an aim in itself. Rather, it should be integrated with other sectoral development priorities, complementing them and helping them to meet their objectives.

It is still early days in these interesting initiatives, and it would be a reason for justified pride if some of these countries, poor as they are, were to make a first major breakthrough in applying communication to development on a national scale.

Bringing Communication into National Development

Politicians understand the value of communication better than most people; they use it in their election campaigns, and they continue to use it to bolster their personal prestige after they have been elected. If they appreciate communication for their personal ends, it seems logical for them to apply it to development as well. And indeed, when top politicians can be reached with a concrete proposal in the area of communication for development, they are usually receptive to the idea. The late James P. Grant, the executive director of UNICEF until 1995, told us that he never had any difficulty convincing heads of state and other politicians of the need for communication to achieve specific targets in the interests of children. The problem was with the technical people in government, he said.

The politicians' interest and instinct for communication has another side, and that is where the risk lies: they will often try to appropriate what is supposedly communication for development for their personal interests. We have seen several communication units of ministries that devote most of their energies to press coverage and video footage of the minister on ceremonial occasions, such as cutting the ribbon to open a fair, building, or whatever.

Nor should it be forgotten that there have been classic cases in quite recent history when governments' main information aim was to brainwash their people and feed them only selected information. Goebbels' Ministry of Propaganda in Nazi Germany was perhaps the most odious form of this ever seen, although the Kremlin in the past, and many other repressive regimes, have followed a similar strategy. However, feeding selected information to people is not the sole domain of repressive regimes. As recently as 'Operation Desert Storm' to expel the Iraqi forces from Kuwait, there was major manipulation of the information fed to the general public in Western countries. Many people believed that they were fully and accurately informed with regard to progress in the war, but information specialists have since commented that never had there been so much television coverage of a war, with people knowing so little of what was truly happening. For example, all the film footage of smart bombs in action was broadcast repeatedly. The public saw those bombs go down air-vents on roofs, and saw them zigzag across Baghdad and explode in their target buildings, but they never saw footage of the numerous and generally unsuccessful attempts to destroy bridges over the Tigris in Baghdad with conventional bombs. In this way, people were left with a false impression of the accuracy of the bombing in general.

In conclusion, although politicians may well be open to proposals to use communication to help solve national development problems, the risk that they may want to appropriate the system for political ends, or manipulate the information, must be taken into account. An institutional arrangement that spreads control of the communication system over a number of stakeholders – in the form of a committee or commission as in Mali – can guard against political take-overs by a self-interested minority. This is also the strategy being used by the Tambuli Community Media project (Chapter 7) at a local level to ward off take-overs.

Communication policy and appropriate legislation

A systematic use of communication for development obviously requires an initial policy-level decision, followed by the sort of process that Mali has been undertaking. Many countries do not even have a statement of principle in their legislation concerning their communication sector, one that defines and guarantees the rights of society and individuals to information and communication. Nor does their policy define and ensure the social and public service character of their national communication media.

In effect, a prerequisite is that the recognition of the communication sector include not only its power in the economy, but also its power in shaping attitudes, values, and behaviour patterns, and in non-formal education and development. To clarify those points is obviously a first necessity in planning a role for communication in national development.

At a more operational level, the policy decision might require that communication, consultation, and participatory planning be used to establish needs and guidelines *prior* to formulating new development proposals. For governments who felt unable to enter into democratic processes of consultation, a less ambitious policy could be the systematic use of communication activities and media to guide and promote the objectives of development programmes that are already established, even if sustainable development would be less likely in those circumstances.

Whatever the emphasis, communication should be conceived and planned as a function that cuts across all sectors, because people need information based on an integrated view of their situation. For example, nutrition and agriculture are closely related in rural areas, and schools can play a major supporting role in informing children, and through them their parents, about these topics. So the ministries of health, agriculture, and education would need to coordinate their communication efforts to obtain the best results and to avoid disseminating incomplete, and perhaps contradictory, information.

In addition to reaching the people with maximum effect to help them towards changes in attitude and behaviour, such inter-sectoral coordination and cooperation also favours effective action programmes at the field level. For example, we might see the agriculture, health, and education sectors working hand in hand to promote and create good school gardens in the interests of better nutrition.

The policy should also formally integrate the activities of the country's communication system into the national development objectives, whether the system is state-owned, commercial, or mixed, and identify mechanisms for doing so. New legislation may be needed to put these policy decisions into practice. For example, not all countries grant licences to commercial radio and television stations with the condition that they provide some free air-time regularly for programmes of public or social interest. Some countries that do lay down this condition – say for one hour of free air-time a week – do not specify at what time of day. The result is that the public and social interest items may go on air when hardly anyone is watching or listening. This is also demotivating for the people entrusted with the production of the programmes, and quite often, the institutions that should be taking advantage of the free air-time give up completely and stop producing programmes.

Since community and local radio stations can be very effective in creating communication processes to speed change and development, there should be legislation in their favour. In many countries, especially in Africa, where state-run broadcasting along the old French and British models was established, it has often been difficult to decentralize broadcasting services. Especially where there are different ethnic groups, with their own languages, the central powers and any majority ethnic groups have been scared out of their minds by the thought of the sedition and revolution that they imagine could spread from some tiny community radio service out in the bush. We mentioned, in Chapter 7, the Allard transmitter at Homa Bay in Kenya, which was closed down after a few months of operation because the authorities said it was increasing tribal tensions.

Fortunately, however, these attitudes are changing in many African countries. For example, there are now several of the small transmitters like the one installed in Homa Bay working freely in different parts of Burkina Faso. In other continents, where ethnic differences may be less widespread, or where the mass media are essentially commercial, there has been less political resistance to setting up decentralized broadcasting services.

Institutional arrangements

In the past, large development programmes have sometimes had their own communication units, with complete capacity for communication research and planning, for the production of media, and for training. An example of this was PRODERITH, described in Chapter 4. In other cases, a central communication unit of a technical ministry has been used to support development programmes, sometimes using the media infrastructure of the ministry of information in addition.

Technical ministries, governmental, and non-governmental institutions quite often have their own communication units, which they use to support their development programmes. This separate communication work by different ministries and institutions has certain drawbacks; it may be wasteful of resources, and the lack of cross-sectoral coordination may cause a loss of effectiveness. A major improvement could be achieved if there were a policy framework and an organizational structure for coordinating communication work, but with each ministry or institution continuing to do its own within that policy and coordinating framework. Indeed, as in Mali, every development ministry or institution should be encouraged to create its own communication capability, but subject to overall policies and coordination.

One step that could be the cornerstone of a suitable institutional arrangement would be the creation of what we might call a Development Communication Policy and Programming Unit at central decision-making level. In many countries, the ministry of planning, or its equivalent, has a certain authority over the others, and this would be a natural location for the unit. In some cases, where the head of state has advisory offices for such things as human rights, women's affairs, and the like, the unit could be added to that circle. But at that level, the risk of political interventions and distortions would be greater.

The Communication Policy and Programming Unit would not have an executive function. From its position at a policy-making level in government, it could keep abreast of the most recent national policies and objectives, advise decision-makers about communication issues and their importance, and set the overall priorities for communication work in the light of the needs and opportunities. Staffing of the unit could be small in numbers but it would need to be high in professional quality. Its overall function would be to guide and support ministries, development institutions, people's organizations, and other participants in the development process in the planning, implementation, and evaluation of their communication work.

Among its specific activities, it could organize and convene a Steering and Coordination Group made up of a high-level representative from each of the sectoral ministries and institutions and the head of the Communication Unit of each. This group would meet on a regular basis to review the communication needs and activities of each sector, and to coordinate and integrate activities whenever possible. The purpose would be to make best use of the available resources and ensure optimum effectiveness of the communication programmes.

In addition, the staff of the Policy and Programming Unit could provide advice and technical assistance to each ministry's — or other institution's — communication unit, arrange joint training courses, and on request, organize evaluations of the various communication programmes. For the training and for the evaluations, they would call on outside resources such as universities and private-sector organizations.

It would be useful to develop a written mandate for communicators working within the framework of a national policy of communication for development. This mandate would explain clearly that their task was to use communication skills, techniques, and media specifically for participatory situation analysis and planning, for training, and for institutional communication within the framework of change and development. This would delineate the scope of the activities and avoid possible confusion with public affairs, journalism, or even political exercises.

The services for research, planning, and media production could be arranged in different ways, according to circumstances. Where individual communication units were already involved in the production of materials, they might want to continue, but with support, advice, training, and coordination from the Policy and Programming Unit. Alternatively, they might get better quality by sub-contracting part of the media research and production work to stronger and better communication units in other ministries or institutions, to NGOs, or to the private sector, as is happening increasingly in the field of health. Small countries could decide to establish a single communication service to handle all of their development needs.

Training in communication for development

The world is packed with universities and other educational establishments providing training in 'communication' or even in 'social communication'. However, almost without exception, the courses they provide are in journalism, public relations, advertising, or various aspects of media production. A survey conducted in Latin America in 1985 by FAO showed that there were more than 400 institutions providing training in 'communication'. Not one of them was providing courses specifically linking communication to social and economic development.

There has been some progress since then, but courses in communication for development are still very rare. Those who started working in the field when it was first launched in the late 1960s – many of whom are still working in it today – came from a variety of different backgrounds. Since it was a new activity, much of the work was experimental and the practitioners were learning as they went along. Some were lucky to work in a wide variety of situations, using different strategies and media, and came to have a broad knowledge of the whole discipline, but they are not too numerous.

In fact, during the survey about communication for development among senior decision-makers in international agencies that we conducted in 1994, a majority of interviewees said there was a severe shortage of competent people who could apply strategic communication within development programmes. In addition, many commented that it was a field calling for special skills. They were of the opinion that there was no shortage of media specialists, such as photographers, radio or video programme producers, journalists, and so on, but people with an overall understanding of communication in a development context were difficult to find.

We would add that, since the training of most of the media producers is for news, advertising or for other productions with a commercial focus, their thinking is based on different criteria from those needed in communication for development. For example, one of us (S.R.-E.) was producing a series of educational videos on child care and nutrition with a professional cameraman. Initially, his main concern was the visual balance and artistic effect of each shot, rather than its clarity of message and its likely educational impact among mainly illiterate mothers. What he was required to do was a totally new concept for him, but after it had been explained to him in detail, he became fully interested and involved.

The other author (C.F.) was once working with an educational photographer making a film-strip to help train illiterate or semi-literate tractor drivers in developing countries in how to operate a complex tractor model. We worked solidly, day after day, on the manufacturer's premises. We carefully set up each shot to show, for example, the hydraulic controls with the operator's hand in different positions. We staged each scene to exclude anything that was not relevant to the message we wanted the photograph to convey, and we used bounce flash to eliminate reflections from the bright paintwork that might confuse the eye and reduce the educational impact.

The manufacturer's professional photographer passed by regularly on his way to the canteen for a cup of tea or a meal. He simply could not believe how much time we were taking in our work. On each occasion that he came past he said, 'Good God! You're not *still* taking photographs of that same tractor, are you?' He was an excellent photographer, but his work and the criteria he applied were quite different. For the most part, when the manufacturer's sales department wanted attractive photographs for advertisements or for a publicity brochure, he would go into the field with the piece of machinery in question, shoot four or five rolls of film, and be done in less than half a day.

Such media producers can, of course, be given the appropriate orientation for working in development, which often calls for putting educational criteria ahead of artistic ones. However, it does take time and working experience to become skilled in the new approach. Practical courses are needed for media producers interested in applying their skills to social and educational communication.

University-level courses are needed in the overall concepts of strategic planning, implementation, and evaluation of communication for development. These could be added as a distinct field of specialization towards the end of courses in general communication. Alternatively, they could be at postgraduate level for people with first degrees in other disciplines.

In any case, the course would need to be an amalgam of a number of disciplines. In outline, it should begin with an introductory part about development itself, and then it should take elements from sociology, from learning theory, and from individual and group psychology as they relate to change and to non-formal education. The central section should cover communication theory and practice as they relate to development, including an overview of each of the media, with their strengths and weaknesses, not forgetting traditional media. Case studies of past experience would form a major part of this section. Finally, the student would be able to specialize in an area of choice such as communication planning or evaluation, or in working with a particular medium.

With stimulus and support from UNICEF, Tulane University in New Orleans has quite recently started to offer courses in social mobilization. Ideally, such courses would take place in developing countries, but so far, contacts between international development agencies and some universities in these countries to try to set them up have not reached conclusions. The issue needs wide follow-up, for it will not be possible in the future to rely on essentially self-taught specialists as in the past. The training needs to be formalized to ensure its quality, and also to make available more people with the necessary knowledge and skills.

Furthermore, university training in communication for development will help to establish the professional identity of the activity. This was neatly, if vulgarly, summed up by a forthright Norwegian woman in a formal UN meeting of development communicators who were seriously discussing this issue of training. 'If you have a university training in the subject,' she declared, 'other development specialists may still shit in your hat, but they can't make you put it on your head!'

Financing

There have been serious problems with the financing of communication for development as part of government services. The problems have become more difficult as structural adjustment programmes in many countries have forced governments to cut back on central spending. An indication of the gravity of the situation is that many countries, especially in Africa, have been forced to reduce spending on essential services that will affect their future, such as education and health.

In these austere circumstances, the constitution of many public broadcasting services in Africa was changed; they became corporations that had to earn their living through commercial advertising, as well as through charging for programme production services and air-time. Just one example of this is Zambia, which privatized its public radio and television services in the late 1980s. As a result, the new Zambian National Broadcasting Corporation began to charge government ministries for services that had previously been free. This provoked an immediate crisis because no special budget allocations had been made to the various ministries to allow them to buy services and air-time from the National Broadcasting Corporation. The ministries had to scrape together funds from other parts of their budgets to buy services and air-time, with the result that they were unable to ensure regular programming for health, agriculture, and so on.

When we were last in Zambia in late 1994, the problem had still not been resolved. Specifically, the Ministry of Agriculture could not pay the National Broadcasting Corporation for air-time, with the result that agricultural radio programmes had been off the air for more than seven months. The secretary for agriculture, an unusually dynamic public functionary, was hoping to find 'funds from somewhere, soon' to pay off the backlog owed to the National Broadcasting Corporation, and to get his farm radio programmes back on the air.

The fact that those responsible for finance in the government had, in effect, eliminated free radio and television services to the various ministries, without allocating funds for them to buy those services, is again indicative of the lack of understanding of the role of the mass media in national development. Even if the quality of Zambia's farm and rural programmes could probably be improved, they were nevertheless being missed by the people in late 1994. In our numerous discussions with groups of farmers in the extremely poor Northwest Province at that time, many complained spontaneously about the farming programme being off the air for months.

Budgetary problems have always plagued communication units within ministries too, even before structural adjustment programmes began. Many of these communication units were started with the help of aid programmes, but they frequently lacked operational budgets from their governments for supplies, such as paper, film, and recording tape, and for the repair of equipment.

These past problems, and the wave of neo-liberalism now sweeping the world, have led to the conviction that communication units must aim to become financially autonomous. In practice, this means that they must charge development programmes for their services, and this introduces some important issues. For example, it means that the communication services have to be professionally good, otherwise they will not find clients; and it also means that they will need a special juridical status in many countries. This is because, if they are normal government services, regulations in most countries stipulate that any money they earn must be paid to the national treasury. To get the funds back to the communication unit that earned them, so that it can continue to operate, is usually a bureaucratic process that takes enormous staff time and effort, and may not always succeed.

To overcome this problem, a few countries have created, or are thinking of creating, parastatal institutions for their communication units. This generally allows them to function like a commercial operation, retaining the funds that they earn so that they can finance their own operations, purchase supplies, and pay for repairs and spare parts for their equipment.

Operating as a parastatal institution has a second major advantage related to the career and salaries of staff. As already mentioned, it is typically very difficult to attract and keep creative staff in bureaucratic structures and on normal government pay scales. Skilled people can normally find better conditions in the private sector. However, a parastatal structure normally allows the management freedom to set salary scales and incentive payments according to the economic health of the enterprise, rather than according to government pay scales. Obviously, this allows a successful parastatal to pay competitive salaries that will attract and keep good people.

Looking for Allies

The current economic policies imposed by international lending institutions in many developing countries are cutting state spending so much that it would be unrealistic to expect that governments could pay the whole bill for communication for development. Therefore, allies need to be found who can provide support in cash or kind. As we saw in Chapter 3, UNICEF and its government counterparts were able to mobilize support from what might have been thought totally unlikely sectors for child immunization. The army, the police, trade unions, professional organizations, the Scout movement, and the religious sector were among those who became involved in many countries.

Communication for development does not lend itself to support from all these sectors, but certainly the religious institutions, which are already active in communication for development in many places, could be a major ally. So could popular movements and NGOs working in areas such as the environment, women's rights, or in any field in which success depends on helping people to change the way they see and do things.

Natural allies are the commercial media and advertising industries. As we also saw in Chapter 3, UNICEF calculated that, in Brazil alone, these industries *donated* services worth US$30 million in the interests of children in the years 1985–90. In many other countries too, free communication services were obtained. It will also be remembered from Chapter 3 that all the major commercial radio networks in Colombia themselves took the initiative of uniting and providing free services in the interests of child vaccination.

These experiences go contrary to the common opinion that commercial media will provide nothing free. Our experience, of course on a much smaller scale than UNICEF in Brazil and elsewhere, is that the commercial media are often very open to concrete proposals to involve them in social issues, especially if they have a local focus. They are well aware that their image is usually one of outright commercialism. Providing a social service gives them a chance to improve that image, and so they are often pleased to comply with a request for help.

Help may be forthcoming even from the smaller media organizations, even if they are less able to afford it than the larger ones. We were once working in a rural area of Argentina where many milk-producing farms were on the verge of bankruptcy. At our suggestion, a small town radio station devoted hours of studio time to making a special programme about the problem and possible solutions and broadcast it several times at no charge. We went to thank the owner, and we asked her whether her station's commitment to a polemical issue troubled her, especially since it involved the local economic power structure in the form of a large private milk-processing plant. 'On the contrary,' she asserted. 'I'm delighted that my station can help promote a debate that's so important for the community.'

The advertising and promotion industry is an important sector to enlist as an ally. It normally has creative people, insights into human behaviour, and mastery in use of the media. Certainly, for development aims that lend themselves to social marketing, enlisting that industry can give excellent results. In many countries, again probably to improve its image, but also because of a social conscience, the industry has been willing to provide services on the basis of the costs of materials only.

Other allies can also be found in the business sector. UNICEF was also able to catalyse much support from business and commerce for child vaccination, for example the slogans on the 20 million matchboxes sold per month in Bangladesh, and there are many other examples of business becoming involved in development matters. One of these is in Thailand, where Mechai Viravaidya's NGO, the Population and Community Development Association mentioned in Chapter 6, launched a programme in 1988 called the Thai Business Initiative in Rural Development. Its aim is to mobilize the corporate sector to bring its business expertise to rural areas through a scheme under which companies adopt villages. Villagers need abilities in organization, production, finance, and marketing, and these can be found in companies. Therefore, company employees with the appropriate skills regularly visit their adopted village to provide the insights and inputs from business know-how that can increase productivity and income for the villagers. Their work complements that of government and of other NGOs, and at the same time, the company employees gain satisfaction from being involved in a socially useful activity.

To put it bluntly, it is not in the interest of business corporations to have ever-increasing disparities of wealth in societies, and to have so many societies that are economically underdeveloped. The present emphasis on 'the market' in economic development, and so-called neo-liberalism, is marginalizing more and more people in many countries. The paradox in this situation is that as the poor get poorer they are less and less of a 'market' for national and multinational business corporations, because they cannot afford to buy anything beyond their bare necessities.

Nor is the increasing social instability, so evident in many countries as the rich get richer and the poor get poorer, in the interest of business. Companies feel the effects and costs of crime, violence, and corruption similarly to individuals. We know of one quite small retailing company, in the capital city of a developing country, which suffered no fewer than nine armed robberies on its cash tills in different stores in 1996.

Thus the business sector has a vested interest in development and in the elimination of poverty. It should not be impossible, therefore, to stimulate corporate support or sponsorship for programmes of communication for development. In fact, this area of work might be particularly attractive to business corporations because credits in media productions would give their sponsorship and involvement very high visibility among the population, a bonus for their image and prestige.

The extremely wealthy could also be a source of support. Maureen Dowd of the *New York Times* wrote an article, which was also published in the *International Herald Tribune* on 23 August 1996, in which she recounted a conversation she had by telephone with Ted Turner, the owner of CNN. He told her how his hand had shaken a couple of years earlier when he signed the papers to give away $200 million to universities and environmental programmes. Rather than feeling the joy of giving, he was consumed by the fear of falling lower on the *Forbes* magazine annual list of the four hundred wealthiest Americans.

But when he talked to Maureen Dowd, he had learned that giving can be as much fun as making, and he wanted his fellow billionaires to open their purse-strings wider. He said that the super-rich in America refused to give money away because they were frightened of dropping down the scale on the *Forbes* list. He said that he had spoken to Bill Gates and Warren Buffet,[1] the two richest men in the country, who had said they would be inclined to give more if there were a list of 'who did the giving rather than the having'. He pointed out that a billion dollars made little difference to people that rich, and that with such a sum one could build a whole university. He suggested that the mega-rich should sign pacts each to give away a billion dollars and move down the *Forbes* list equally. He also suggested a 'Heart of Gold' prize to honour philanthropists, and an 'Ebenezer Scrooge Prize' to embarrass stingy billionaires.

Maureen Dowd wrote in her article that both Gates and Buffet had promised to give away most of their money, but Gates did not intend to make plans to do so until he was 50 or 60, and Buffet would give most of his money to population control only after he

1. The 1996 Forbes list estimated Bill Gates' wealth to be US$18.5 billion and Warren Buffet's to be $15 billion.

and his wife had gone. An impatient Turner told Dowd that when the environment and population were concerned, 'Tomorrow is not another day. They should do it now!'[2]

To stimulate the involvement of the private sector, governments could create conditions that made it financially attractive for business to contribute in cash or kind to communication for development. For example, there could be tax relief for media company productions that provided information or education focused on human and social development. Similar relief could be granted to corporate sponsors of such programmes, in much the same way that donations to charity are tax-deductible in many countries.

Perhaps prizes could also be arranged for the best media productions covering themes such as population growth, the environment, children's rights, and so on. The awarding of those prizes could, in itself, be a media event that would attract public attention, in the same way that the annual Oscar awards do. A series of 'Oscars' for media productions linked to sensitizing and educating people about the present and possible future situation of humanity could encourage this type of production and set standards of excellence. There could be national and international competitions.

Opportunities of New Technologies?

From the beginning of the period of relatively cheap personal computers and satellite communications, there have been discussions as to how these technologies could be used to benefit the poor in rural and urban areas. As long ago as 1983, there was a meeting in Paris under the title 'A Speculation on the Barefoot Microchip'. It did not conclude very much, and the vision presented by some participants of the health worker or agricultural extension officer sitting in a village, tapping the symptoms of some human or plant disease into a computer, and receiving a diagnosis and suggested treatment from the system, has as yet not materialized.

In India, there is a recent proposal, under the umbrella of the World Bank, to create a network of 'information shops' in rural areas. This idea is not new in itself, for village information centres worked quite well in the Philippines until they were politicized under

---

2. In September 1997, when this book was in page proof form, Ted Turner followed his own advice: he pledged $1 billion to the UN for development programmes, mainly concerning the environment and children.

President Marcos. The basic principle is to create a place where villagers can go for information – either free or for a fee – on agriculture, health, family planning, and other socio-economic topics. The Indian proposal is to provide information through computer links to databanks, through electronic mail contacts with specialists, as well as through a collection of videos and other audio-visual media, books and publications. A novel idea would be to feed information *from* villagers into the system, giving it a two-way function, and also linking villagers to villagers over such topics as people looking for jobs and people looking for labour. But the truly innovative aspect is that the information shops would also sell music records and cassettes, hire out videos and audio-visual equipment, and provide services such as desk-top publishing, photocopying, telephone, and fax.

The underlying principle is to position information as a *product* or *input* that may be free or may be sold at differential prices. For example, information related to storms, disasters, expected outbreaks of crop diseases, health, and family planning topics would be free. A small charge would be imposed for general information about agricultural practices, while information with a commercial significance, such as market information for high value crops, would bear the highest charges.

Income from the commercially viable and high-demand elements of the operation, for example, the sale of music records and cassettes, photocopying, and the like, would go towards covering the costs of the social and technical information services. The objective would be to have the system run as a profit-making operation that would be financially sustainable.

There is now speculation on the role that could be played by information technology in developing countries. As we write this, the government of Canada and the World Bank are planning a conference in Toronto for June 1997 called 'Global Knowledge: Knowledge for Development in the Information Age'. Certainly, today's information technology could be extremely useful for human development. We only have to think of the technical possibility that now exists to deliver interactive learning systems, via computer screens, cheaply to wherever they are needed. In the USA, a model known as the Educational Utility has begun to function in recent years. It consists of three parts: first, there is a central databank from which most of the software regularly used by the system can be made available, but which at the same time serves as a gateway to media producers, video libraries, other databases, and so on; second, there are a number of decentralized storage and processing centres which can download, process, and store software and information from the central storage facility; and, third, there are local systems through which users can access the information stored in the decentralized storage centre nearest to it.

In practice, the decentralized centres are typically found in education or health authorities, universities, schools, hospitals, or wherever there are enough subscribers to access the system. The users are teachers, students, school administrators, doctors and other health workers, parents, and so on. Anyone with a personal computer and a telephone line can subscribe to the system and access it, whether in the office, school or home. The software is available in multimedia, so that for example, one can download an instructional video on a topic of one's choice, or a text with photographs and audio commentary. The software can also be interactive, for example through posing questions that the student answers as a measure of his or her progress. If the student answers incorrectly, the system goes back to the point not properly learned so that it can be revised. In this way, the student enters into a dialogue with the programme, but always learning at his or her own speed.

There are enormous cost benefits of the way this system is structured compared to the more traditional access to central databases, with much of the cost going to the telephone company whose line is being used. The decentralized system used by the Education Utility downloads whole software programmes to the local level, usually at night when telephone rates are lowest. If a user wants some software that is not stored locally, it can be ordered from the central storage facility, and if that facility does not have it, it will work as a gateway so that it can be obtained from wherever it exists. From the cost viewpoint, the system has reduced the charge to under 50 US cents per hour. The principle is similar to having electricity or water on tap whenever required, but in this case it is educational materials that are available, hence the title Education 'Utility'.

The Internet obviously has great potential for putting development organizations and groups in touch with each other and with sources of information. UNDP has been helping to set up Sustainable Development Networks. These allow access to thousands of advocacy groups, many concerned with environmental issues, but others dealing with health, education, and the like. A practical example of the usefulness of such networks occurred in Pakistan in 1994, when two men died after inhaling toxic fumes from some barrels dumped near Karachi railway station. To prevent further deaths, the police rolled the barrels, containing an unidentified chemical substance, into the nearby river. The authorities then sent out an appeal for advice to two international networks, Peace Net and EcoNet. Within 24 hours they had received more than 50 replies by electronic mail and fax from all over the world. They were able to identify the deadly substance and take measures to prevent more death or damage. Pressure groups too will certainly make ever increasing use of the Internet to exchange ideas and experience and further their causes.

Certainly, advances in communication technology have brought great potential for change and development. The tragedy is that technology is not the problem, for in fact, technology tends to develop much faster than we are able to develop the capacity to use it wisely for our own good. Policy decisions are needed. For example, very few countries have so far come even close to using rural and local radio broadcasting to its full development potential. This is because, even when the national population is predominantly rural, the emphasis in almost all countries is on entertainment, news, and commercial or political interests, and primarily with urban audiences in mind. Those sectors of broadcasting therefore attract nearly all the resources, leaving broadcasting for development as a Cinderella.

The opportunities offered by advances in communication technology should not bewitch us; rather, the almost worldwide lack of coherent policies that link communication to change and development should appal us. Without those policies, we will not get far beyond beaming television soap operas produced in faraway places such as Hollywood to billions of people sitting in their rural hovels and urban slums around the world, for whom the style and content have no relevance to their culture or to their needs in social and economic advancement.

CHAPTER 10

A Framework for Action

We turn once again to Paul Kennedy's opinion that nothing less than a 're-education of humankind' is needed to meet the forces of change facing the world. In his book, Kennedy writes about the need for better education in the formal sense of reducing illiteracy and preparing or retraining people for the workplace, but he also goes on to write about education in the broader sense. He states that education:

> also implies a deep understanding of why our world is changing, of how other people and cultures feel about those changes, of what we all have in common, as well as of what divides cultures, classes, and nations ... In the end it is not enough merely to understand what we are doing to our planet, as if we were observing the changes through a giant telescope on Mars. Because we are all members of a world citizenry, we also need to equip ourselves with a system of ethics, a sense of fairness, and a sense of proportion as we consider the various ways in which, collectively or individually, we can better prepare for the twenty-first century.

Kennedy's description of education in its largest sense is in the same general line as Dr Soedjatmoko's. As already quoted, for him, development is 'above all, learning. The learning needed by individuals, communities, and nation states to prepare themselves to live in the future.'

A third authoritative view was expressed directly to us in an interview with Dr Ismail Serageldin, the World Bank's vice-president for sustainable development. This highly articulate man has a broad vision of the world's problems and provided fascinating insights into social development and the role of civil society. (By civil society, we mean that multiplicity of social institutions that allow a society to live in harmonious coexistence by standards and values that it creates itself for individual and group behaviour, rather than having standards imposed from above.)

Serageldin said that communication was the lifeblood of social development. It was essential for social interaction, for democracy, for informal debates, and for the exchange of information and ideas. It was linked to the building of civil societies. And building civil society should be the number one priority as we go into the third millennium. In his opinion, it was even more important than education.

Civil society, Serageldin went on, needed to be helped to take root, and development of this sort was like a tree: you fed the roots to make it grow; you didn't pull on the branches. Societies evolved when they had cohesion and social norms. A society needed to be integrated and integrating, because that allowed initiatives to be introduced and to spread. Building civil society called for a flow of ideas, for communication to promote dynamic change, and to start chain reactions.

Countries in the North should help countries in the South to build civil society. We need to be imaginative. We should use NGOs more. In the coming years, uplinks and downlinks to satellites would open even more possibilities. Computers would become like transistor radios today and we should establish networks and linkages between people. But the information should be relevant to the local conditions and culture. Serageldin concluded that information was the *sine qua non* of a modern state.

These converging viewpoints reinforce the central theme of this book, namely that communication processes that facilitate learning and attitudinal and behavioural changes among individuals and in societies are vitally necessary for human advancement. However, some people may think that such processes would be impossible to launch in the majority of countries, either because their regimes are authoritarian, or because the commercialized media are too frivolous and money-oriented to deal with serious issues of society and development. In fact, Paul Kennedy also wrote in his book:

> In societies where fundamentalist forces block open enquiry and debate, where politicians, to attract the support of special interests, inveigh against foreign peoples or ethnic minorities, and where commercialized mass media and popular culture drive serious issues to the margins, the possibilities that education will introduce deeper understanding of global trends is severely limited.

With regard to commercialized mass media and national values, we have already quoted Jim Hoagland's article in which he identified television and cinema as the most powerful non-military technology ever invented and deplored its failure to help enlighten American society about the choices facing it. He concluded pessimistically, saying that serious debate about fundamental issues and choices is 'too hard in America today'. If Hoagland is right, and given America's present leadership in the world, the implications for our future are bleak.

These rather pessimistic views of the possibilities for 're-education' in many countries and of the media situation merit further consideration, for things may well change, or be changed. In fact, murmurings in favour of change are already being heard in the USA, which is important because that country is a role model for so many others.

For example, another prominent American journalist, William Pfaff of the *Los Angeles Times*, wrote an article published in the *International Herald Tribune* on 8 August 1996 that was highly critical of the US media scene. His article, which was prompted by the way the media presented a totally commercial and materialistic image of America to the world during their coverage of the Olympic Games in Atlanta, called for the 'commercial stranglehold on America' to be broken and for concepts of public interest and public service to be restored in society. He deplored the fact that everyone in the country was 'cast under the juggernaut wheels of commercial entertainment which now dominates all that people see and hear in the United States'. He went on to call for a 'public coalition to fight for a public communications sector freed from commercial pressures, so as to break the present grip of demagogy in politics, news, and public affairs debate'. He also called for politicians 'who will attempt to re-establish civil responsibility and intelligent public dialogue'. He said that there was much existing pressure for change but that it needed to become organized nationally. He pointed out that, in the past, Americans had shown their ability to change in the face of circumstances such as the Progressive Movement, the New Deal, and the Cold War, and he ended by saying, 'whether they will actually change [again now] is the unanswerable question'.

Other articles in the major press, similar to Hoagland's and Pfaff's and which raise issues about cultural values and the media in American society, have been appearing quite frequently since 1996. President Clinton, too, talks about promoting family values via the mass media, so it does indeed seem that there are some stirrings that may bring change. Whether this change, if it comes, will be the result of legislation or public pressure remains to be seen. The traditional attitude of the commercial media in the United States and elsewhere is that any form of government intervention whatsoever is 'censorship'. This was the long-standing position of the US television industry *vis-à-vis* any rating system, until in the end they were forced by public pressure to announce that they would start their own system voluntarily, and before the Federal Communications Commission imposed one.

Public pressure may, in fact, be the best way of persuading commercial media to look beyond the immediate material gains they can obtain from satisfying mass audience appetites for entertainment, and to devote at least some of their attention to education in the wide sense. Another scenario may well be that, in the years to come, the accelerating problems of society and sustainable development, many stemming from *laissez-faire* policies, will finally alarm politicians and media managers into realizing that the media industry has a key role to play in reshaping attitudes, behaviours, and consumption patterns that are affecting the future. This could lead to policies that put much greater emphasis on a public service approach to mass media programming.

Authoritarian regimes will also find themselves under increasing pressure from their populations. Such regimes have always understood the use of communication media for building and maintaining their power base, and they usually control information through media censorship and disseminate only information that is favourable to themselves. However, the control of information will probably slip out of their hands. Satellite broadcasting leaps national boundaries; use of the Internet is expanding everywhere, and even fax machines on people's desks or in their homes can bring in information from outside. Nor should we forget how Ayatollah Khomeini, while he was still exiled in Paris, subverted the Shah's regime in Iran and prepared its overthrow by circulating cassette tapes of his speeches among clandestine resistance groups.

Dr Serageldin expressed the opinion that totalitarian regimes are doomed to failure over the long haul, because, in the end, one cannot keep people away from information in today's world. In his view, the collapse of the Soviet system was brought about largely by the inability of the system to use markets which require free flow of information, including information from outside. Centrally planned economies reach a ceiling of economic activity and efficiency beyond which they cannot improve, expand and compete without technical

commercial information. Once information arrives from the
side, even through fax machines on people's desks, it is difficult
to control its content. Those living in a totalitarian system become
aware of its limitations, and that can be the beginning of the end
of such a regime.

'Re-education', but How?

No one in their right mind today would think of the 're-education
of humankind' as a process to be conducted by 'Big Brother' governments forcing us to learn new behaviour patterns. The very opposite
should be the aim; the process should be democratic, with people
being helped to learn for themselves.

Unfortunately, there can be no universal recipe for how to use
communication to help re-education and change. This is partly why
specialists in communication for development are sometimes accused
of being too general when talking about their subject. This criticism
usually comes from policy-makers and technicians who often want
clear-cut recipes or pre-cooked solutions to cover all situations. So,
when they ask communicators how communication could, in principle, help their programmes, they are frustrated by the lack of
definition from our side. As a result, they often consider the field
imprecise and untidy.

The reason for this failure of the minds to meet is that there can
never be tidy recipes for communication for development. We are
dealing with the human condition with all its complexities and
variations, rather than with the physical and technical laws that govern,
say, irrigation, construction, or soil conservation. For communicators,
every single situation is different, beginning with differences in the
audience groups to be reached, their location and distribution, their
characteristics and needs, and their existing attitudes and behaviour.
Then, the behavioural objectives will be different, and so will the
messages needed, the formats for presenting them, the media that
are available or most appropriate, the quality and effectiveness of
interpersonal contacts from field personnel, and so on. The list is
almost endless, and every situation calls for an analysis, audience
research, and a strategic communication plan. Thus development
communicators cannot be precise until they have been called in to
complete the analysis and research, and have drawn up a strategic
plan.

Any framework for action, such as the one we will propose here, is bound to be equally general, but some broad principles can be set down. Obviously, those broad principles would need to be adjusted to the individual situation and needs.

First, we will outline a possible framework of action for the major issues that have implications for the future of humankind and the planet, and which call for concerted efforts to facilitate change at national, regional, local, family, and individual level. Typical of these issues are population, environment, children's rights, and building civil society in general.

Second, we will consider the different situation linked to specific development projects, which may have their origins in needs identified at the community level or in national policy needs. In both cases, they require the active and informed participation of the local population if they are to succeed and be sustained.

Mobilizing People around Major Issues

Information and experience are, of course, the principal basis for all learning and decision-making, but people normally go through several stages of exposure to information and its internalization before it actually affects their attitudes and behaviour.

The first stage is when people are exposed to information that creates an awareness of a situation or problem. This information may well have a global focus. For example, television documentaries and press coverage on themes such as population growth and its likely effect on global natural resources, or the impact of industrialization on greenhouse gas emissions, could be expected to create general awareness of these issues. A national focus could also be taken in presenting such information.

The tone of media presentations should not be merely alarmist, for that approach can also provoke rejection by audiences. Rather, the attempt should be to provide an objective analysis of the situation and its implications for the future, incorporating debate and discussion at the same time. For example, although most scientists support the hypothesis of global warming, there are others who disagree. For the most part, the debates between them have taken place in meetings of specialists on the subject, but the general public should know all sides of the argument. The debate could be brought much more into the public domain through TV documentaries and the popular press. This would help to prepare people so that when, and if, mounting evidence leads to the need for urgent action to reduce greenhouse gas emissions, they would be readier to understand and accept measures that may be unpopular. For example, environmentalists are already talking about global energy taxes to reduce the use of hydrocarbon fuels, and certainly this would be unpopular in countries where cheap fuel for private cars is seen as a right.

Entertainment mixed with education is most certainly one of the best media strategies to reach mass audiences and arouse awareness of issues. We have already seen the success of *The Archers* (Chapter 5) for agricultural and rural development, and of TV dramas, and of involving musicians in population education (Chapter 6). However, there have been many other uses of combined entertainment and education in recent years. Popular musicians have been involved in writing and performing songs with messages that have covered a range of issues, many of them linked to children. A series of songs written and performed by the most popular group in the Congo promoted breastfeeding, oral rehydration therapy, and growth monitoring of babies in the late 1980s. The songs were so attractive that they became national hits. They must surely have had an important effect in promoting the actions they covered, but as is so often the case, no scientific impact evaluation was conducted.

Some communicators in UNICEF had an interesting idea in the early 1990s. It was based on the popularity that television drama series – soap operas – now command, and the influence they have in promoting lifestyles through their role models. Many drama series reach huge audiences in their country of origin, and sometimes millions more in other countries because the better ones are exported. For example, Hollywood productions often get worldwide distribution; series made in Cairo get shown throughout the Arabic-speaking world; and productions from Mexico and Brazil are avidly followed in many other countries of Latin America. Therefore, the UNICEF communicators reasoned, why not try to introduce scenes into these series that would influence behaviour with regard to children.

In pursuit of this idea, they organized a training workshop in Brazil in 1993 for a number of the most important television drama scriptwriters in Latin America. The workshop went exceedingly well, and the scriptwriters were seized by the importance of what they could help to achieve by weaving social messages into their work. For example, it would be easy to insert a short conversation about the benefits of breastfeeding, or of any other child-care measure. Even better would be to show such measures actually being taken, but always as a natural part of the story-line.

Sadly, putting this idea into practice was ambushed by budget and organizational problems. Quite understandably, the scriptwriters wanted technical support from UNICEF. Specifically, they wanted a hotline or other way of obtaining authoritative information urgently when they were in the middle of writing a script to a deadline. For example, how long after birth should a child be vaccinated against measles? Or how much should a healthy infant weigh at eight months? Or does the Convention on the Rights of the Child say anything about corporal punishment, and if so what?

UNICEF was never able to set up this service, so sadly this ingenious initiative never got properly off the ground. However, the principle remains valid, and lends itself to many social and development themes. In fact, this strategy of mixing entertainment with education to influence behaviour is already expanding, in both industrialized and developing countries. It deserves the widest possible use, but in a subtle fashion, so as not to create audience rejection.

Whether through documentaries or messages integrated into entertainment, the mass media have a key role to play in creating general awareness about the need for change and development, and that is why we believe that government policies and legislation should promote and facilitate the work of the media in this direction.

Localized information to create self-interest

Self-interest, in one form or another, is usually what makes people introduce change into their lives, or take certain actions. There are obvious topics of immediate self-interest to almost everybody. Health is a principal one, and general awareness created mainly by mass media of how to improve health does bring about behavioural change. For example, the promotion of breastfeeding, mainly by television, has been very successful in many developing countries. In the industrialized world too, reductions in heart disease have been achieved through promoting healthier life and eating styles via the electronic media and the press. Educational use of media in this way is especially effective if health staff reinforce the messages during their personal contacts.

There are other issues, however, that require much more effort to facilitate change. Those issues are ones that do not have an apparent immediate appeal to self-interest, such as greenhouse gas emissions, or drug abuse in other people's families. A first need for communication work on such issues is still the creation of a climate of awareness – through documentaries or drama series, or in any other way – but people will be unlikely to change until they see the issue in terms of its present or likely future effect on their personal situation. An initial step towards achieving this can be to translate macro-level information into the local context and circumstances. This is important because global and national problems, and plans for resolving them, may be meaningless to local authorities, groups, and individuals.

Let us take a problem in Italy, where people dump rubbish, plastic, and unwanted things such as old mattresses and domestic appliances over the edge of the road into rivers and streams. If the government wanted to stop this age-old habit because it was trying to clean up its rivers, seas and beaches for tourism, or as part of some pro-gramme to reduce pollution in the Mediterranean, it would probably make little progress with generalized information about the millions of tons of rubbish dumped in this way nationally, and its effects. Part of the problem would be that the sea is usually quite far from the hill and inland areas where the practice is common. But if people were informed about the local dimensions of the problem and about its negative effect on the local environment, and possibly on their health, they would be more likely to take the matter seriously and change their behaviour. In practice, the more localized the problem or the development target becomes, the more stimulus to action there will be, simply because people see the problem or target as being immediately relevant to their own situation.

This was precisely the strategy, invented by one of us (S.R.-E.), for the vaccination posters in Colombia, described briefly in Chapter 3. The national target of reaching 80 per cent of the country's children under the age of one had been set by the *central* government, and therefore it would be easy for those at community level to believe that the main responsibility for reaching the target lay with the Ministry of Health in the capital. But the contrary was true because the recently launched decentralization programme had passed the responsibility for vaccination to the mayor of each municipality and his local health service.

The way around this problem, and to stimulate local action, was to provide each of the municipalities in the country with information about the immunization coverage in that particular municipality, specifying how many children were *not* covered for each of the pathogens. This brought the national target of 80 per cent coverage down to specific local figures, requiring specific local actions. At the same time, by providing the data in the publicly displayed form of posters, the whole community was made aware of the number of their children still unvaccinated and whether this was good, average or poor coverage. This rating was an indication of the performance of the mayor and his team and of parental commitment, and when the coverage was classified as poor, pressure soon built up on parents and the authorities to take action.

Colombia was the first country in the world to implement such a strategy of localized information, but it has since been adopted by Canada in its community-based health programmes. The Colombian and Canadian experiences show that the strategy can be applied to a wide range of health topics, especially those that have a close link with behaviour patterns or with awareness of the need for preventative health care. Just some of the examples would be work-related accidents, lung cancer, complications during pregnancy and delivery, heart disease, AIDS, and so on. The strategy works particularly well when the local situation can be compared to the regional or national situation.

Without doubt, the same strategy could be used for many aspects of human and social development, provided that statistical data are available. For example, in the area of the environment, many measurable standards could be made locally public. Some of these could be: levels of pollution in the local waterways or lakes, or in the air; levels of pesticide use and their residues in harvested crops and in the land; deforestation rates; land degradation, and so on. These could be set against the figures for other communities or regional and national averages, in effect either to shame people into taking action or to give them a sense of pride and a desire to stay ahead.

Many other themes also lend themselves to the approach. Among them could be: juvenile delinquency, cases of domestic and street violence, abuse of women and children; school enrolment and dropout; population growth and fertility rates; drug and alcohol abuse, etc.

The need for analysis and discussion

Localized information is most effective when it becomes the subject of analysis and debate within a community, and when groups form to take action. This is in part because individuals acting alone are often resistant to change. How often have we heard people, who are doing something that has negative effects on society, say that they have no intention of changing because 'everybody else does it, and my changing won't make any difference'?

Change may also be difficult for the individual because there are always constraints and risks involved. The constraints can be social – for example, an action that goes against tradition may be objectionable to the rest of the community, or making a change that does not produce good results may expose the person to ridicule. There may also be real risks involved, for example, investing in expensive technology or new production methods which turn out not to be economically or technically viable.

Naturally, there is strength in numbers, and for that reason, change takes place more easily and rapidly when groups, even small ones, become involved in analysing information, discussing its relevance to their particular situation, internalizing it, and making decisions to take action. It is in this way that movements and pressure groups build up. This could result, for example, in community-level groups interceding with local industries about the effect of pollution from their factories on the community.

We once saw an exhibit that had been put up by the local students in the main square of the town of Modena in northern Italy. It included photographs of such things as pipes discharging waste from factories into streams. Each photograph showing a case of industrial pollution had an accompanying text giving the name of the factory, describing where the discharge was located, and explaining the effect it was having on the stream or other aspects of the local environment. The exhibit was arousing a great deal of popular interest and a fair degree of indignation.

Such popular pressure on local industry must surely bear fruit over time, as has been shown in Chattanooga in the state of Tennessee in the USA. Only a few years ago, the city suffered from such serious air pollution that the sun was hardly ever seen clearly. Most of the pollution was being caused by local industry. The authorities promoted a civil debate on the issues. There was meeting after meeting to discuss the problem and to arouse the interest and commitment of the population. Those mainly responsible for the pollution became involved and, step by step, actions were taken. Today, the situation has been transformed beyond recognition, and there is a general sense of community achievement.

Information materials with local content to stimulate interest, analysis, and discussion can be presented in a variety of forms – video or audio recordings, photographs, or even written reports.

People exposed to information material may understand its significance in different ways, but the analysis and discussion that follows
will help to clarify the issues and lead towards a consensus view.

Once a clear diagnosis of the local situation or problem has been
achieved, the path is open to consider solutions and actions to
improve matters. For example, if a community analysed the problem
of drug abuse among its youth, there could be several results. The
first could be to bring the problem out from under the carpet so
that it was openly discussed as a problem of the community, and
not just of the drug-abusers and their families. This could lead to
de-stigmatizing drug-abusers. From this, a concerted community
action programme might be created involving parents, teachers, ex-
drug-abusers, local police, and other members of the community.
The continued discussions, and the involvement of the drug-abusers
themselves, could lead to a clearer understanding of the phenomenon
and to agreed proposals for tackling it.

This may sound an idealistic process, but we saw it working in
villages in northern Thailand in 1995. Worldview International Foundation, an NGO working in communication for development with
funding mainly from Norway, had launched a programme to help
fight drug abuse in Thai villages close to the border with Burma.
These villages had been traditional opium poppy growers, but they
had stopped in the last decade as the result of successful crop
substitution and rural development programmes. However, traffickers
carrying heroin from over the nearby border were passing through
the villages on their way south, and were luring people, mainly the
young, into the drug trap.

The centrepiece of the communication initiative in each village
was a community sound system similar to the ones described in the
Mexican case study (Chapter 4). Among its various functions, the
sound system was the forum for discussion about the drug problem.
Gradually, the exposure of the problem led people to realize that it
was a community issue, and that no blame should be attached to the
drug-abusers or their families. As the subject was brought into the
open, and all its aspects were discussed, the numbers of people who
were drug-abusers, and who they were, also emerged. This led to
the creation of support groups to try to wean them from the habit
or to persuade them to go to a rehabilitation centre in the region.
Obviously, they have not been successful in every case, but significant
progress was being made, especially in reducing the number of new
drug-abusers.

Mobilizing communities

Governments are usually good at mobilizing resources, but NGOs can be good at mobilizing people, as was mentioned in Chapter 3. Even if central or major media networks have a natural role to play at the macro level, local media and NGOs are more effective at the community level.

Governments are increasingly recognizing that NGOs have an important and useful function that they themselves cannot perform. Not so many years ago, people in governments and international development agencies often thought that NGOs were made up of do-gooders involved in matters about which they knew almost nothing, and that they were generally a nuisance factor. However, things have changed and today there is a general acceptance of their usefulness. Thus many governments and development agencies are now entering into joint ventures with them, for they can be their fingertips in the communities in a way that the official sector seldom can be. Of course, care is needed in selecting partner NGOs, for not all are equally competent and effective.

NGOs and popular groups are well placed for mobilization at the community level and should be encouraged to assume a role in conjunction with government institutions and civil society. They may need orientation and training to be able to play their part effectively, and governments and development agencies should make sure they receive it.

Traditional media, especially popular theatre groups, can also play an important role in most countries. Drama, which has always existed in human society, is a natural form of expression that reflects daily life. It is based in reality but it interprets it, in dramatic or humorous form, and passes it back to the audience. In this way, the theatre becomes like a mirror in which people and communities can see themselves from a certain distance and in a different light, so gaining new perceptions of their reality and of ways to change it. For example, there may be a traditional attitude or behaviour pattern that is blocking progress in certain communities. A humorous skit or dramatic presentation about it can make people see its negative side and open the door for change.

The Gram theatre group in Bangladesh, mentioned in Chapter 3, became involved in promoting children's health and other social themes in the late 1980s. Popular theatre has been effectively used for similar themes in Nigeria, for environmental protection in Melanesia, for civil rights in Argentina and Chile, for population education in Burundi, to help develop strong popular organizations in Brazil, to gain better conditions for the 'untouchables' in India, and for AIDS education in Jamaica. These are just a few examples from around the world. There are many more. Theatre, and other forms of popular art, such as puppets, can be powerful communication tools when creatively used.

The most effective communication to mobilize people to participate in the solution of the major problems would use a combination of national or large-scale mass media with local and traditional media, supported by NGOs and government development agents at the community level.

Communication for Development Projects

Development projects are normally created to solve local and national needs, and at the same time to improve standards of living. After decades of conceiving development projects in ministry offices or in international development agencies, with little or no consultation with the intended beneficiaries, the principle of involving people in analysing the problems and planning accordingly is finally gaining acceptance.

A few donors for development go even further: they now seem to believe that *no* initiative should be taken that does not originate in expressions of need by communities. This is going too far in the opposite direction from previous practice, for although it might be an ideal objective in some ways, it fails to take into account national development and the needs of other sectors of society. For example, a government might analyse the nutritional level of people in the cities, and the market for fruits and vegetables, and decide that more production could increase consumption at reduced prices and improve urban nutrition levels. Another example might be to reduce the cost of imports of a certain commodity that could be easily produced nationally.

Communication processes are also important in such cases because the government's proposals to solve a national need should be discussed in detail with those whose support and actions are required. The purpose should be to ascertain how the communities see their potential role, what they would need to fulfil it, and what benefits would accrue to them. In other words, there would be negotiations, starting from the point of where government interests and community and individual interests overlapped.

In practice, such a communication process could begin with a video programme about the national need, explaining its causes and possible solutions. This video could set the scene for group discussions in the community to elicit the true opinions and ideas of the participants. Video could be used to record the ideas and opinions of the villagers for feedback to the planners, and also as a record for future use. However, all the above process assumes a genuine desire to listen to what people in the community have to say, to take their ideas and opinions into account in the planning, and to reach an agreement that will satisfy both national and community needs.

For other types of project – those that do not have a national interest as their departure point, but start out with the purpose of improving a local situation – the communication process for planning the project should be open-ended. The communicators should begin their task with no preconceived ideas; their only objective should be to start and facilitate a process of situation analysis, of identification of the causes of problems, and of options for solving them. From this, action plans can be drawn up for what the community itself will do, and for what outside support and inputs are needed. Thus a project can become a partnership between the community and the development agency. Unfortunately, this does not always work out as planned because of traditional 'we-know-best' attitudes in government echelons, or because there is no real appreciation or respect for farmers' opinions, which is what we experienced in Uganda, as described in Chapter 9.

Any development project almost invariably calls for people to acquire new knowledge and skills: rural people may need to learn for the first time about irrigation techniques, or agro-forestry, or soil conservation, or how to use new tools; mothers may need to learn about family nutrition, or about new arts and crafts as part of an income-generation programme; and community and group leaders may need to know more about organization, management, and simple accounting.

The list of possible subjects is endless, but in all cases, communication materials and processes can be of fundamental importance for helping people to learn. Anything from videos to slide-sets, flip-charts or pre-recorded cassette tapes will make new information more comprehensible, especially to people of low educational levels. And simple printed materials that they can keep at home will serve as a reminder for the future. Field development agents who are going to use the materials need to know how to present them and lead the discussion that follows in such a way that the people can begin to internalize the new information.

The monitoring and evaluation of projects that are partnerships between communities and development agencies require the participation of all concerned. People from the community and the development agency need to see and analyse the successes and failures in their own efforts. Again, this process requires group communication techniques. In addition, stimulating the discussions with audio-visual reports can add insight and depth to the process. For example, if one of the project elements were not succeeding properly, a video showing its physical situation, and interviews with those involved in it, could open discussions in order to analyse what was going wrong.

As we have seen, many development projects need to involve different technical sectors of government in a coordinated way. First, and especially when dealing with poorly educated people, these sectors need to be able to respond to development problems as the beneficiaries see them, that is to say in a holistic and interconnected way; and second, during the implementation of the project, the different sectors need to continue to coordinate their work.

Since in most governments the sectors are compartmentalized, this presents a communication challenge. Mechanisms need to be set up for information exchange and coordination, but just as important, the jealousies and rivalries that often exist between government services need to be overcome. The best way to achieve this is by creating a common understanding among the services involved of the importance of the project, of its objectives, and of what needs to be done by each sector to achieve them. If a collegiate and team spirit can be created through communication in this way, with the importance of the role of each partner properly recognized, most of the rivalries will usually vanish. The project will be perceived as a joint endeavour from which all will gain credit and satisfaction if it succeeds.

The style in which official meetings are run also plays a crucial part in building a sense of teamwork. It is astonishing how often meetings are badly prepared and conducted. In fact, they are often not prepared at all. Usually the senior person present runs the meeting, regardless of whether he or she has any skills in this area. Clear objectives and a good moderator are essential. The moderator must know how to stimulate members of the meeting to get the best out of each, but at the same time keep the meeting on track towards its objectives. Otherwise, the time wasted, and the frequent failure to reach conclusions, generates frustration and bad feeling, the very antithesis of what is required for good teamwork. Training in meeting skills is available: it would be used much more if policy-makers and senior staff realized the enormous cost of poor meetings in wasted time and in failure and delay in making important decisions properly.

Of all the major development projects that have taken place to date, PRODERITH probably came closest to achieving the optimum use of communication in all its functions, and as an integral part of the programme – at least before Mexico's economic problems parti-ally crippled it. In the early years of PRODERITH, Eric Miller, a British rural development specialist who had visited it, wrote: 'I do not know of any other rural development programme that has dedicated so much attention, not only to the technical and economic aspects, but to the social dimension as well.'

Communication, Yes – but not Alone

It has not been our intention to give the impression that communica-tion alone can solve all the problems of change and development. People may be fully motivated and willing to change, but if the physical possibilities for that change are not present, the process will be stillborn. A couple may want to limit the number of their children, and know about contraception methods, but if the services are not available locally, at a price they can afford, they will be able to do little about it. The Italians who throw their rubbish over the roadside will go on doing so, however aware they may be of the local environmental damage, if there are no public tips charging a reason-able fee. Working with farmers to motivate them to improve their production will serve no purpose if the necessary farm inputs are not readily available at a price that makes their use economically viable. On the other hand, communication can help to create demand in certain circumstances and thus put pressure on the services to perform. This was UNICEF's hypothesis for child immunization, and it proved correct in many countries.

Certainly, change and development indeed need various com-ponents. Our point is that communication should be an equal among them, and an integral part, right from the stage at which plans are being drawn up. Only in this way will those plans reflect the needs and possibilities of people, enlist their participation, and provide them with the skills and knowledge they need. Anything less and the initiative will not be sustained.

The driving force for writing this book was that communication for development has been so seriously neglected as a part of policies for development, by both national governments and most development agencies. It can no longer be treated like the fifth wheel on a car – nice to have, but something of a luxury. Communication needs to be converted into the steering wheel to help guide the enormous changes necessary by those responsible for national policies, by institutions, societies, communities, and groups. The forces of society need to be unleashed for the changes necessary for sustainable development in the next century, but in the final analysis, it is individual change and action, multiplied many thousand million times, that would make the large-scale impact we need to take us down the right path.

Democratic communication processes and the media hold the key to creating awareness, new values and behaviour patterns, and to the spreading of knowledge and skills on the scale necessary to empower individuals and groups to control their own destiny, and that of future society.

Bibliography

Books

Anzola, Patricia (1988) *Hacia un diagnóstico de la Comunicación social en Colombia.* Bogotá: Mincomunicaciones, DNP, UNICEF.

Bernal Alarcon, Hernando (1971) *Educación fundamental integral y medios de comunicación social: El uso sistemático de los medios masivos de comunicación en programas de desarrollo.* Bogotá: Acción Cultural Popular, 1971.

Brumberg, Stephen F. (1978) *Acción Cultural Popular: Mass Media in the Service of Colombian Rural Development,* for the International Council for Educational Development, April 1972 (Chapter VI, 'Major lessons of ACPO's experience', pp. 42–203) in *Acción Cultural Popular.* Bogotá: Acción Cultural Popular, pp. 37–41.

Freire, Paulo (1972) *Pedagogy of the Oppressed.* London: Penguin.

Gore, Al (1993) *Earth in the Balance: Ecology and the Human Spirit.* New York: Plume.

Gumucio-Dragon, Alfonso (1994) *Popular Theatre.* Lagos, Nigeria: UNICEF.

Gumucio-Dragon, Alfonso and Cajias, Lupe (eds) (1989) *Las radios mineras de Bolivia.* La Paz: CIMCA-UNESCO.

Harrison, Paul (1993) *The Third Revolution: Population, Environment and a Sustainable World.* London: Penguin.

Kennedy, Paul (1993) *Preparing for the Twenty-First Century.* London: Fontana.

Leakey, Richard and Roger Lewin (1996) *The Sixth Extinction: Biodiversity and its Survival.* London: Weidenfeld and Nicolson.

Manoff, Richard K. (1985) *Social Marketing: New Imperative for Public Health.* New York: Praeger.

Meadows, D. H., D. L. Meadows, J. Randers and W. Behrens (1972) *The Limits to Growth.* New York: Universe Books.

Morgan, Robert M. et al. (1982) *Evaluation of Acción Cultural Popular: An Integrated System of Rural Non-formal Education for Colombia, South America.* Tallahassee: Florida State University Learning Systems Institute.

Musto, Stefan (1978) *Communication Media for Rural Development: Comunidades* (Año V, septiembre–diciembre, no. 15, pp. 7–31, Instituto Alemán de Desarrollo June, 1971) in *Acción Cultural Popular.* Bogotá: Acción Cultural Popular, pp. 45–65.

Musto, Stefan A. et al. (1971) *Los medios de comunicación social al servicio del desarrollo rural: Análisis de eficiencia de 'Acción Cultural Popular-Radio Sutatenza' (Colombia),* prólogo y glosas de Acción Cultural Popular, Bogotá: Instituto Alemán de Desarrollo.

Oepen, Manfred (ed.) (1995) *Media Support and Development Communication in a World of Change: New answers to old questions?* proceedings from an international conference, Berlín, 19–20 November 1993, organized by ACT 'Appropriate Communication in Development', Freie Universitat Berlin, Worldview International Foundation. Bad Honnef: Horlemann Verlag.

Rogers, Everett M. (ed.) (1976) *Communication and Development: Critical Perspectives.* London: Sage.

Sadick, Nafis (ed.) (1994) *Making a Difference: Twenty-Five Years of UNFPA Experience.* London: Banson.

Singh, Rahul (1994) *Family Planning Success Stories (Asia, Latin America, Africa).* New Delhi: UBSPD Publisher's Distribution.

Woods, Bernard (1993) *Communication, Technology and the Development of People.* London: Routledge.

Zalamea, Luis (1994) *Un Quijote visionario.* Bogotá: Jorge Plazas S., Editor.

Institutional Documents

Connections: Newsletter on Communication, Environment, Rights of People and Sustainable Development (1995) Sri Lanka: Mihikatha Institute, November.

Curtin, Leslie B. et al. (1992) *Indonesia's National Family Planning Program: Ingredients of Success.* Washington: DUAL Incorporated and International Science and Technology Institute (occasional paper, 6/Report, 91-134-136).

Food and Agriculture Organization (1994) *Mali: Politique Nationale de Communication pour le Développement.* Rome: FAO, PNUD; République du Mali. Ministère de la Culture et la Communication.

— (1992) *Roundtable on Development Communication: Rome 3–6 September 1991.* Rome: FAO.

— Development Support Communication Branch (1989) *Guidelines on Communication for Rural Development: A Brief for Development Planners and Project Formulators.* Rome: FAO.

Fraser, Colin (1994) *How Decision Makers See 'Communication for Development': Report of a Survey Commissioned by the Development Communication Roundtable.* New York: UNICEF/WHO.

Fraser, Colin and Jonathan Villet (1994) *Communication: A Key to Human Development.* Rome: FAO.

Hamijoyo, Santoso S. (1992) *Some Thoughts on IEC Strategy for the '90s.* Jakarta: National Family Planning Coordinating Board.

International Conference on Population and Development (1994) (Cairo: 5–13 September). New York: United Nations, 1995 (A/Conf.171/13/Rev. 1)

Ögün, Bilge and Karen Houston Smith (1991) *Inocenti Global Seminar: Participatory Development Summary Report 21–29 May 1990.* Florence: UNICEF.

Servaes, Jan and Patchanee Malikhao (1991) *Concepts: The Theorical Underpinnings of the Approaches to Development Communication.* UNFPA/UNESCO

Project Integrated Approaches to Development Communication Study and Training Package, New York: UNFPA/UNESCO.

UN (1995) *The Copenhagen Declaration and Programme of Action 6–12 March 1995*, World Summit for Social Development. New York: United Nations.

UN Conference on Environment and Development (1992) *Agenda 21: Adoption of Agreements on Environment and Development*. New York: United Nations, 1992.

UNDP (1996) *Human Development Report 1996*. New York: Oxford University Press.

UNFPA (1993) *Developing Information, Education and Communication (IEC) Strategies for Population Programmes*. Technical Paper 1, New York: UNFPA.

— (1993) *Male Involvement in Reproductive Health, Including Family Planning and Sexual Health*, Technical Report 28. New York: UNFPA.

— (1995) *The State of World Population 1995*. New York: UNFPA.

— (1996) *The State of World Population 1996*. New York: UNFPA.

UNICEF (1990) *Children and Development in the 1990s – a Unicef Sourcebook: On the Occasion of the World Summit for Children 29–30 September 1990*. New York: UNICEF.

— (1994) *The Progress of Nations 1994*. New York: UNICEF.

— (1995) *The Progress of Nations 1995*. New York: UNICEF.

— (1994) *The State of the World's Children 1994*. Oxford and New York: Oxford University Press.

— (1995) *The State of the World's Children 1995*. Oxford and New York: Oxford University Press.

— (1996) *The State of the World's Children 1996*. Oxford and New York: Oxford University Press.

US Agency for International Development (1993) *The Substance Behind the Images: AID and Development Communication*. Washington: US Agency for International Development.

World Conference on Women (1995) (4: Beijing 4–15 September) (Doc.A/Conf. 177/20). New York: United Nations.

Case Studies

Adhikarya, Ronny (1994) *Strategic Extension Campaign: A Participatory-Oriented Method of Agricultural Extension. A Case Study of FAO's Experiences*. Rome: FAO.

Aragon, Angela et al. (1995) *DWTL-FM: Has Laurel Lost Its Voice? A Case Study*. Thesis presented to the Department of Communications, Ateneo de Manila University, Manila.

Bernal Alarcon, Hernando et al. (1978) *Acción Cultural Popular: Pioneer Radiophonic Education Program of Latin America 1947–1977 (Bogotá, June 1977): A Case Study*, in: *Acción Cultural Popular*. Bogotá: Acción Cultural Popular, 1978, pp. 1–34.

Brumberg, Stephan F. (1975) 'Colombia: A Multimedia Rural Education Program', in *Education for Rural Development: Case Studies for Planners*. New York, Washington and London: Praeger, pp. 1–61.

FAO, Development Support Communication Branch (1994) *Applying DSC Methodologies to Population Issues: A Case Study in Malawi*, by Agnes Kavinya, Sultana Alam and Anamaria Decock (Development Communication Case Study 12). Rome: FAO.

— (1987) *Education Through Entertainment: The British Radio Drama Series 'The Archers, an Everyday Story of Country Folk'*, by Colin Fraser (Development Communication Case Study). Rome: FAO.

— (1987) *The Paradigm of Communication in Development: From Knowledge Transfer to Community Participation – Lessons from the Grameen Bank, Bangladesh*, by Andreas Fugelsang and Dale Chandler (Development Communication Case Study). Rome: FAO.

— (1987) *A Rural Communication System for Development in Mexico's Tropical Lowlands*, by Colin Fraser (Development Communication Case Study). Rome: FAO.

— (1990) *Towards Putting Farmers in Control: A Second Case Study of the Rural Communication System for Development in Mexico's Tropical Wetlands*, by Colin Fraser (Development Communication Case Study 9). Rome: FAO.

Fraser, Colin (1992) *Harnessing the Power of Ideas: Communication and Social Mobilization for UNICEF-Assisted Programmes. A Case Study*. New York: UNICEF.

Fraser, Colin and Sonia Restrepo-Estrada (1997) *Communication for Rural Development in Mexico: In Good Times and in Bad* (Development Communication Case Study). Rome: FAO.

— (1994) *Juanita: Putting Children in the Electoral Arena. A case study of advocacy and social mobilization for children linked to decentralization and elections in Colombia*. New York: UNICEF.

Articles

Begley, Sharon (1996) 'He's Not Full of Hot Air'. *Newsweek*, 22 January, pp. 42–6.

Bernal, Hernando (1989) 'Requiem por Sutatenza'. *Chasqui*, no. 32, octubre–diciembre, pp. 64–7.

Dowd, Maureen (1996) 'A "heart of gold" challenge to Ol'Skinflints'. *International Herald Tribune*, 23 August.

Friedman, Thomas (1996) 'Japan's Top Priority: Decent Jobs'. *International Herald Tribune*, 26 February, p. 8.

International Herald Tribune (1996) 'U.S., in Switch, Targets Global Warming: It Urges Firm Commitments and Quicker Action to Fight Pollution', 18 July, pp. 1, 7.

Manne, Alan S. (1995) 'Are "Greenhouse" Talks Premature Hot Air?'. *International Herald Tribune*, 23 August, p. 9.

Mifflin, Lawrie (1996) 'TV Networks Seek to Set Up Own Sex-and-Violence Code'. *International Herald Tribune*, 16 February.

Paye, Jean-Claude (1995) 'Economic Growth Will Fail Us Unless Our Societies Grow, Too'. *International Herald Tribune*, June.

Pfaff, William (1996) 'The Commercial Stranglehold on America Has to Be Broken'. *International Herald Tribune*, 8 August.

Speth, James Gustave (1996) 'Two Worlds in Counterflow, or 358=2.3 Billion and Counting'. *International Herald Tribune*, 23 August.

Stevens, William K. (1996) 'A Skeptic Asks, is it Getting Hotter, or is it Just the Computer Model?' (profile of Dr Richard S. Lindzen). *New York Times*, 18 June, pp. C1, C8.

Watson, Russell (1996) 'Weird Weather'. *Newsweek*, 22 January, pp. 38–41.

Yoder, Edwin M. Jr (1996) 'Smut on the Tube is a Real Issue'. *International Herald Tribune*, 6 March.

Index

Aabenhus, Ole, 196
Acción Cultural Popular (ACPO), 144–61, 237; becomes ecclesiastical body, 154; collapse of, 156–61; danger of politicization, 154; mobilization of peasants, 158; newspaper, 160; philosophy and work of, 150–3; position on birth control, 157; publishing house, 155; training centres, 161; usefulness to peasants, 155–6; withdrawal of support for, 158
advertising industry, 259, 260; drawing on resources of, 87–8
advocacy, 68, 69, 73, 86
African Bee Control Programme (Mexico), 124–5
Agenda 21, 34, 38, 238
agriculture: broadcasting about, 130–44, 225, 226, 257; deterioration of, worldwide, 11
AIDS, 3, 24, 27, 59, 176, 178; information about, 27; prevention of, 25 (in Zimbabwe, 26); spread of, 25–6
Allard, Martin, 194, 195
alliance building, 69, 88–91, 258–6
Aquino, Corazon, 194
The Archers, 130–1, 142, 161, 177, 224, 272; and firefighting use of ponds, 142; as medium for information, 142; creation of characters, 135–9; portrayal of foot-and-mouth disease, 141, 144; producing of, 139–40; success of, 140–2
Argentina, 46, 57, 166, 278; milk-producers' project, 259
Arnaldo, Carlos, 194, 195
audience research, 47, 189, 223, 224
audio-visual technology, use of, 47, 60, 64, 101, 281

Baghdad, bombing of, 250
Bangladesh, 82–3, 84, 85–6, 89, 91, 93, 183, 278; falling fertility rates, 176; rat-reduction project, 233; threat of rising sea levels, 9

Bangladesh Rural Advancement Committee (BRAC), 89
Baseley, Godfrey, 130–1, 132–5, 138, 222
Bernal, Hernando, 160, 161
bilharziasis, 20; aetiology of, 43–4
Bolivia, 15, 16, 20, 23, 57, 175, 185; soil erosion in, 10
Bolivian Institute for Agricultural and Livestock, 10, 20
Boyd Orr, Lord, 11–12
Brazil, 11, 31, 87, 88, 164, 165, 166, 188, 259; death squads in, 30; fertility rates in, 187
breastfeeding, 68, 227; campaigns to promote, 87, 234–5, 272, 273
Buffet, Warren, 261
Burkina Faso, 196, 248, 252; Operation Commando, 94
business sector: as allies, 260, 261, 262; sponsorship in family planning campaigns, 179

Canada, 63, 263, 275; radio programming in, 61
Caracol radio network (Colombia), 76, 84, 159
Catholic Church, 154, 171; and contraception, 172, 173, 174; and José Joaquín Salcedo, 157; and media systems, 200
change: among policy-makers, 6–14; among individuals, 22–34
Child Survival and Development Revolution (CSDR), 68, 70, 73, 87, 88
childbirth: cash incentives for, 166; in Bolivia, 16; in Indonesia, 17
Childers, Erskine, 43, 44, 45, 46
children: diseases of, 108; employed in factories, 31; involved in armed conflict, 30; rights of, 32, 271; situation of, 27, 30 *see also* mortality, child
Chile, 28, 103–4, 108, 278
civil society, development of, 266, 267, 271
Cob, Don Clotilde, 106–7

289